Radical Criminology

issue six ✳ fall 2016

ISSN: 1929-7904
ISBN 10: 0-9982375-2-3
ISBN 13: 978-0-9982375-2-7

a publication of the
Critical Criminology Working Group
at Kwantlen Polytechnic University
(12666 72 Avenue, Surrey, BC V3W 2M8)
www.radicalcriminology.org

Ⓟ punctum books ✳ earth, milky way
www.punctumbooks.com

Radical Criminology ✳ Issue 6
November 2016 ✳ ISSN 1929-7904

General Editor: Jeff Shantz

Advisory Board: Olga Aksyutina, Institute for African Studies of Russian Academy of Sciences, Moscow; **Davina Bhandar** (Trent U.); **Jeff Ferrell** (Texas Christian U.); **Hollis Johnson** (Kwantlen Polytechnic U.); **Michael J. Lynch** (U. of South Florida); **Mike CK Ma** (Kwantlen Polytechnic U.); **Lisa Monchalin** (Kwantlen Polytechnic U.); **Heidi Rimke** (U.Winnipeg); **Jeffrey Ian Ross** (U.Baltimore); **Herman Schwendinger,** independent scholar

Production Editor: PJ Lilley

Cover Artist: *Artact QC*   (see pg. 324)

Unless otherwise stated, contributions express the opinions of their writers and are not (necessarily) those of the Editors or Advisory Board. Please visit our website for more information.

✳ Contact Us ✳

email: editors@radicalcriminology.org

website: http://journal.radicalcriminology.org

Mailing address: Kwantlen Polytechnic University, ATTN: Jeff Shantz, Dept. of Criminology
12666   72 Avenue
Surrey, BC, Canada V3W 2M8

*

Our website uses the Open Journal System,
developed by the Public Knowledge Project at
Simon Fraser University:

journal.radicalcriminology.org

Here, you may create your own profile to contribute to this
project, or simply subscribe your email address to our low
traffic mailing list, to receive notifications of important new
content added to the journal. Use of your address is limited
to matters relating to the journal, and we will not be sharing
our subscribers list with other organizations.

*

As an online, open access publication,
all our content is freely available to all researchers
worldwide ensuring maximum dissemination.

*

Printed paper copies with full color cover
are available at cost through

punctum books ✶ earth, milky way
"spontaneous acts of scholarly combustion"
www . punctumbooks . com

radicalcriminology.org/issue6

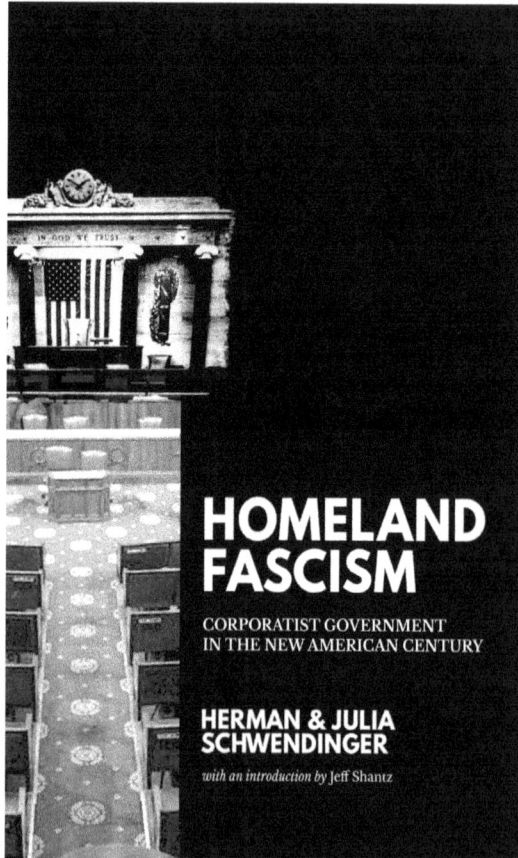

INSIDE

editorial /

features /

editorial

Insurgent Criminology in a Period of Open Social War

Jeff Shantz

C riminology has throughout its history been a dualist field of knowledge proceeding along distinct, often separate tracks. On the one hand is academic criminology based in institutions of post-secondary education or public policy. On the other hand is a community criminology, often insurgent, coming from and expressing the experiences of people and communities subjected to the violence of the state and institutions of criminal justice. This goes back to the early days of criminology when the first and sharpest criticisms of academic criminology—such as that of Lombroso, for example—were being provided by insurgent criminologists, primarily anarchists like Peter Kropotkin and criminalized rebels. Today these dual tracks stand in somewhat stark contrast as community movements opposing state violence and brutality, from Black Lives Matter to Idle No More to new poor people's movements, are developing and asserting some of the strongest and most incisive analyses and opposition to systems and institutions of criminal justice in liberal democracies like Canada and the US.

The struggles of the present period are stripping the cover off of policing as military institutions for social war waged against the working class, especially racialized and poorest sectors, in defense of statist management, capitalist ownership, and accumulation. The police are increasingly revealed as agents of pacification and regulation (as they have always been) rather than of public safety or security.

There is an insurgent criminology—lively, engaged, informed, vital, analytical, honest, brave—emerging not in the halls of the academy nor in the sessions of academic conferences but rather in the streets and neighborhoods of those who are targeted by the state for ongoing punishment, repression, violence. That insurgency is bringing with it important critiques of criminal justice as well as the beginnings of compelling challenges and alternatives, moving through and beyond reformist demands. One of the most important and promising developments has been the posing and pondering of alternatives to policing and the raising of abolitionist perspectives, responses, and projects. These are the voices academic criminology must hear and must heed. And the movements they must support as active allies, even more as accomplices and public defenders.

TAKING SIDES

When Black Lives Matter Toronto (BLMTO) stopped marching during the Toronto Pride parade and demanded that police be kept out of Pride parades they were openly, courageously, with clear sight affirming that police are not part of communities of the oppressed. That the police are in fact oppressors. This position moves vibrantly, vocally, beyond liberal (and even too many critical) approaches in criminology that seek conciliation, compromise, or accommodation with police (often on supposedly "realist" grounds). Yet the BLMTO approach is a profoundly realist one. It identifies and acknowledges and opposes the reality of policing as a historic force of brutality, harm, inequality, and injustice in the day to day lives of oppressed and exploited people and communities.

Criminologists need to follow the courageous, principled example set by BLMTO in the Pride parade and openly challenge the attempts to normalize the presence of active police officers in sites of social life such as university departments. Active officers must be openly opposed, their presence in university departments as active agents of surveillance and repression rejected. Not only the demilitarization of campus police[1], but the full call for "Cops off Campus" as raised in the civil rights and student struggles of the 1960s and 1970s[2] must once again be taken up in movements of engaged,

---

[1] Movement for Black Lives: Demilitarization of Law Enforcement policy brief: https://policy.m4bl.org/wp-content/uploads/2016/07/Demilitarization-of-Law-Enforcement-Policy-Briefs.pdf

critical criminology today. Criminologists need to challenge openly all attempts by police (border security, state intelligence, police, etc.) to recruit students behind the cover of faculty positions. University campuses and departments must not be transformed into recruitment offices. An appropriate response would also include opposing recruitment tables at job fairs and other events on campus. At the same time police must not be allowed to gain the ideological benefit of presenting police propaganda—let's call it *copaganda*—from the respected status conferred by a faculty posting—neither from a position at the front of a classroom, nor through media appearances nor via "public advocacy" efforts such as townhall meetings designed to promote growth of snitch culture in working class communities.

Academic criminologists need to stop the subservience to a false collegiality with oppressors in their own departments or schools and recognize that social struggle does not stop at the doors to the academy or on the pavement outside campus. Social war infuses, pervades institutions of higher learning as it does all areas of social life. This is true perhaps especially within criminology departments. It is true in funding, programming, co-op and practicum

---

[2]   See also the Schwendingers' "*Who Killed the Berkeley School? Struggles in Radical Criminology*" an open publication from our Thought|Crimes press imprint at
    http://thoughtcrimespress.org/BerkeleySchool
    For more on the recent campaign in London (in historical context), see "How to Get Cops Off Campus":
    http://www.workersliberty.org/story/2014/01/15/how-get-cops-campus or on twitter, look for #CopsOffCampus

placements (which go overwhelmingly to systemic institutions), boards of governors, advisory committees, research grants, etc.

The insurgent criminologists of the community uprisings are in many ways far ahead of even the critical criminologists in their analysis of the nature of policing, incarceration, the prison-industrial complex, and in understanding how to mobilize to confront these. In many respects, they are also out front in their willingness and preparedness to consider and develop alternatives. And they are doing so from the direct, experiential position of those who have felt the power of the state levelled against them, their families, their communities, even over generations. In this, the insurgent criminologists, members of oppressed and exploited communities, put the lie to so called realists who again and again seek to link the oppressed to "better" policing (as part of a "realist" desire for safety and security, of which the police provide neither).

This is increasingly a time for critical criminologists to take sides with the insurgents to actively support the resistance forces in this social war. Time to abandon allegiances and alliances with the dominant structures. The last few years have shattered the façade of consensus in neoliberal democracies and thrown the social war that always rages beneath state capitalism out into the open to be properly viewed and confronted. From the police killings of civilians, particularly Black and Indigenous people in the US and Canada, to the fascist mobilizations in the wake of Trump, to the more obvious military trappings of policing in municipalities large and small alike. Trenchant new analyses are required to openly, honestly and publicly challenge unprecendented new surveillance regimes which increasingly concern themselves with predictive policing and the development of algorithmic governance and control mechanisms which tighten racial and class profiling, from the constantly shifting redlining of whole neighborhoods down to even personalized, individualized containment.

Criminology has a great opportunity now to shift its positioning within the social war of neoliberal capitalist regimes. It has a chance to situate itself in solidarity with the insurgent criminologists of Black Lives Matter, Idle No More, and the new poor people's movements, anti-borders movements and asylum seekers defense, those organizing inside (or outside support) such as the Prisoners Strike[3] etc. To continue to press for systemic change alongside those many who have struggled for years demanding a full inquiry into the hundreds of Missing and Murdered Indigenous Women, even while we recognize along with them that the current "Terms of Reference" are too vague, and not holding police accountable, and much further action will be necessary.[4]

Criminologists can provide real resources including community material resources (meet-

---

[3]   The prison strike (across US private and public jails) was called for September 9th 2016 (45th anniversary of the Attica Rebellion.) See SupportPrisonerResistance.net or http://iwoc.noblogs.org

[4]   "Coalition Calls Federal Plan for National Inquiry too Vague." http://www.bwss.org/coalition-calls-federal-plan-national-inquiry-vague/

ing space, technology, equipment, etc.) and immaterial resources (analytical skills, software, methodological practices, engaging with processes to access information, making matters of public record, etc.) which can very tangibly support movements. As well criminologists have decades of research and case analysis, practical assessment of alternatives from transformative justice, community safety, community healing, and various approaches in abolition (whether police, prison, or systemic abolition). These can be brought into conversation with insurgent criminologists provided the academic criminologists do so as allies willing to listen to and learn from the insurgents.

AN HONEST REALISM
(AGAINST AN IDEOLOGICAL DISCIPLINE)

Criminology has been in many ways a classically ideological discipline. That is, it has served the dual functions of covering up inequality and injustice while legitimizing or justifying the actions of ruling groups. Criminology does this in part by putting forward various appeals to a "realism" that accepts the existing institutions of criminal justice as proper, appropriate, necessary instruments of security, safety, protection —that is, of justice. Every time criminology accepts state definitions of crime, notions of justice, or forms of punishment it plays an ideological role.

An honest realism, however, is one that pulls no punches in describing, and explaining, the brutality of criminal justice system practices as the everyday, regular, expressions of those systems, not as atypical, irregular, or divergent. Such a realism would not seek to reform systems that, history has shown us, cannot be reformed and, in fact, were designed to do exactly as they are doing. An honest realism would not seek excuses to compromise with such systems and especially would not seek excuses from the political left (as in various forms of left realism). An honest realism would say openly and unflinchingly that to be against police brutality is *at its core* to be against police—given that the institution itself is inherently and thoroughly one of brutality. An honest realism would situate this brutality in the regimes of control, accumulation, exploitation, regulation, and pacification that it upholds, and was always designed to uphold. An honest realism will also recognize and state that the police have always been militarized, rather than militarizing recently, and have been always been deployed to secure social war (for the state and capital) rather than social peace. This is the realism reflected in and expressed by the insurgent criminologists of Black Lives Matter, Idle No More, and the new poor people's movements.

Conclusion

During the recent protests against the killings by police of Alton Sterling and Philando Castille, I was part of a network, mostly community organizers and activists, sending regular reports and criticisms of police across social media. Many were contributing analyses of very high caliber. Interestingly there were two major criminology conferences happening at the same time. So my social media timeline was interspersed, strangely, with messages from academic criminologists (mainly critical and progressive ones) about the fancy conference meals and swank settings, while insurgent criminologists were sending urgent messages of great insight and analysis from the midst of often brutal struggle and direct, systemic mass violence. This was a visual expression of the duality of criminology. The messages of the insurgent criminologists showed where criminology needs to be more fully. In the streets and organizing centers of the neighborhoods. Not in the bistros and ballrooms.

The promise of this moment will relate in part to connections critical criminologists are willing and able to make with insurgent criminologists in the streets and communities. And criminologists must take the initiative of acting to support and defend those whose bodies are quite literally on the line. Criminologists should seek guidance from the movements in terms of resources and labors that are needed and that criminologists might be uniquely capable of providing (research, writing, meeting spaces, popular defense, court defense, anti-ideological work, etc.). Criminologists can look to the recent reaction of librarians who vehemently protested against managerial directives their profession should be "neutral" on Black Lives Matter, reminding all that "At their best, public libraries exist to comfort the afflicted and afflict the comfortable" and of course that "to stay neutral in situations of injustice is to choose the side of the oppressor."[5]

JEFF SHANTZ, AUGUST *2016*,
SURREY, B.C. (UNCEDED COAST SALISH
TERRITORIES)

IF WE WASH OUR HANDS OF
THE CONFLICT BETWEEN THE POWERFUL
AND THE POWERLESS WE SIDE WITH
THE POWERFUL - WE DON'T REMAIN NEUTRAL

Photo: via "Banksy" in Gaza

---

[5] See their "badass tweetstorm" of reaction at #NoNeutralLibraries;
http://aplus.com/a/black-lives-matter-storytime-underground]

[features]

A Radical Grounding for Social Disorganization Theory:
A Political Economic Investigation of the Causes of Poverty, Inequality and Crime in Urban Areas

Michael Lynch
& Lyndsay N. Boggess

This article examines specific observations about crime produced by social disorganization theory (SDT) related to the relationship between urban poverty, inequality and crime, from the perspective of radical criminological. As we note below, the development of radical criminological explanations of crime entered a state of dormancy by the 1990s at the same time that increased attention was being paid to expanding critical alternatives to the kinds of class-based and political economic approaches preferred by radical criminologists in other disciplines. Since 1990, that tendency to shy away from class and political economic analysis has also pro-

duced a lack of critical investigation of orthodox theories of crime and the avoidance of
class-based critiques of those theories. While
this observation applies to all contemporary
orthodox theories (e.g., there has been limited
or no radical critique of life-course theory
[for an exception see Lynch 1996], self-control
theory, developmental theories, general theories [for an exception see, Lynch and Groves,
1995]), it is also applicable to the continued
development of a critique of social disorganization theories of crime (Lynch and Groves
1986; Lynch and Michalowski 2006).

In line with the above observations, the argument below examines how radical criminological theory can be used to critique and extend the assumptions of SDT in ways that are
consistent with a political economic analysis
of the relationship between crime, poverty
and inequality. Of particular concern in this
analysis is an exploration of the association
between poverty, inequality and crime
posited by social disorganization theory,
which marks a useful starting point for a
more radical analysis of these associations.
From a radical perspective, SDT lacks an
analysis of the origins and the distribution of
poverty and inequality in urban areas. That
missing theoretical description can be addressed by the assumptions inherent in political economic approaches used to address the
production of crime.

To be sure, poverty and inequality are two of the more persistent correlates of crime in SDT research, and the ability of radical approaches to explain the differential distribution of poverty and inequality in urban landscapes—an issue that SDT does not address theoretically, and rather begins with the existence of poverty and inequality—extends our ability to conceptualize and understand how capitalism produces crime through the intermediary appearance of visible social and economic outcomes such as poverty and inequality. In short, the focus of this work is explaining the emergence and distribution of poverty and inequality in capitalist societies, their transference to urban space, and their connection to crime. The goal is to radicalize social disorganization theory and capture its many insights in ways that are consistent with a radical explanation of crime. In doing so, we are able to identify the ways in which radical criminology and SDT complement one another.

The primary focus of a radical extension of SDT focuses on providing a political economic explanation of the origins of poverty and inequality. SDT begins with an assumption that in any society, poverty and inequality exists, and that these social factors are distributed unequally within urban areas. With few exceptions (Sampson and Wilson 1995; Sampson 2012; Wilson 1987), SDT does not offer an explanation of the geography of poverty and inequality, and hence cannot explain *why* crime is distributed the way that it is except with reference to the assumed unequal distribution of poverty and inequality. Radical explanations can deepen the arguments of SDT by illustrating how poverty and inequality are produced and distributed within capitalist systems of production and within urban areas in ways that are consistent with and reproduce the structural tendencies of capitalist systems to promote inequality and produce poor, economically marginal populations.

To explore this issue further, we begin with our background assumptions and provide additional support for the type of argument offered here. In the sections that follow, we review the general assumptions of SDT and its findings with respect to poverty, inequality and crime. Next, we begin our discussion of the radicalization of SDT. Finally, we include a discussion of some of the limitations of our argument and suggestions for additional theoretical exposition of a radical perspective on social disorganization.

BACKGROUND

The radical tradition in criminology, by which we mean the preference to employ political economic analysis and structural orientations for the analysis of crime, law and justice, has been largely dormant in the 21st century. To be sure, critical criminology which includes theoretical analysis outside of political economic theory, has rapidly expanded in recent decades. Many of those explanations, however, overlook the relevance of political economic theory for explaining crime, including, for example, the decade long decline in crime (Lynch 2013b), and instead have helped promote a cultural turn in criminology (Farrell, Hayward and Young 2008; Jones 2013; see more generally, Jameson 1998).

Efforts to remedy the neglect of radical criminology and its political economic emphasis have been undertaken in recent years. In addition to the current journal, *Radical Criminology*, a recent issues of the *Journal of Crime and Justice* (2013) calls attention to political economic explanations and to emerging explanations and orientations designed to help reinvigorate radical criminology (Michalowski 2013; Kramer 2013; Lynch 2013b; Carlson et al. 2013; Stretesky et al 2013; Barrett 2013). As noted in articles in the *Journal of Crime and Justice* (Lynch 2013a), the neglect as well as the critique of the radical criminological approaches and the preference for class-based analysis is ideologically situated in orthodox criminological assumptions about the causes of crime. Orthodox critics, for example, have historically rejected the initial assumptions of radical explanations, comparing the theoretical assumptions of radical explanations of crime and justice to the doctrine of communist states. As a consequence, those critiques reject radical criminology both out of hand and ideologically, and fail to appreciate the contributions radical theory can make to explanations of crime and justice. In doing so, a wide variety of orthodox theories reject radical explanations of crime and justice without a thorough-going analysis of its assumptions or the related empirical research (see Lynch, Schwendinger and Schwendinger 2006, for discussion). Criminologists largely avoid radical explanations, and have framed the critiques of that approach around a series dated, largely invalid criticisms (Lynch 2013b). Those criticisms, for example, depict radical explanations as abstract, anti-empirical, as unquantifiable, and questionable because of their assumed political orientations (for review see Lynch and Michalowski 2006). As noted, this type of criticism is dated and has not kept pace with the development or application of radical criminology, and especially its empirical applications to the study of crime (Lynch, Schwendinger and Schwendinger 2006).

While those criticisms have become irrelevant to the nature of more contemporary versions of radical criminology, there are, to be sure, limitations in the radical criminological literature, and those limitations have facilitated the neglect of radical criminology. Chief among those limitations has been the failure to continue a radical critique of orthodox theories of crime that once stood center stage in radical criminology (e.g., Taylor, Walton and Young 1973; Chambliss 1975; Krisberg 1975; Quinney 1980). During the hey-day of radical criminology in the 1970s and 1980s one could locate references to radical criminological approaches in a number of orthodox criminological studies. That is to say, despite the critique of radical criminology that had been developed by orthodox criminologists, orthodox criminologists still made reference to the important insights of radical criminology especially in relation to political economic analysis and discussions of class bias with respect to crime, law and justice, and the role of institutionalized power as an important issue to consider when explaining crime, law and justice. This critique was especially relevant to class bias and the neglect of the crimes of the powerful (Lynch and Michalowski 2006). References to radical criminological literature, however, have largely disappeared from the orthodox criminological literature, and in part, that outcome is a consequence of the neglect of the further development of political economic and class-based explanations and the development of multiple alternative critical criminological approaches that neglect class-based analysis and critique (Lynch 2013b).

To facilitate further development of radical explanations of crime and contribute to reinvigoration of that approach, in the present work we draw attention to political economy and its intersection with one of the major structural approaches employed by orthodox criminologists—social disorganization theory. Following a review of social disorganization theory, we explore how the orthodox version of social disorganization can be attached to more radical theoretical premises, and how doing so changes the nature of social disorganization theory.

Review: The Core Elements of Social Disorganization Theory

Developed from the 1920-1940s, and expanded during the 1980s through the present, social disorganization theory (SDT) has become the major structural explanation for crime, particularly within the context of urban areas from an orthodox criminological perspective. SDT frames its assumptions against historical trends in urban development and industrialization, the nature of urban geography and the distribution of social institutions with respect to visible relations and patterns in the urban landscape. The main features of this explanation are reviewed below.

The origins of social disorganization theory can be traced to several approaches for explaining the origins of urban networks and relationships including the work of Park (1915), Thomas and Znaniecji (1920), Park, Burgess and McKenzie (1925), Thrasher (1927) and Wirth (1928). One of the contemporary versions of social disorganization theory originated when researchers recognized that high crime endured in specific locations within the city despite changes in the population that lived there (Shaw and McKay 1942). Building on this observation, Shaw and McKay (1942) sought to explain crime as a consequence of neighborhood structure, and not as a characteristic of the individuals living there. Specifically, they argued that low economic status, residential instability, and racial/ethnic heterogeneity disrupted forms of community organization necessary for crime control. Whereas socially organized communities are able to establish effective networks of informal social control, structural factors in socially disorganized communities tend to inhibit socialization (but not always, Mazerolle, Wickes and McBroom 2010). As a consequence, social disorganization impedes the formation of common goals among residents and limits the capacity of a neighborhood to control behavior, which contributes to higher rates of crime and delinquency (Kornhauser 1978; Bursik and Grasmick 1993; Kovandzic, Vieratic and Yeisley 1998; Sampson, Raudenbush and Earls 1997).

Research on social disorganization theory has shown a consistent relationship between negative community attributes such as poverty, economic inequality, residential instability and family disruption and high crime rates (e.g., Boggess and Hipp 2010; Krivo and Peterson 1996; Sampson and Groves 1989). In particular, research has focused on the role of poverty and economic inequality, especially as experienced by the Black urban poor. Income inequality can impact crime rates in two primary ways. First, crime will increase as residents in impoverished neighborhoods compare themselves with others who are more affluent or have more resources. As a consequence of this perceived injustice or strain, violent crime may flourish. Second, in general the economic differential among residents leads to reduced interaction and thus lower levels of informal social control necessary to prevent crime, with the exception that impoverished communities with high collective efficacy tend to have lower rates of offending (e.g., Rukus and Warner 2013; Sampson, Raudenbush and Earls 1997; for variations for Latino communities see, Burchfield and Silver 2013; for rejection in Netherlands see Bruinsma et al. 2013). Indeed, Hipp (2007) determined that overall income inequality is associated with higher crime rates, especially violent crime. Sampson and Wilson (1995) recognize that the brunt of this violence is borne out by poor Blacks who are more likely to live in economically and socially disadvantaged neighborhoods when compared to Whites.

Radicalizing Social Disorganization Theory

Above, we reviewed the core elements of SDT. That approach offers a rich inspection of various factors that contribute to crime at the geographic level. SDT is a structural explanation to the extent that it focuses on the distribution of structural manifestations of social arrangements within geographic space, or how larger economic relations are reflected and distributed in urban geography. Largely missing from the SDT explanation of the factors that produce crime, however, is a theoretical explanation of the sources of disorganization that explores how larger structural forces shape urban ecology and the appearance of disorganization. One exception is Sampson and Wilson (1995) who argued that macrostructural forces shaped cities by concentrating black poverty in the city center. Though the authors briefly discuss governmental policies that contributed to urban decay and planned segregation such as deindustrialization, white-flight, lax code enforcement, and the construction of freeways and public housing in predominantly black neighborhoods, they do not fully explore the motivations of these governmental decisions from a radical perspective. As Lynch and Michalowski (2006) previously argued, it is by grafting a larger political economic explanation onto SDT that a more contextualized and structural explanation of SDT can be created to explain the origins of social disorganization.

In taking such an approach to the impact of social disorganization on crime, we begin with an assumption that the empirical results produced by social disorganization research studies are valid, and that the findings of that view have utility for explaining crime and its distribution. What we seek, then, is a radical explanation for the empirical facts produced by SDT that connects those results to political economic relations and organization—that is, to the broader political economic structure of capitalism.

In taking this approach to crime and social disorganization, our work is informed by what we hold out as one of the most noteworthy modern theoretical arguments on the production of radical social theory, C. Wright Mills' (1959) *The Sociological Imagination*. Drawing on the classical sociological tradition, Mills argued that adequate social explanations must pay attention to the role social structure plays in organizing social life. With respect to the SDT tradition, that means being able to explain the urban processes that impact crime develop (i.e., poverty and inequality), and being able to situate the forms of social disorganization that develop and in which people are enmeshed within the core relations found within a social system's economic, political and social arrangement. Below, we illustrate how this can be accomplished to create a political economic explanation of SDT in ways that provide radical criminologists the opportunity to explain the missing connections in SDT—the unequal geographic distribution of social disorganization—opening the opportunity for radicals to contribute to that structural orientation for explaining crime.

THE POLITICAL ECONOMY OF POVERTY AND INEQUALITY

Two important concepts in SDT that have long been associated with the geographic distribution of social disorganization and crime are poverty and inequality. Missing from that empirical set of observations, however, is the rationale that explains *the origins* of poverty and economic inequality. In other words, SDT takes the existence of poverty and inequality as a starting point for empirically analyzing how those conditions relate to crime, and offers only a very general observation that poverty and inequality are related to the process of industrialization (for an exception, see Sampson and Wilson 1995). What SDT fails to offer, however, is an explanation for the existence of poverty and economic inequality, the distribution of poverty and inequality throughout geographic space, and how industrialization generates poverty and economic inequality. Such an explanation of the origins of poverty and inequality is central to radical theory, and it is by referring to political economic theory that the geographic distribution of poverty and inequality and the origin of poverty and inequality can be explained. In this more radically oriented approaches, SDT provides the superstructure of the explanation (the empirical evidence of the visible relationship outcomes between crime, poverty and inequality, or social disorganization and crime), while political economic theory contributes the infrastructure for the explanation—the explanation of the origins of poverty and inequality within the normal operation of a capitalist economy.

In order to frame this type of radical explanation of crime, we must begin with the following questions: why are people poor? And why are economic resources unequally distributed? There is no general explanation to those questions, since the factors that produce poverty and economic inequality vary across historical eras and are different for unique forms of economic relations, and emerge in different ways within any urban area. Thus, to narrow those conditions, any radical/political economic explanation of poverty and economic inequality must begin by first specifying the structural conditions to which the explanation applies. Here, we select as our historical frame of reference contemporary capitalism, and note that our explanation is, therefore, relative to locations in where capitalism is the primary form of economic, political and social organization.

Having selected capitalist economies as the starting point for our analysis, we must turn to Marx's (1974) theory of capitalism to expose and understand the origins of poverty and inequality in capitalist systems of production. Generally, Marx's theory of capitalism (1974) remains the most appropriate theoretical explanation for the general organization of capitalism and the processes and effects of capitalist production. In the Marxist view, capitalism is based on the inherent existence and need for inequality between classes, first at the level of ownership of the means of production. The proposition that the means of production are unequally distributed in a capitalist system is not simply an assumption, it is an empirical observation concerning how ownership of production is actually distributed within capitalist systems of production. Empirically, this means that a small portion of the population owns the majority of the stake in the productive mechanisms found within society. A number of studies confirm this observation with respect to ownership patterns in capitalist nations (Wolff 2002; Thompson 2012).

Ownership inequality is related to other forms of economic inequality found within society. Thus, for example, it can be illustrated that inequality in ownership is related to inequality in both income and wealth (Autor, Katz and Kearney 2008). These latter forms of inequality, however, are merely expressions of the more general form of inequality related to the ownership of the means of production, and do not themselves serve as a sufficient explanation of the structural processes and dynamics that promote and maintain inequality in the first instance. To be sure, the existence of these additional forms of economic inequality such as income and wealth inequality are important to the reproduction and extension of inequality more generally within a capitalist system (Peet 1975). That is to say, income and wealth inequality reinforce ownership inequality, and are empirical indicators of the extent of inequality. They are not, however, in themselves the causes of inequality, but rather are consequences of other forms of structural inequality inherent in capitalist systems of production.

In order to explain the origins of inequality in capitalist systems of production, we must refer to Marx's argument that inequality in ownership of the means of production is, in the first instance, a necessary requirement of capitalist economic relationships. Capitalism cannot exist within out this form of class inequality. In other words, in a definitional sense, identifying capitalism requires that the means of production is unequally distributed. This inequality is not only a class based relationship between the owners and non-owners of the means of production, it is one that must, by its nature, extend throughout society. The nature of capitalist inequality requires that it extends to other productive, social and political relations as well. This means that inequality is, for example, expressed in work relations between the classes with respect to the control of the labor process, and with respect to the unequal distribution of the proceeds of production. The secret behind this latter part of the explanation concerning the unequal distribution of the proceeds of production is found in the Marxist theory of surplus value under conditions of capitalism.

To begin, it is necessary to state the obvious: that the goal of capitalist production is to generate profit, and not only to generate profit, but for the owners of production to maintain the majority of the profit generated from production—that is, for income from production to be unequally distributed. In a capitalist system, the generation of profits hinges on the ability of the capitalist to exploit labor, or as Marx (1974) also noted, to extract surplus value from the laboring class. In simple terms, surplus value is the excess value labor produces above the wages it receives for labor. It is this labor surplus that comes to define the nature and extent of inequality between classes within society.

Modern reinterpretations of the extraction of surplus value linked to Marxist ecology or Marxist ecological economics (Foster 2000; Foster, Clark and York 2010; Burkett 2005), helps us appreciate that this process begins with the exploitation of nature. That is to say, human labor cannot be exploited unless nature's labor is first exploited by extracting the raw materials for production from nature. While this approach for understanding the entire process of exploitation in capitalist systems has relevance to other applications of radical criminology (Stretesky, Long and Lynch 2013), especially those related to the production of ecological destruction in capitalist economies, for the present work we need to simply acknowledge that capitalism must also exploit nature without probing that argument extensively as it bear little relevance to the explanation of crime in the SDT approach (see below for additional comments on this point related to the definition of crime).

Beginning with the exploitation of nature, the capitalist seeks to extend the exploitation process by extracting surplus labor from the working class by manipulating various aspects of the process of production (Marx 1974). The relevance of this argument to radical criminology has been previously established with respect to crime and punishment (Lynch 1987, 1988, 2010; Lynch, Groves and Lizotte 1994). To summarize this view, the capitalist extracts surplus labor from the worker, paying the worker less than the value of the labor performed (Marx 1974). In short, the worker receives less in wages than the value of the labor they applied and the value of the commodity they produce. The surplus labor the worker generated becomes part of the price of the commodity. When sold, the capitalist retains the surplus valued realized from the sale of the commodity. The proportion of the retained surplus value, or the rate of surplus value extracted from the labor process, contributes to the production of economic inequality (e.g., income and wealth differentials) between the capitalist and the worker.

POVERTY

Above, we have illustrated how radical economic explanations locate one source of economic inequality in the basic functional operation of the capitalist process—the extraction of surplus value. In this section, we turn our attention to poverty, another important empirical correlate of crime in the SDT approach.

In radical economics, poverty outcomes emerge from any number of operational processes associated with capitalism. One such process is economic marginalization, which is also driven by the capitalist's interest in profit and the process through which surplus value is extracted from the labor force. Here, we must also introduce the concept of the organic composition of capital (g), which is the ratio of technical to variable capital (c), or the value composition of capital comprised of expenditures on machinery, raw materials, rent and other expenses, versus the proportion spent on labor (variable capital, v). Following Marx's description, the organic composition of capital, g, is equal to c/v, and provides an objective means of measuring the organization of capital's distribution.

Theoretically, the organic composition of capital is important because it impacts the extraction of surplus value. In an effort to drive up the proportion of surplus value extracted from the labor process, the capitalist invests in labor saving technology (c), driving up investment in the technical component of capital relative to investment in its variable component (v). Theoretically, the result is that as the capitalist invests more in technical capital, less variable capital investment is required to either produce the same volume or a greater volume of commodities (the exception is when both c and v rise while g rises). In other words, investment in technical capital including machinery increases the productivity of the workforce, and requires less investment in labor to generate the same or an expanding volume of product. Over time, investment in technical capital leads to a reduction in the need for labor, producing unemployment. In the long run of capitalism, this expansion of unemployment means that fewer workers are required for production, and a permanent level of unemployment is established once capitalism matures, producing a permanent marginal population. That unemployed population is not simply out of work, they are unemployable or economically marginal because there is an insufficient volume of work available. This means that the marginal population cannot obtain work because the volume of work has been diminished by investment in labor saving technology. It is from the extraction of surplus value and manipulation of the organic composition of capital, then, that the marginal population emerges, and from which the ranks of the poor are formed.

This process reoccurs continually throughout the history of a capitalist economy, and cycles within and across the stage of the social structure of accumulation found within a capitalist system that manifests itself at any point in time (Carlson and Michalowski 1997). Thus, over time, we *may* see poverty cycles related to economic marginalization. That is, poverty may, under certain conditions, increase or decrease over time. But, despite the rise and fall of poverty, the overall trend in poverty under capitalism is one of rising poverty, and each successive social structure of accumulation fails to reduce poverty to its previous level. Thus, while poverty may fall within a given segment of a social structure of accumulation (SSA), over the long run or across SSAs it should rise or drift upward (whether or not it does so is an empirical question). This is difficult to illustrate with official data on poverty given that the official poverty rate may not be an adequate indicator of the extent of poverty, and that such measures may not align appropriately with the Marxian description of this process.

Tʜᴇ Gᴇᴏɢʀᴀᴘʜʏ ᴏғ Pᴏᴠᴇʀᴛʏ ᴀɴᴅ Iɴᴇϙᴜᴀʟɪᴛʏ

From the perspective of political economy, one of the limitation of SDT and especially its intellectual roots in the Chicago School of Sociology is that it SDT is "so deeply immersed in free market reasoning that its practitioners seem not to have been aware that there was even an alternative approach" to urban geography and human ecology (Logan and Luskin 2007, 4). In making that point, Logan and

Luskin draw attention to alternative political economic explanations of urban geography. Despite various critiques of urban geography posited by those employing political economic explanations, the essential Marxist argument that urban geography is a reflection of class conflict and struggle and suggests an alternative starting point for the analysis of the urban landscape and relations (Castree 1999) has not been widely adopted generally, and has been completely absent from criminological examinations of urban relations.

With respect to Marxist political urban ecology, a defining work is Castells's (1977), *The Urban Question: A Marxist Approach.* Not easily summarized due to its length and complex detail, one of the important political economic observations offered by Castells was that the city is the spatial expression of larger political economic relationships that define capitalism as a system of production. Following Castells, it can be argued that the physical space of the city reflects the forms of class conflict, class exploitation, power relations between classes, and the organizational routine of the capitalist system of economic production in which an urban area is located. In sum, we can say that under capitalism urban spaces are, in other words, divided along the same lines as capitalist economic relations and express the vertical forms of power found within capitalism horizontally or across the plane of urban space.

As noted earlier, SDT has no underlying explanation for the physical structure of urban centers. Originally guided by the well-known concentric zone model and assumptions about the growth of organisms borrowed from biological sciences, Chicago School researchers depicted the city as an organism with different phases of growth. The center of the city as an organism was the business sector, and all other aspects of the city as organism were depicted as being arranged around this center. Each area of the urban center is, we suggest, "taken for granted" in this view, meaning that the SDT approach begins with rather than explains why the city has different ecological segments.

Historically, this view of the city was developed from concentric zone models developed from observations made by early Chicago School researchers on the city of Chicago. The concentric zone model itself is a description of urban space in Chicago, and is not universally evident in other urban areas. That is to say, other urban growth and organizational patterns are seen across cities (Harris 1997) and there is nothing inherently advantageous to the traditional concentric zone approach to urban organization.

In light of Castells's observations about capitalism and urban space briefly reviewed above and observations produced by SDT in relation to crime, we are now in a position to describe the geography of cities and the production of crime as an expression of economic relationships. Here, we pay particular attention to geography and crime in relation to poverty and inequality since these are the central empirical predictors of crime in the SDT tradition.

Urban Geography, Poverty and Inequality in a Radical Perspective

To begin, it is important to note that as we argued above, poverty and inequality in various forms (i.e., economic, access to production, income, wealth, and political) are outcomes generated by the organizational structure of capitalism. That is to say, within a capitalist system, the normal operation of the system of capitalist production generates forms of poverty and inequality that do not otherwise simply exist as a natural consequence of human social organization. Rather, within capitalist economies, the organization of urban areas reflects the organizational nature of capitalism. Thus, we do not begin with poverty and inequality as givens as SDT does, but as we illustrated above, must first demonstrate how capitalism produces poverty and inequality. Since we have already undertaken that task, the issue that remains is to explore concerns related to the geography of poverty and inequality in the urban landscape, and their intersection with crime.

There is nothing in the theory of capitalism which states that poverty and inequality must be located in specific places within the urban geography of a city. That is to say, the exact location of poverty and inequality cannot be explained as necessarily emerging in a given location or space within urban areas. What this view suggests is that urban poverty and inequality must result from the progression of capitalism, and that specific urban locations become the physical locations of poverty and inequality in capitalism's urban geography. How poverty and inequality are distributed within any specific urban location requires knowledge concerning the historical development of capitalism in a given location. Nevertheless, some general observations on this point can be offered.

For example, urban poverty and inequality are likely to be located near industrial locations since these areas, as SDT notes, take on the appearance of disorder relative to other forms of organization in the urban space of capitalism. Over time, these disorganized areas can move, expand and recede depending on how the capitalist form of production within any urban location changes and how capital is invested and reinvested within urban area within different eras of capitalism's development. One can expect, however, a long term association between the geography of poverty, inequality and class in urban spaces within a capitalist system. Under capitalism, the hierarchy of class power tends to be replicated across urban space, creating identi-

fiable urban spaces where poverty and inequality stand out.

Like classes, power, production and other
dimensions of the economic relations of capitalism, poverty and inequality *must exist*
within capitalism. Moreover, poverty and inequality exist within capitalism as outcomes
of and mechanisms for replicating the nature
of capitalist order and its inherent tendency
toward inequality. As a result, poverty and inequality must be unevenly distributed within
urban space so that the hierarchy of capitalist
relations can be made visible and social
groups can be differentiated and regulated
differently (i.e., in relation to concepts of
power and discipline as described by Foucault
1979). Moreover, as some suggest, these visible
signs of group differentiation are also expressed in the psychological attitudes and
perspectives of members of the working class
(Sennett and Cobb 1972). We can conceptualize this spatial distribution of poverty and inequality as one of the dimensions of the horizontal, multi-directional plane of power that
replicates the vertical axis of class or economic power in a capitalist economy. In this
view, the spatial distribution of poverty and
inequality reinforces vertical power (the class
hierarchy of capitalism), but is laid out across
the landscape of the city. In terms of income,
for example, poverty occupies the lowest
space on the vertical distribution of incomes
for all residents and classes within an urban
area, and geographically, the urban poor are

isolated by their lack of economic, political and social power within urban geography. Geographically, however, the spatial dynamics of poverty can be dispersed and may be widely or narrowly distributed in any urban location depending on how class struggle and urban space intersect with one another within the historical context of a given urban location as affected by the development of capitalism in specific cities. This means that any discussion of the spatial dynamic of poverty (or inequality) within an urban area will tend toward abstraction where it is not tied to the specific historical dynamics of an identifiable urban location. In the present discussion, we have chosen to stick to this more abstract discussion rather than attempt to illustrate our points with respect to any particular urban location.

POVERTY AND URBAN GEOGRAPHY

Geographically, as anyone familiar with any urban location can attest, pockets of poverty form in urban centers. These are the physical locations of the most impoverished members of an urban area—the economically marginalized—where the capitalist landscape separates the economically marginal from the remainder of the population, and to which the signs of poverty become attached, confined and segregated. The poor are not segregated in these locations by choice, as these locations certainly contain the most undesirable conditions with the fewest resources and opportunities for employment and healthy lifestyles or as meaningful locations for achieving human potential (Sennett and Cobb 1972). As a result, these areas constitute locations no one would choose given a real choice concerning where to live. In this view, the poor do not cluster together, as some early or even latter cultural theories linked to some SDT research might suggest, because of their shared values, norms, beliefs and cultures (i.e., as in the lower class subculture of poverty, Banfield 1970; Hyman 1977; Lewis 1963, 1968; Rainwater 1970). Rather, the poor cluster together and become fragmented into these enclaves of poverty because this is where they can afford to live in the urban landscape of capitalism. That among the poor, ethnic minorities may cluster together is certainly an empirical fact. Yet, the clustering of the ethnic or immigrant-poor is not evidence of the power of culture to draw together people with similar values, but rather is evidence of the power of economic organization as the key structuring force behind residential segregation in urban areas. Significant evidence of income, class and racial segregation exists in the US, for example, with studies indicating an increase in class segregation over time (Fischer 2003). Some portion of class and race segregation is due to neoliberal policies or policies of the welfare state (see chapters in Musterd and Ostendorf 2013), indicating the potential for further development of Wacquant's (2012, 2011, 2009) analysis of the neoliberal state and the punishment of poverty as one path for redirecting radical criminological explanations of crime.

It is in the urban neighborhoods of the poor, where, indeed, social disorganization (and as certain forms of social control) is the greatest. But, this cluster of poverty is not a form of social disorganization caused by the "culture of the poor," but rather the manifestation of the organizational forces of capitalism. On this point, some versions of social disorganization theory misinterpret the empirical evidence concerning the concentration of poverty in urban areas. This is a mistake that some, such as Shaw and McKay, did not make. Rather, as Shaw and McKay (1942) noted in their analysis of crime, when the immigrants who once occupied a disorganized area move from those locations, crime does not follow but remains in the disorganized communities immigrants leave behind. This would imply that it is not the culture of those populations that produces and organizes crime, but rather the economic context in which they were situated and the disorganized nature of capitalism as manifest in the segregation of the urban poor. What remains the same about those disorganized, high crime areas despite who lives there is that they continue to reflect the forms of disorganization capitalism produces, and despite who lives in those areas, continues to produce crime as a consequence of the economic disorganization found in those areas promoted by capitalism.

As described above, in the ordinary path of its development capitalism produces an economically marginal population. As a productive system, not only does capitalism produce the economically marginal, it also produces conditions that maintain that population in marginal economic circumstances and in segregated communities. In this way, capitalism produces a surplus of labor and a surplus laboring population that depresses the wage rate as far as possible (theoretically, as close to the minimum as possible, with the minimum being defined by the subsistence wage relative to other prevailing economic conditions, Marx 1974). Moreover, as Castells indicates, the physical location of the poor in areas of concentrated poverty allows the poor to also be used for ideological purposes—to spread a message about poverty to the working class to facilitate their compliance with the requirements of capitalism, and to create negative messages about their fate should they fail to work hard and adhere to disciplinary regimes (see also Wacquant 2009).

The ideological use of the poor is not limited to its ability to persuade those with work to work harder, and to value employment. In his influential book, *The Undeserving Poor*, Katz (1989) argues that the vocabulary of poverty that identifies mainstream political discussions has "channeled discourse about need, entitlement and justice within the narrow limits bounded by the market" (1). He goes on to suggest that "these historic preoccupations have shaped and confined ideas about poor people and distributive justice in recent American history" (1989, 1). This description of the poor, however, is not merely a discourse, but a practice. As a practice, political discourse about the poor regulates the physical space the poor are allowed to occupy within urban areas. Isolated in their "pockets of poverty," the poor serve an ideological purpose for the system of capitalist production. The poor are maintained in their geographic space where they are isolated and serve as example of the consequences of failing to abide by the disciplinary regimes of capitalism (Foucault 1979). They are periodically rediscovered, made visible, and interpreted as deserving of capital investment when the system of production experiences a legitimation crisis (e.g., see Habermas 1975) and needs to use images of the poor to maintain its legitimacy (Zurn and Leibfried 2005) or when it needs to transition the marginal population into employment when the labor market is tight and wages are rising, as in welfare-work state mechanisms (Esping-Andersen 2006).

In orthodox criminological theory, the existence of the poor in the urban landscape is typically accepted as a normal condition, and simply as the modern expression of the historical tendency for a population of the poor to exist in urban areas across various types of economic and social organization (Katz 1989). That view of the ever-presence of the poor is now so widespread, even in academic literature, that it seems natural to imagine that the poor are a required part of the urban landscape (Katz 1989), and that all societies have been burdened by the poor, or that poverty is a natural state of human existence. To the contrary, this image of the poor which is promoted in modern times and especially by orthodox economics is far from true when one considers the anthropological evidence of the poor across historical epochs. One of the most influential works on this subject, Marshall Sahlin's (1972) *Stone Age Economics*, posits that circumstance such as poverty as conceived in modern times was largely unknown in the original affluent society of the hunter-gatherer. In opposition to the modern assumption that human nature produces unlimited wants and patterns of behavior that make some individuals "lazy" and therefore poor, employing evidence from hunting-gathering societies, Sahlins suggests that the reverse is true among hunter-gatherers: there are limited wants amidst the bounty provided by nature, and human wants are easily met leaving significant leisure time and the general absence of poverty. This empirical observation about equity and poverty in hunter-gatherer life is opposed by the stereotype of the brutish conditions others assert to have existed in pre-modern societies, including, for example, the constant need to search for food to ensure survival that has often been described in other literature (for discussion see, Stoczkowski 2002). According to Sahlins, in the hunter-gatherer society, poverty in the modern sense is unknown. Thus, we can conclude that in contrast to the social form in which humans lived the vast majority of their existence (hunting-gathering), the poor are a product of more modern settlements in which ownership has become a central feature of access to the means of production, and that the poor are produced and reproduced by capitalism.

In the radical view, the emergence of urban poverty is not the result of deficiencies in cultures, values and norms; it is not the product of human nature; it is not, as, Edward Banfield (1958, 1970), Oscar Lewis (1963, 1968) and a generation of scholars and politicians argued, a consequence of a culture of poverty, of personal preferences for isolation, or the lack, as some criminologists might argue imbuing these antiquated ideas with modern currency, of impulse controls (for a critique and empirical analysis on some of these points see, Grove and Corrado 1983). Rather, in the approach taken here, poverty is an essential feature of the political economy of capitalism, and some portion of the population is plunged into poverty by the ordinary development of capitalism and isolated into disorganization and poor neighborhoods, not by their preference for poverty or culture, but by the very nature of capitalist political economic arrangements. In this view, poverty is not an indicator of some individual pathology, but rather is a structural deficiency produced by capitalism.

Inequality and Urban Geography

The explanation of the geography of inequality is much the same as the explanation of poverty as far as political economy is concerned. Inequality is a core feature of capitalism, and the vertical hierarchy of capitalist inequality or its class structure is, like poverty, distributed across the space of the city and reappears in the horizontal space built by capitalism as a reflection of its class (vertical) hierarchy of power. In the SDT view, the distribution of inequality is taken as the nature of things—that is, as a real, existing phenomenon that is taken as real by its very existence and requires no special explanation of its origins. If an explanation of inequality is offered by this type of orthodox view it is that inequality may reflect and result from variations in human ability, aptitude, hard work or perseverance. Such a view of inequality provides an individual level explanation for a structural problem and constitutes an ecological fallacy in this type of explanation.

In contrast, in the radical political economy view the origin of inequality in the modern city is associated with the inherent forms of structural inequality required and produced by capitalism. Thus, in the structural view of political economy, inequality is not interpreted as reflecting the characteristics of individuals, but rather the characteristics and structure of capitalism. Inequality, in this view is part of the basic organization and nature of capitalism. Thus, because capitalism generates inequality, that inequality must be distributed unequal across both the vertical hierarchy (e.g., the division between owners and workers; between the wealthy and the impoverished, etc.) and horizontal planes (the geography) of capitalism (Browett 1984; Peet 1975). As prior research indicates, spatial inequality may also reflect other aspects of capitalism such as the mobility of capital and different types of capital (Walker 1978), as well as the effects of class struggle and labor struggles (Strope and Walker 1983). The latter observations imply that it is important to acknowledge that labor struggles and responses to labor struggles and class conflict can shape both the vertical and horizontal nature of inequality in any particular system of capitalism and any given urban areas. These, then, are additional issues that a radical political economy addresses which are omitted in the traditional SDT approach and which have important ramifications for not only understanding the distribution of inequality in urban areas, but the forces that transform urban inequality.

In short, the city's division into unequal regions where inequality, poverty or wealth are contained and isolated or where resources are unequally distributed, is not a mere empirical fact about the geography of the city. Rather, that form of urban geography is a consequence of the distributional requirements of capitalism, and urban space is the spatial manifestation of the inherent forms of inequality capitalism produces. In this view, capital itself cannot be evenly spread across the space of the urban landscape when it is unevenly spread across classes or other divisions within a capitalist system of production (Peet 1975).

From Capitalism to Crime

If SDT correctly identifies the ways in which poverty, inequality and crime are related, this is the result of the fact that the empirical distribution of poverty and inequality reflects the vertical structure of capitalism in ways that are not perceived by SDT itself. That is to say, SDT empirically identifies the real outcomes or the reality of how poverty and inequality is distributed in relation to crime, but not because it uses a theoretical position that accurately describes how poverty and inequality should be distributed in urban areas or because it forwards a theory concerning the origins and dispersion of inequality and poverty. In other words, the empirical results from SDT research sit well with the theoretical expectations generated from a radical criminological and political economic perspective, but not for theoretical reasons.

This outcome—the ability of SDT to theoretically link poverty, inequality and crime to the political economic structure of society—is somewhat of an "empirical accident" from the theoretical vantage point of political economic theory. This empirical accident results from the fact that SDT correctly identifies how the outcomes produced by capitalism such as poverty and inequality are distributed and contribute to street crime in urban locations. Thus, it is clear that empirically, SDT research shows a connection between poverty, inequality and crime, yet at the same time fails to explain the forces that produce poverty and inequality or explain why these negative consequences of capitalism are unevenly distributed in the urban space of capitalism. In short, this correct empirical finding is not the result of SDT's *correct theoretical identification* of the causes of poverty and inequality, for on that account, SDT fails to specify the forces that cause poverty and inequality to emerge in the first instance, or which force it to be distributed in some manner. As noted above, SDT assumes the existence of poverty and inequality, and beginning with that assumption and those outcomes (the existence of poverty and inequality) constructs a useful explanation of the links between poverty, inequality and crime. In this sense, the SDT explanation of crime is much like an explanation of climate change which states that an increase in temperature produces climate change, leaving the causes

of temperature increases unidentified and un-
explained.

In contrast to the SDT view, a radical analysis allows the causes of poverty and inequality
to be identified. In the radical view, it is insufficient to suggest that poverty and inequality exist, or that they are related to crime.
What is important in the radical view is to explain how poverty and inequality are, in the
first place, produced by political economic arrangements, and how those political-economic arrangements sets the rest of the
process—the production of crime—in motion. In addition, because the radical view of
social disorganization and crime is also much
different than the SDT view, both lead to
quite different policy implications. SDT approaches would hold poverty and inequality
reduction programs as essential elements that
could be employed to reduce crime, a natural
choice from the SDT view since this is the beginning of the explanations of crime. These
poverty reductions programs might include
investing resources in poor and unequal urban locations, and to be sure, such policies
have had better success than the individual
level forms of reform suggested by other orthodox approaches to crime.

To some, the radical policy approach would
appear to suggest the same things as the SDT
view—that is to say, poverty and inequality
reduction policies. This, however, would be a
misinterpretation of the radical policy impli-

cations related to crime control (Lynch and Michalowski 2006). In the radical view, the central policy issue would be related to addressing the cause of poverty and inequality, not the appearance of poverty and inequality. In the radical view, to change the causes or appearance of poverty and inequality requires altering the basic political economic relations behind the causes of poverty and inequality—that is, reconfiguring political economic relationships. That means transitioning beyond capitalism and its inherent forms of inequality. Radicals understand that you cannot invest in impoverished neighborhoods and expect that those policies will be sufficient to transform poverty and inequality in the long run. Why? Because of the way the system of production and ownership is organized, the tendency of the political economic arrangement will be to re-create poverty and inequality. Eventually, the force of political economic organization will undo efforts to create surface equity, and this must be so because the capitalist system of production is based on promoting inequality in the first place. Thus, while SDT draws attention to the correct concerns (poverty and inequality), the lack of an explanation for poverty and inequality in the SDT view leads to policies that will have only short-term effects on crime.

The observations offered above should not be taken to imply that the surface associations between crime and poverty and inequality are irrelevant and unrelated. Rather, for radicals what is more relevant than the empirical association between crime/poverty/inequality is the explanation of the origins of poverty and inequality and therefore crime in the organization of capitalism's political economic relationships. If, for example, poverty and inequality produce crime, this relationship only exists because it is produced by capitalism. That these relational intersections make sense in the context of capitalism's political economy is not surprising. Whether the poor steal because they are deprived and want, as Engels (1845) described in his analysis of the working class in England, or whether one accepts more contemporary expressions of similar ideas in absolute and relative deprivation theories (Blau and Blau 1982) is in itself rather irrelevant to a more radical theoretical description of the causes of poverty and inequality, and how those processes are endemic to capitalism.

Limitations and Future Research

No explanation of crime is so well specified that it is without its limitations. The current discussion of a political economic model of urban crime, or the radical political economic approach to SDT taken here, is limited by two primary conditions. First, the argument built here was designed as an example of one way in which radical criminological explanations can be employed to deepen the underlying assumptions of SDT. As noted, SDT contains no theory that explains the distribution of social relations such as poverty and inequality within urban space. SDT simply accepts that poverty and inequality are empirical outcomes of the dispersion of social relations across urban areas. While we have attempted to illustrate how the distribution of poverty and inequality in urban spaces is impacted by political economic relations, one weakness of our argument is that its focus is limited to only these two dimensions of SDT explanations of crime and does not address other issues, such as collective efficacy, that have become more common to specific applications of social disorganization theory (Sampson, Raundenbush and Earls 1997). Additional theoretical discussion, therefore, is needed to address other aspects of SDT and the political economic foundations of other social forces such as the distribution of, for example, formal and informal social control within urban space. On this point, we suggest that the work of Foucault (1979) can be of some use. Of particular relevance in that work is Foucault's analysis of discipline, and the role social institutions play in rendering bodies docile. Geographically, docile bodies can be expected to have specific locations within urban space depending on the density of social relations and institutional mechanisms employed to render bodies docile. Thus, where formal and informal social control is "thickest," the likelihood of bodies being rendered docile is greatest. One should not, however, confuse this idea with the more traditional criminological assumption that the density of social control is best measured by criminal justice mechanisms alone. Indeed, from the perspective of Foucault, one could argue that the spatial distribution of criminal justice control is inversely related to dominant forms of social control that are associated with the "ordinary routines" of political economic organization that generate the overall disciplinary regime of capitalism and how that disciplinary regime is carried out in various social institutions and social relationships. Thus, where political economic organization is at its weakest, such as in zones where poverty is prevalent and areas where inequality is great, supplemental social control such as the form of social control offered by criminal justice mechanisms will be greatest. It should also be noted that these observations are empirically testable, and that future research can address the empirical utility of this view and could be related to arguments about collective efficacy—that is to normative social networks. Doing so, however, is beyond the scope of the current analysis, and requires extensive discussion beyond the space available for this discussion. Here, too, one might weave in Wacquant's (2012, 2011, 2009) views on the association between poverty and social control.

Second, because our argument is designed as an extension of SDT, we have accepted the SDT argument without devoting any extensive criticisms to its assumptions. On this point, one of the primary criticisms that ought to be exposed is that in the SDT tradition, crime is defined as an offense against the criminal law. As radicals well know, that criticism implies that there are a wide range of offenses that SDT does not address. From a radical perspective, most important among these offenses is the exclusion of a range of crimes committed by the powerful: white collar crime, corporate crime, green crimes, and state and state-corporate crimes. Social disorganization theories do not apply to these behaviors, and have limited utility for explaining these behaviors to the extent that they only address the distribution of street crime within urban space. At the same time, however, there is sufficient reason to believe that a radical revision of SDT could be constructed to account for these omitted offenses. That is to say, since radical theory offers an explanation of the political economic of urban space, it can also be used to specify conditions and the expected locations of the crimes of the powerful. Elucidating that explanation, however, is the subject for future research. Clearly, one can state, for example, that the distribution of green crimes will cluster around industries, and that those most affected by green crimes will be the working and marginal classes as well as racial and ethnic minorities—observations that have already been well supported by environmental justice research (for a criminological discussion, see, Burns, Lynch and Stretesky 2008).

Final, one might argue that the theoretical explanation developed here is insufficient to the extent that it fails to address the long term relationship between poverty, economic inequality and crime, and especially the fact that over the past two decades there has been world-wide evidence of falling crime rates despite the continued production of inequality and poverty. Addressing that issue is no small task, and doing so requires, as Lynch (2013b) has suggested, revising some of the general political economic assumptions of radical criminology and addressing how political economic relations have changed and altered the relationship between poverty, inequality and crime over time. Second, in the present work, we have focused attention on the spatial relationship between crime, poverty and inequality, and evidence on that account does not suggest that these spatial relationships have changed. The fact that over time the relationship between poverty, inequality and crime changes should not be startling, and one could argue, is not outside of political economic analysis since it is not necessarily poverty and inequality themselves that generate crime from a political economic perspective. Crime is, as we have noted above, "produced," meaning that it is an interaction of circumstances that can generate (but does not always do so) crime through the interaction of forces that cause crime, the construc-

tion and application of law, and forms of social control (such as policing and other mechanism that control the poor). Additional effort
is required to work towards such an explanation that begins with the political economic
analysis of social disorganization theory reviewed in this work. It is possible that the intersection of these factors varies over time
and may require the kinds of social structures
of accumulation arguments Carlson and
Michalowski (1997) apply to explain the varia-
tion in the relationship between unemployment and crime across the historical development of capitalism.

CONCLUSION

One of the contributions radical criminology made to the criminological literature
during its emergence was a through-going
critique of orthodox theories of crime. The
primary form of critique radical criminology
posed was of the class-bias prevalent in orthodox theories. Since those early critiques, a
more extensive critique of orthodox criminology failed to develop sufficiently and has
not been widely applied to the scope of orthodox theories that now exist within criminology.

In the present work we have explored the
extension of a radical critique of orthodox
criminology from a radical perspective, drawing on the suggestion that such a critique can
help both strengthen the radical analysis of

crime and contribute to new radical explanations of crime, some of which have the potential to re-direct orthodox theories and perhaps undermine their arguments (e.g., Lynch and Michalowski 2006; Lynch and Groves 1986). Here, we have taken up that approach focusing our analysis on social disorganization theory.

As noted above, one of the trends that limited the development of a more extensive radical critique of orthodox criminological theory was the development of alternative critical criminological approaches which largely abandoned class analysis. In the context of more contemporary critical versions of criminology and the shift away from radical criminology, the critique of class bias in orthodox theories was lost, and further refinement of radical critiques of orthodox theories failed to appear in the criminological literature. In place of more developed radical critiques of orthodox criminological theories, critical criminologists tended to introduce much more abstract critiques of orthodox theory, many of which drew upon post-modern approaches of various types. The relevance of those more abstract critical criminological critiques were essentially lost on orthodox criminological theorists who began to ignore the critical criminological critique of orthodox criminology (Lynch 2013b). In the end, the in-roads made by radical criminology through class-based analysis seem to have been undermined by the development of the more abstract critique posed by critical criminology since the early 1990s.

Above, we have attempted to return to the radical critique of orthodox criminology initiated in the 1970s—a critique which never fully materialized and was derailed by a preference that left-leaning criminologists expressed for approaches that developed alternatives to radical criminology and the preference for class based and political economic analysis. At the same time, the declining significant of radical criminology allowed orthodox theory to regroup and return to explanations that either purposefully ignored or became indifferent to existing radical criminological critiques based in class analysis and political economic theory. In the context of a weaken radical critique and the abstract nature of the new critical criminological critique, orthodox theory development was allowed to continue unabated without having to face a form of radical critique that once helped tempered orthodox criminological theory and required it to address the class-based critique posed by radical criminologists.

In the present analysis we have returned to the radical critique of criminology and here we have offered up a new radically situated critique of social disorganization theory. We have not done so to reject the lessons learned from SDT, but rather to illustrate that radical criminological can, (1) explain some of the central features of SDT research within the context of a radical approach and (2) deepen and replace some of the ungrounded assumptions of SDT. As Lynch and Michalowski (2006) argue, such efforts are theoretically subversive to the extent that the findings produced by orthodox theory can be shown to comport with radical expectations. Doing so produces a serious threat to orthodox theories that are incapable of aligning their expectations with the alternatives radical criminology poses.

In posing the critique of SDT found above it is not, however, our intention to undermine SDT completely—that is, to reject the insights of SDT as completely irrelevant for criminology. Rather, our critique points out that many of the empirical results from SDT sit well with radical criminological expectations, and extend SDT by explaining how factors such as poverty and inequality in urban areas are produced by the structure of capitalism. This type of radical extension of SDT—and other orthodox theories of crime—creates a more complete explanation of the processes that generate crime in urban areas in contemporary capitalist economies. Whether the approach outlined here is treated as a hybrid theory that emerges from an integration of orthodox and or radical views or as orthodox or radical theory is of little consequence. More important is that the resulting explanation contributes to criminological knowledge concerning how economic, social and political forces intersect to produce crime and to illustrate a more complete structural explanation of crime.

In the present article, we have argued that SDT misses an important point because it does not adequately address how social structure, and more precisely, political economy, explains the emergence of poverty and inequality and their distribution in urban areas. To be sure, SDT has a valid point to make about the connection between poverty, inequality and crime. At the same time, the SDT approach fails to appreciate that poverty and inequality cannot be taken as givens but that their existence must be explained to produce a well-rounded explanation of crime in urban areas. In the present work, we have illustrated that radical political economic theory can fill in that void in SDT.

With respect to policy, it is also useful to briefly comment on one of the core issues that this journal promotes—namely, that radical criminology needs to become more insurgent and active in its struggle against capitalism (Shantz 2014). How, for example, is the type of theoretical analysis posed here insurgent? If by insurgent we mean revolutionary, then one might suggest that the present analysis is, at best, a weak form of insurgency since it promotes the coupling of radical and orthodox analysis rather than the immediate revolutionary step of overthrowing orthodox analysis. In contrast to that view, however, we pose that the pathway to revolution is sometimes long, and that incremental steps can help facilitate future insurgency. The step taken here, for example, is also insurgent because it takes the first step in undermining the hegemonic domination of orthodox theory within criminology. Beyond that, our approach can also be considered insurgent to the extent that it fosters policy responses to factors such as poverty and inequality as causes of crime that can only be successfully addressed by changing the economic, social and political structure of capitalism.

In closing, we would like to point out that this article is also insurgent in an unexpected way. As a collaboration between a radical criminologist and a structural criminologist who has made contributions to the SDT literature, the insurgent nature of the current work identifies areas of compatibility between radical and orthodox explanations of crime which can be explored through collaborative efforts. That collaboration has required that both of us temper our approach at different points in the above discussion, and struggle with presenting issues related to radical and SDT approaches in ways that are not objectionable to either side. Such collaborations can be employed to advance the views of both sides in ways that reasonably reflect both positions and in the end, produces a new approach that both sides can respect. That collaborative effort is in itself revolutionary and illustrates how criminology can be advanced by mutual understanding and cooperation as opposed to one-sided opposition. Such collaborative effort allows the radical/critical to emerge in ways that are respectful of orthodox sensitivities and facilitates greater acceptance of radical criminological theory, which would indeed be a revolutionary step within criminology.

REFERENCES

Autor, David H., Lawrence F. Katz, and Melissa S. Kearney. 2008. "Trends in US wage Inequality: Revising the Revisionists." *The Review of Economics and Statistics* 90(2): 300-323.

Chambliss, William J. 1975. "Toward a Political Economy of Crime." *Theory and Society* 2(1): 149-170.

Banfield, Edward. 1970. *The Unheavenly City*. NY: Little, Brown.

Barrett, Kimberly L. 2013. "Bethlehem Steel at Lackawanna: The State-Corporate Crime that Continue to Victimize the Residents and Environment of Western New York." *Journal of Crime and Justice* 36(2): 265-284.

Boggess, Lyndsay N., and John R. Hipp. 2010). "Violent Crime, Residential Instability and Mobility: Does the Relationship Differ in Minority Neighborhoods?" *Journal of Quantitative Criminology* 26:351-70.

Browett, John. 1984. "On the Necessity and Inevitability of Uneven Spatial Development under Capitalism." *International Journal of Urban and Regional Research* 8(2): 155-176.

Bruinsma, Gerben JN, Lieven JR Pauwels, Frank M. Weerman, and Wim Bernasco. 2013. "Social Disorganization, Social Capital, Collective Efficacy and the Spatial Distribution of Crime and Offenders: An Empirical Test of Six Neighbourhood Models for a Dutch City." *British Journal of Criminology* 50(3): 942-963.

Burchfield, Keri B., and Eric Silver. 2013. "Collective Efficacy and Crime in Los Angeles: Implications for the Latino Paradox." *Sociological Inquiry* 83(1): 154-176.

Bursik Robert and Harold Grasmick. 1993. *Neighborhoods and Crime: The Dimensions of Effective Community Control.* New York: Lexington Books.

Blau, Peter, and Judith Blau. 1982. "The Cost of Inequality: Metropolitan Structure and Violent Crime." *American Sociological Review* 47: 114-129.

Burkett, Paul. 2005. *Marxism and Ecological Economics: Toward a Red and Green Political Economy.* Chicago: Haymarket Books.

Burns, Ronald G., Michael J. Lynch and Paul B. Stretesky. 2008. *Environmental Law, Crime and Justice.* NY: LFB Scholarly.

Carlson, Susan M., Elizabeth A. Bradshaw and Carrie L. Buist. 2013. "Bringing the Poor Back in: Regulation and Control of Surplus Populations in Finland and the Netherlands." *Journal of Crime and Justice* 36(2): 196-234.

Carlson, Susan M., and Raymond J. Michalowski. 1997. "Crime, Unemployment, and Social Structures of Accumulation: An Inquiry into Historical Contingency." *Justice Quarterly* 14(2): 209-241.

Castells, Manuel. 1977. *The Urban Question: A Marxist Approach.* Cambridge, MA: MIT Press.

Castree, Noel. 1999. "Envisioning Capitalism: Geography and the Renewal of Marxian Political Economy." *Transactions of the Institute of British Geography* 24(2): 137-154.

Engels, Frederick. 1973[1845]. *The Conditions of the Working Class in England.* Moscow: Progress Publishers.

Esping-Andersen, Gosta. 1990. *The Three Worlds of Welfare Capitalism.* Oxford: Polity Press.

Ferrell, Jeff, Keith Hayward and Jock Young. 2008. *Cultural Criminology.* Sage: London.

Fischer, Mary J. 2003. "The Relative Importance of Race and Income in Determining Residential Outcomes in US Urban Areas, 1970-1990." *Urban Affairs Review* 38(5): 669-696.

Foster, John Bellamy. 2000. *Marx's Ecology: Materialism and Nature.* NY: New York University Press.

Foster, John Bellamy, Brett Clark, and Richard York. 2010. *The Ecological Rift: Capitalism's War on the Earth.* NY: New York University Press.

Foucault, Michel. 1979. *Discipline and Punish.* NY: Vintage.

Groves, W. Byron, and Charles Corrado. 1983. "Culture as a Metaphysic: An Appraisal of Cultural Models." *Crime and Social Justice* 20: 99-120.

Habermas, Jurgen. 1975. *Legitimation Crisis.* Boston: Beacon Press.

Harris, Chauncy. 1997. "The 'Nature of Cities' and Urban Geography in the Last Half Century." *Urban Geography* 18(1): 15-35.

Hipp, John R. 2007. "Income inequality, race, and place: Does the distribution of race and class within neighborhoods affect crime rates?" *Criminology* 45: 665-697.

Jameson, F. 1998. *The Cultural Turn: Selected Writings on the Postmodern 1983-1998.* London: Verso.

Jones, David W. 2013. "Putting the Psyche into 'Cultural Criminology': A psychosocial understanding of looting, masculinity, shame and violence." *Journal of Psycho-Social Studies Volume* 7(1): E-journal ISSN: 1478-6737

Rodman, Hyman. 1977. "Culture of Poverty: The Rise and Fall of a Concept." *The Sociological Review* 25(4): 867-876.

Katz, Michael B. 1989. *The Undeserving Poor: From the War on Welfare to the War on Poverty.* NY: Pantheon.

Kovandzic, Tomislav V., Lynne M. Vieraitis and Mark R. Yeisley. 1998. "The structural covariates of urban homicide: Reassessing the impact of income inequality and poverty in the post-Reagan era." *Criminology* 36(3): 569-599.

Kramer, Ronald. 2013. "Carbon in the Atmosphere and Power in America: Climate Change as State-Corporate Crime." *Journal of Crime & Justice* 36(2): 155-172.

Krisberg, Barry. 1975. *Crime and Privilege: Toward a New Criminology.* Englewood Cliffs, NJ: Prentice-Hall.

Krivo, Lauren J., and Ruth D. Peterson. 1996. "Extremely disadvantaged neighborhoods and urban crime." *Social Forces* 75: 619-648.

Kornhauser, Ruth. 1978. *Social sources of delinquency.* Chicago: University of Chicago Press.

Lewis, Oscar. 1968. "The Culture of Poverty." In D. Moynihan (ed), *On Understanding Poverty: Perspectives from the Social Sciences.* NY: Basic Books.

Lewis, Oscar. 1963. "The Culture of Poverty." *Transaction* 1(1): 17-19.

Logan, John R., and Harvey Luskin. 2007. *Urban Fortunes: The Political Economy of Place.* Berkeley, CA: University of California Press.

Lynch, Michael J. 2013a. "Reexamining Political Economic and Crime and the Crime Drop." *Journal of Crime and Justice* 36(2): 250-264.

Lynch, Michael J. 2013b. "The Political Economy of Crime and Justice: An Introduction." *Journal of Crime and Justice* 36(2): 138-140.

Lynch, Michael J. 2010. "Radical Explanations of Penal Trends: The Rate of Surplus Value and the Incarceration Rate In the United States, 1977-2005." *Journal of Crime and Justice.* 33(2): 63-94.

Lynch, Michael J. 1996. "Race, Class, Gender and Criminology: Structured Choices and the Life Course." In M. Schwartz and D. Milovanovic (eds), *Gender, Race and Class in Criminology.* Hamden, CT: Garland.

Lynch, Michael J. 1988. "The Extraction of Surplus Value, Crime and Punishment: A Preliminary Empirical Analysis for the U.S." *Contemporary Crises.* 12:329-344.

Lynch, Michael J. 1987. "Quantitative Analysis and Marxist Criminology: Old Answers to a Dilemma in Marxist Criminology." *Crime and Social Justice* 29:110-127.

Lynch, Michael J. and W. Byron Groves. 1995. "In Defense of Comparative Criminology: A Critique of General Theory and the Rational Man." *Advances in Criminological Theory.* Volume 6. New Brunswick, NJ: Transaction.

Lynch, Michael J., and W. Byron Groves. 1986. *Primer in Radical Criminology (1st Edition).* NY: Harrow & Heston.

Lynch, Michael J., W. Byron Groves and Alan Lizotte. 1994. "The Rate of Surplus Value and Crime:

Theoretical and Empirical Examination of Marxian Economic Theory and Criminology." *Crime, Law and Social Change* 21(1): 15-48.

Lynch, Michael J., Herman Schwendinger and Julia Schwendinger. 2006. "The Status of Empirical Research in Radical Criminology." In F. T. Cullen, J. P.Wright, and K. R. Blevins (eds), *Taking Stock: The Status of Criminological Theory. Advances in Criminological Theory, Volume 15*. New Brunswick, NJ: Transaction.

Lynch, Michael J. and Raymond J. Michalowski. 2006. *Primer in Radical Criminology, 4th Edition*. Boulder, CO: Lynne Reinner.

Marx, Karl. 1974[1867]. *Capital, Volume I*. NY: International Publishers.

Mazerolle, Lorraine, Rebecca Wickes and James McBroom. 2010. "Community Variations in Violence: The Role of Social Ties and Collective Efficacy in Comparative Context." *Journal of Research in Crime and Delinquency* 47(1): 3-30.

Michalowski, Raymond J. 2013. "Ethnic Cleansing, American Style: SB 1070, Nativism and the Contradictions of Neo-Liberal Globalism." *Journal of Crime and Justice* 36(2): 173-195.

Mills, C. Wright. 1959. *The Sociological Imagination*. NY: Oxford University Press.

Musterd, S., & Ostendorf, W. (Eds.). 2013. *Urban segregation and the welfare state: Inequality and exclusion in western cities*. NY: Routledge.

Park, Robert E. 1915. "The City: Suggestions for the Investigation of Behavior in the City Environment." *American Journal of Sociology* 20: 579-83.

Park, Robert E., Ernest Burgess and Roderick McKenzie. 1925. *The City*. Chicago: University of Chicago Press.

Peet, Richard. 1975. "Inequality and Poverty: A Marxist-Geographic Theory." *Annals of the Association of American Geographers* 65(4): 564-571.

Quinney, Richard. 1980. *Class, State and Crime.* NY: Longman.

Rainwater, Lee. 1970. "The Problem of Lower Class Culture." *Journal of Social Issues* 26(2): 133-148.

Rodman, Hyman. 1977. "Culture of Poverty: The Rise and Fall of a Concept." *The Sociological Review* 25(4): 867-876.

Rukus, Joseph and Mildred E. Warner. 2013. "Crime Rates and Collective Efficacy: The Role of Family Friendly Planning." *Cities* 31: 47-46.

Sahlins, Marshall. 1972. *Stone Age Economics.* NY: Aldine de Gruyter.

Sampson, Robert J. 2012. *Great American City: Chicago and the Enduring Neighborhood Effect.* Chicago: University of Chicago Press.

Sampson, Robert J. and W. Bryon Groves. 1989. "Community Structure and Crime: Testing Social-Disorganization Theory." *American Journal of Sociology,* 94, 774-802.

Sampson, Robert J., Stephen W. Raudenbush, and Felton Earls. 1997. "Neighborhoods and violent crime: A multilevel study of collective efficacy." *Science* 277(5328): 918-924.

Sampson, Robert J. and William J. Wilson. 1995. "Race, crime, and urban inequality." In J. Hagan and R. Peterson (Eds.), *Crime and Inequality* (pp. 27-54). Palo Alto, CA: Stanford University Press.

Sennett, Richard, and Jonathan Cobb. 1972. *The Hidden Injuries of Class.* NY: Vintage.

Shaw, Clifford and Henry McKay. 1942. *Juvenile Delinquency in Urban Areas.* Chicago: University of Chicago Press.

Stoczkowski, Wiktor. 2002. *Explaining Human Origins: Myth, Imagination and Conjecture.* Cambridge, UK: Cambridge University Press.

Stretesky, Paul B., Michael A. Long and Michael J. Lynch. 2013. "Does Environmental Enforcement Slow the Treadmill of Production? The Relationship Between Large Monetary Penalties, Ecological Disorganization, and Toxic Releases within Offending Corporations." *Journal of Crime and Justice* 36(2): 235-249.

Storper, Michael, and Richard Walker. 1983. "The theory of Labour and the Theory of Location." *International Journal of Urban and Regional Research* 7(1): 1-43.

Taylor, Ian, Paul Walton and Jock Young. 1973. *The New Criminology: For a Social Theory of Deviance.* NY: Harper and Row.

Thomas, W. I., and F. W. Znaniecki. 1920. *The Polish Peasant in Europe and America.* Chicago: University of Chicago Press.

Thompson, Michael J. 2012. *The politics of inequality: A Political History of the idea of Economic Inequality in America.* NY: Columbia University Press.

Thrasher, Frederick. 1927. *The Gang: A Study of 1,313 Gangs in Chicago.* Chicago: University of Chicago Press.

Waquant, Loic. 2012. The Punitive Regulation of Poverty in the Neoliberal Age. *Criminal Justice Matters* 89(1): 38-40.

Wacquant, Loic. 2011. "The Wedding of Workfare and Prisonfare Revisited." *Social Justice* 38(1-2): 123-124.

Wacquant, Loic. 2009. *Punishing the Poor: Neoliberal Government and Social Insecurity.* Durham, NC: Duke University Press.

Wilson, William Julius. 1987. *The Truly Disadvantaged: The Inner city, the Underclass, and Public Policy.* Chicago: University of Chicago Press.

Wirth, Louis. 1928. *The Ghetto.* Chicago: University of Chicago Press.

Wolff, Edward N. 2002. *Top Heavy: The Increasing Inequality of Wealth in America and what can be done about it.* NY: The New Press.

Zurn, Michael and Stephan Leibfried. 2005. "Reconfiguring the National Constellation." *European Review* 13, sl: 1-36.

COERCIVE OCCUPATIONS AS STATE FACILITATION: UNDERSTANDING THE U.S. STATE'S STRATEGY OF CONTROL

VINCE MONTES

The continuation of structural inequalities cannot be understood based solely on the power of the elite, such as conceived as a 1% and 99% dichotomy; it needs to be understood within the complex and sophisticated system that is supported and carried out by many non-elite. Central to this argument is the idea that segments of the population, including some of the most exploited and oppressed, derive material and ideological benefit from the misery associated with the inequalities that are rooted in the current established social arrangements.[1] It is this phenomenon that demands an explanation that can move beyond simple dichotomies (e.g., elite

---

[1] The established social arrangement is the result of cultural and material forces that combine to bring about a stable social order. Stability in this sense is the byproduct of combinations of value consensus that are precariously propagated by the dominate ideology, economic, and coercive means.

vs. non-elite, white vs. black, etc.) to a greater understanding of how individuals collaborate with a system that is rooted in inequality. This article examines one of the ways that the U.S. state facilitates the incorporation of millions of individuals into the rank-and-file of policing, correctional, national security, and military organizations.

According to many leading theorists (such as Christie 1993; Garland 2001; Parenti 2008; Wacquant 2008a), the economic and political changes that have occurred starting about forty years ago lead to increases in the surplus population and a growth in the "dangerous class." The economic crisis of declining profits and racial and class rebellion contributed to a move away from the politics of the carrot (a Keynesian welfare state) and the labor/capitalists compromise to the politics of the stick (i.e., the police build up and mass incarceration) (Parenti 2008, 240). According to Parenti, the implementation of neoliberalism in the 1980s and the 1990s re-established profit margins for the capitalists, while the state went about managing "the excluded, and castoff classes" (2008, 241). Yet, as the state relied more on policing and imprisonment of particular sectors of the population, there was also a parallel growth in coercive occupations. Had it not been for this boom in coercive employment many more individuals would have more than likely joined the surplus population and dangerous classes.

The basic premise in this article is that the above circumstances created a positive correlation between the implementation of neoliberal policies and increased inequality and the increasing dependency on a vast amount of coercive forces required to sustain it. In understanding U.S. state power, we must understand its role as the enforcer of the status quo —i.e., unequal relationships that primarily benefit a national and a global network of elites, which the global and domestic repressive apparatuses are tasked with maintaining. A preliminary account of the pervasive coercive forces below illustrates a glimpse into the rise and pervasiveness of coercive occupations.

The role of state coercion in disrupting and neutralizing the mobilization of contentious action and the managing of marginality cannot be minimized.[2] Yet, what is often missed and is of equal importance is the role that the state plays in facilitating large segments of the population into the established order as enforcers of the status quo (Christie 1993; Katz 2007). As we will see, the U.S. state utilizes a multitude of strategies in order to maintain stability. This article is concerned with one particular state strategy: the use of employment in coercive occupations as a means to neutralize contentious action by incorporat-

---

[2] For Katz (2007), the marginalized are people who are largely excluded from the rewards associated with full citizenship, including employment, housing, consumption, social benefits, and equal justice.

ing individuals into the system as a compliant and loyal member employed in one of the various coercive forces. There are over 10 million people employed in policing organizations, correctional, and military types of occupations. The U.S. has the largest number of coercive forces in the world, especially when you examine the actual versus official figures. One needs to consider coercive forces as the premier job suppliers, from law enforcement officers, prison guards, soldiers, to members of Homeland Security and in addition, all the supportive civilian and private contractor jobs that comprise its employment matrix. Incalculable millions of communities and families are also dependent on these organizations for their livelihoods. If we add the approximately 23 million military veterans, many of whom remain connected to military service through their active participation in veterans' organizations and/or through veteran benefits, we can begin to see the larger implications of this particular strategy.[3] Furthermore, coercive institutions have far-reaching influence in academia as being benefactors of research funding and employment, which also offers a partial explanation for why critical analysis that addresses this phenomenon is largely absent. Upton Sinclair may in fact have been correct when he stated: "It is difficult to get a man to understand something when his

---

[3] "Projected Veteran Population 2013 to 2043," Prepared by the National Center for Veterans Analysis and Statistics (2014).

salary depends upon him not understanding it" (in Parenti 2011, 2).

Understanding coercive forces such as policing, correctional, and military organizations is important because they employ large numbers of people with stable and secured jobs; this is increasingly true in the current times of employment insecurity. The U.S. Department of Defense alone, for example, is the world's largest employer, with the Chinese military being a distant second (Ruth 2012).[4] Moreover, the U.S. has only 5% of the world's population, but accounts for more than 40% of the world's military spending (Quigley 2010). When one combines all the budgets of all the coercive organizations—i.e., policing, corrections, national security, and the military—it is nothing less than astonishing in terms of the degree of spending and employment it spawns, from direct and indirect employment, as we will see below. In addition, these organizations are, to varying degrees, highly bureaucratic hierarchical organizations, which instill strict discipline and demand a greater degree of obedience than other occupations found either in the public or the private sectors. The common denominator that links these coercive occupations is that they function to a large extent as arms of the state to protect and enforce the status quo.

---

[4] According to Ruth (2012), the world's largest employers are the following: the U.S. Department of Defense, 3.2.; the Chinese military 2.3; and Walmart 2.1 (in the millions).

Explaining loyalty and allegiance cannot be reduced to economic motives and interests. Loyalty and allegiance are also culturally contrived with feelings of group solidarity, sense of duty, and patriotism. In fact, many employed in coercive occupations receive elevated status not because they possess stable employment, but because many of these occupations are awarded high degrees of esteem. The elevated status granted to the members of coercive occupations is orchestrated by the state and other agents of socialization such as the media and educational institutions. For Glen Greenwald, the U.S. military receives a tremendous amount of veneration from U.S. society and can be seen as the central religion, which "is by far the most respected and beloved institution among the U.S. population" (2012). This is hardly an exaggeration when one considers the degree in which society is saturated with the political socialization to respect and honor the military (e.g., in the mainstream media, in schools, and in all sporting events, especially at the professional level). Yet, the worship of "all things military" appears to be just a tip of the iceberg. Law enforcement and national security, in many ways, appear to also be afforded the same veneration when it comes to the mainstream media and formal educational systems. The police, for example, are often portrayed by the media as heroic crime

fighters (Surette 1998; Reiner 1985).[5] This is
not to say that the corporate media are not at
times critical of the police and the military or
that these institutions do not have their critics, but on the whole, much of the coverage
either in the news, movies, or TV programing
appears overwhelmingly supportive. As a result, critical analysis of coercive occupations
is a difficult endeavor because U.S. society
does appear to worship all things coercive, especially when they represent the U.S. and are
sanctioned and rationalized by the state.

What also appears to be a salient feature is
that these coercive organizations tend to foster a type of master status in which their
members primarily identify themselves and
are identified by others by their occupation—
e.g., as a police officer or as a soldier. In fact,
these identities tend to trump all other identities such as social class, ethno-racial, and gender and develop a sense of group solidarity
amongst those in coercive occupations. The
"we versus them" mindset permeates
throughout these professions, which hinders
attempts at creating a more unified and just
society and world that is based on solidarity
and commonality. Rather than mitigate inequalities within the U.S. or between nation
states, the U.S. state instead allocates endless

[5] Lovell argues that police departments view the media as both
supportive and adversarial and as a result developed specialized
public information officers to insure that the pro-police message
of professional crime fighting and how the brave men and women
put their lives on the line every day to make the streets safe
remain the dominant view (2010).

amounts of expenditures, resources, and lives in upholding the system of capitalism, the very system that simultaneously generates vast amounts of inequality, creates insecurity, and dysfunction at home and abroad, which then lays the groundwork for disruption— e.g., crime and organized/unorganized forms of resistance (e.g., Hagan 1994; Linebaugh 1976; Piven and Cloward 1977; Quinney 1977; and National Advisory Commission on Civil Disorders 1968).

This paper is organized in the following manner. First, its theoretical framework is presented as a means to contextualize coercive forces within the larger context of the U.S. state strategy. Secondly, the U.S. coercive forces are mapped out in order to illustrate their sheer size and the pervasive nature of their employment matrix. Thirdly, an analysis is presented that focuses on the capability of the hegemonic bureaucratic state's ability to develop, in many cases, esteemed identities that are ideologically sanctioned and operate like master statuses because they hinder solidarity among the oppressed and exploited and isolate its members from social movements and protest.

Theoretical Framework

The concept of facilitation has largely been absent in the analysis of state repression and when it is applied it is often interpreted as merely the flipside of repression. Although social movement research has been insightful in understanding the nuanced relationships between social movements and state repression (della Porta and Reiter 1998; Davenport, Johnston, Mueller 2005),[6] it has not focused on the complex and multifaceted repressive and facilitative modes of the state; whose actions extend beyond protest policing and are not limited to mobilization phases.

In fact, understanding the strategies of the state goes beyond the policing of protest during periods of mobilization, because states cast wider nets that target larger segments of society and operate more as a permanent strategy (Montes 2008). The U.S. state, for example, should be conceptualized as having various modes of repression, which include such actions as covert counterintelligence operations (e.g., COINTELPRO) and the use of legal procedures such as federal grand juries that target political dissidents (Blackstock 1988; Churchill 1988, 1990; Davenport 2005; Deutsch 1984). In addition, Pamela Oliver attempts to expand the concept of state repression by understanding its connection to crime control (2008, 8). She argues that once we understand that one of the major functions of criminal law is to protect unequal distributions of resources, we can begin to see crime control as a form of state repression (2008,

---

[6] These theorists focus on what is coined the repression and mobilization nexus, which analyzes how repression does not always produce demobilization; it in fact sometimes inspires greater resistance and wider participation in protest.

13). The use of state repression continued way after the riots in the 1960s and the demise of the social movements, but its aim was not preventing unrest by repressing riots but preventing unrest by repressing potential rioters (Oliver 2008). These potential rioters are seen as the ones who can start a revolution. The state and the supporters of the "law and order" agenda have linked ordinary crime with riots and social movements and pursue crime control policies that make no distinctions between these categories (Oliver 2008). This is an important contribution because it expands the state strategy beyond a narrow focus on political dissent to include crime control as a form of repressing of the poor and racial minorities, many of whom the state perceives as a threat to the social order (Marx 1970a; Marx 1970b; Oliver 2008; Parenti 2008).Yet, we know that no state, even the most authoritarian, rules with just only force and violence. Understanding the U.S. state requires an understanding of its complex and sophisticated strategies that are designed to maintain the status quo. Under the general rubrics of the concept of facilitation, facilitation can be seen as a series of non-coercive mechanisms such as co-opting and bribing, or what Charles Tilly (1978) referred to as any action carried out by a state that lowers the cost/consequences for collective contentious action.[7] In this modified version of the concept, the state

---

[7] Tilly provides examples to how the U.S. state authorities repressed some social movement groups, while protecting others and providing political access to them (1978, 100).

continues to be viewed as complex and as a strategic agent, but a facilitative measure is not reserved for only contentious actors or social movements. Gary Marx provides an example of a broader definition of this concept when he wrote that the U.S. "legal system, with the protected freedoms of the Bill of Rights and local ordinances regarding parade permits, is a more distant form of facilitation and control" (1979, 95). In this context, we define facilitation as any state action that is designed to persuade contentious or potentially contentious actors from targeting the state or elite with disruption. Some of the ways this is accomplished are by providing: employment; social aid (Piven and Cloward 1971); elite promotion, i.e., co-opting oppositional leaders into positions as intermediaries; and channeling movements' grievances into electoral processes (Tarrow 1998; Tilly 1978).

Not all state facilitative actions are meant to co-opt or integrate the dangerous classes. In fact, some facilitative actions are intended to appease contentious and potentially contentious individuals, groups, and segments of populations. Although the state utilizes many facilitative strategies, employment is but one; it may very well be one of the most effective strategies because like social aid provisions it addresses subsistence and material needs, which have served as one of the key impetuses for mobilization. Employment in coercive occupations goes beyond the general objective of filling empty bellies in exchange for compliancy. As we will see, employment in coercive forces is a deliberate strategy designed to integrate individuals more firmly into the social order. Besides economic reward, members receive greater levels of institutional socialization that transcend a job into a duty, which is in many cases honorific and virtuous.

By situating coercive forces within the context of the U.S. state strategy framework, we will attempt to analyze coercive forces, which appear to be a critical component of it. Coercive forces overlap with repressive and facilitative modes and serve dual functions: one as enforcers of the social order and second as facilitation (see Chart 1).

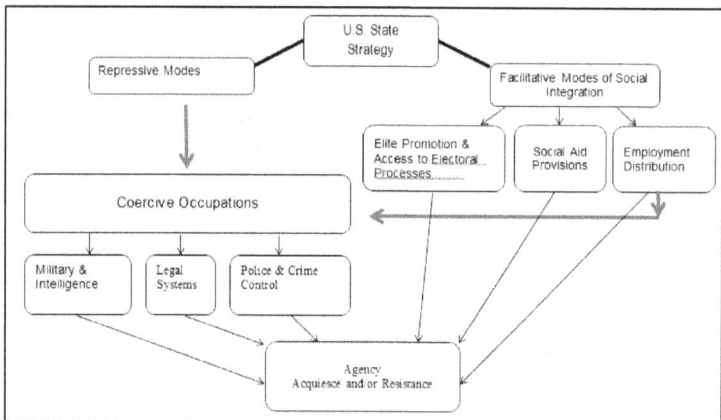

Chart 1: The State Strategy

Because of the paramilitary and military bureaucratic structures in which these occupations are embedded are highly sanctioned and esteemed by the legitimacy of the state, we will analyze the state's legitimacy below. For many of the members and supportive personnel employed in coercive forces, to act in a contentious manner that seeks change to the social order, amounts to not only acting against one's job security and benefits, but acting against one's sworn duty and oath. In addition, unlike other occupations that can be seen as having facilitative qualities, coercive occupations are the pillars and bedrock of the social order because they are directly responsible for upholding it. Their elevated status and honorific pride are sanctioned by the state and therefore contingent on the continuation of the status quo.

MAPPING COERCIVE FORCES

Mapping the far-reaching tentacles of the coercive state is a difficult enterprise, and mapping its pervasive coercive employment matrix is even more difficult. It is one thing to locate accurate data on the numbers of individuals in the various occupations and entirely another to account for the all the supportive personnel and private sector employees that serve to supplement them. Of course, the sketches below do not begin to address all of the industries, communities, and families that economically depend on coercive occupations as their lifeblood.

POLICE COERCIVE FORCES

We will begin with crime control and what is often referred to as an industry. Nils Christie wrote, the problems facing Western societies are that:

> Wealth is everywhere unequally distributed. So is access to paid work. Both problems contain potentialities for unrest. The crime control industry is suited for coping with both. This industry provides profits and work while at the same time producing control of those who otherwise might have disturbed the social process" (1993, 13).

This appears to be an accurate statement because it largely captures the multiple roles that the criminal justice system plays in managing inequality and the lack of employment. Christie explicitly states that the criminal justice system is required to maintain relations of inequality. This observation can be verified by the fact that most of the 7,053,977 adults supervised by correctional systems (Glaze and Bonczar 2010) are poor. Fewer than half of those incarcerated held a full-time job at the time of their arraignment and two-thirds were from households with annual income amounting to less than half of the official poverty line (Wacquant 2008b, 61).

When the data for mass incarceration are aggregated by race, mass incarceration really appears to look like racial mass incarceration (Alexander 2010; Bobo and Thompson 2012; Loury 2008). The U.S. population consist of approximately 12% Black and 15% Latino, however some reports illustrate that these two groups represent about 60% of these incarcerated. In 2012, the incarceration rate per 100,000 was 2,841 for Blacks, 1,158 for Latinos, and 463 for Whites per 100,000 (Carson and Golinelli 2013). The rate of incarceration by race appears to demonstrate racial disparity within the criminal justice system. As noted above, the U.S. incarceration rate is the highest in the industrial world, but it is even higher when aggregating for race. Yet, Bruce Western (2006) illustrates that mass incarceration affects the poorest of the African American population, which points to the class element in racial disparity in those who are incarcerated.[8] In short, one can argue that mass incarceration really involves the containment of the most marginalized: the ones with the greatest distance from wealth and privilege and who are perceived as the greatest threat to the social order.

There is a sizable amount of the U.S. population under the control of the criminal justice system (see Table 1). For example, 1 in every 35 adult residents in the U.S. is under some form of correctional supervision in yearend 2012 (Glaze and Bonczar 2010). In fact, the U.S. leads the world with the highest incarceration rate, with approximately 716 per 100,000 (Walmsley 2011). One of the reasons why this has not generated popular moral outrage is because the prison population and those under its surveillance do not reflect the greater population (Cole 1998). Yet, Table 1 illustrates a fuller picture of those incarcerated. By calculating together Immigration and Customs Enforcement (ICE) detentions, and military, Indian country prisons, juvenile detentions, and territories/colonies' incarceration with all those in state and federal prisons and all the individuals under correctional su-

---

[8] According to Western, the highest rates of incarceration among blacks and whites males are among those who do not possess high school degrees: for black males it tripled to reach over 58% and for white males it more than doubled to 11.2% during the period between 1979 and 1997 (2006, 26).

pervision the overall number increases to 7,142,563. Of course, these numbers do not include all the individuals that are held in Iraq, Afghanistan, Guantanamo, CIA black sites or other nations in which the U.S. military is involved with counterinsurgency operations. Besides the containment of the most marginalized that are perceived as posing a threat to the status quo, Christie argues that the crime control industry also provides employment for many who are without jobs (1993).

Table 1: Estimated number of persons supervised by adult correctional systems, by correctional status, 2012

Probation	3,942,800
Parole	851,200
Federal and State Prisons	1,483,900
Local jails	744,500
ICE	9,957 (2008)
Military facilities	1,651 (2008)
Jails in Indian country	2,135 (2008)
Juvenile facilities	92,845 (2008)
Territorial prisons	13,575 (2008)
Total	**7,142,563**

Sources: Glaze and Herberman (2013) and Sabol, West, and Cooper (2009)

This can be seen in numerous ways such as the fact that in 2014, there were 469,500 correctional officers, which required a minimal educational requirement of a high school diploma or equivalent for entry level employment.[9] In addition, in 2012, there were approximately

---

[9] U.S. Bureau of Labor Statistics. *Correctional Officers: Occupational Outlook Handbook*, Jan/2014.

90,600 individuals employed in probations and parole, as mainly probation and parole agents.[10]

In fact, the management of the "dangerous class" has also created economic opportunities to the private sector in the form of privately run prisons, programs, and labor. In 2010, there were 128,195 state and federal prisoners housed in private facilities. Corrections Corporation of America, the largest private prison corporation, housed 70,000 prisoners, operated over 60 facilities, and ran 600 inmate programs.[11] They have approximately 17,000 employees (370 in corporate offices and 16,630 in facilities and transport businesses).[12] The second largest for-profit correctional and detention management corporation is the GEO Group Inc. (formerly known as Wachenhut), which has approximately 65,949 active beds, operates 106 facilities, and employs 19,000.[13] Edwin S. Rubenstein's research discovered that investors in these for-profit companies, which trade on the New York Stock Exchange "have a financial interest in keeping private prison cells filled. Industry experts say a profitable private prison must have a 90 percent to 95 percent capacity rate" (2014). Private prisons are the most profitable in the prison industry complex (Palaez 2014; Parenti 2008).

According to Scott Cohn, "Small towns are trying to get in on the boom, along with architects,

---

[10] U.S. Dept. of Labor Statistics. Bureau of Labor Statistics. *Probation Officers and Correctional Treatment Specialists*, January 8, 2014.

[11] See Corrections Corporations of American website: www.cca.com.

[12] See the Public Interest website:
http://www.inthepublicinterest.org/organization/corrections-corporation-america

[13] See Geo Group, Inc. 2012 Annual Report.

health care providers, and technology companies. They're all after their piece of the billions behind bars" (2012). In addition, many private corporations contract prison labor. The following corporations utilized prison labor such as "IBM, Boeing, Motorola, Microsoft, AT&T, Wireless, Texas Instruments, Dell, Compaq, Honeywell, Hewlett-Packard, Nortel, Lucent Technologies, 3Com, Intel, Northern Telecom, TWA, Nordstrom's, Revlon, Macy's, Pierre Cardin, Target Stores, and many more" (Palaez 2014). In this context, prison labor is highly profitable because labor is cheap and as Palaez states corporations don't have to worry about labor strikes or paying unemployment insurance and vacations (2014). Yet, the prison industrial complex has not provided a Keynesian stimulus comparable to the military industrial complex with its extensive spin-off industries and employment (Parenti 2008, 216). Nevertheless, a CNBC reported that there are 700,000 individuals working in city, state, and private prisons; approximately 450,000 as correctional guards and the other 350,000 workers working at various personnel levels.[14] Prisons appear to be a mini-jobs program, employing many with the promise of high salaries, good benefits, and minimal education requirements.

Besides correctional officers, parole and probation agents, and all its supportive personnel, the policing matrix includes various law-enforcement officers, which operate at the city, state, and federal levels and are attached to traditional policing and national security. According to a 2011 Bureau of Justice Statistics report, in 2008, state and local law enforcement agencies employed more than

---

[14] See "Billions Behind Bars—Inside America's Prison Industry." CNBC. NBC Universal. 2013.

1.1 million persons on a full-time basis, including about 765,000 sworn personnel (defined as those with general arrest powers) (Reaves 2011). These organizations also employed approximately 100,000 part-time employees, including 44,000 sworn officers. (Reaves 2011). There are approximately 120,000 federal full-time sworn law enforcement officers (Reaves 2012). Not all of the federal enforcement officers are assigned to crime control; their role in policing varies. In all, there are 73 federal law enforcement agencies, which are divided into two branches: the Department of Homeland Security (e.g., U.S. Secret Service, U.S. Customs and Border Protection, and Homeland Security Investigation) and the Department of Justice (e.g., FBI, DEA, ATF, and Federal Bureau of Prisons). Both departments combined employ approximately 120,000 sworn officers: this figure is up from 69,000 since 1993 as a result of the USA Patriot Act and the creation of the Department of Homeland Security.

When factoring the official figures of city, state, and federal police, which are approximately 929,000, this number is relatively average when making international comparisons with advanced countries based on number of police per 100,000 (population) ratios.[15] However, this number, is highly deceptive when one considers all the other coercive forces that serve as auxiliary members meant to augment the coercive arm of the state. By including prison guards (493,100), probation

---

[15] See "The Tenth United Nations Survey of Crime Trends and Operations of Criminal Justice Systems" (Tenth CTS, 2005-2006), United Nations Office On Crime and Drugs. In this survey, the U.S. reported that it had a police size of 683,396, which is 225.66 per 100,000, which is very similar to Canada's ratio of 191.73 per 100,000. https://www.unodc.org/unodc/en/data-and-analysis/Tenth-CTS-full.html

and correctional agents (90,600), private police (2,000,000), Transportation Security Agency (TSA) (60,000)[16] we arrive at an entirely different figure, which is approximately 3,572,700 million.

Studies on private security suggest that there may be as many as 90,000 private security organizations employing roughly 2 million security officers in the United States.[17] The Transportation Security Agency (TSA), with approximately 60,000 agents, whom are not sworn officers yet comprise of the increasing coercive apparatus, which is coordinated by the Department of Homeland Security and serve as an example of the increasing policing and its centralization. The reason for the inclusion of all the above categories is because the main objective of these organizations is to augment policing efforts. This is the case, regardless of whether they are sworn or not; they function to maintain the social order.

According to a 2012 U.S. Census Bureau report that in 2006, there were 424,946 (368,668 full-time and 56,278 part-time) civilian employees (i.e., nonsworn) in city and state policing organizations.[18] In addition, the two federal law enforcement branches: the Department of Homeland Se-

---

[16] See Department of Homeland Security website.
https://www.dhs.gov/

[17] See "Building Private Security/Public Policing Partnerships to Prevent and Respond to Terrorism and Public Disorder" (2004), Office of Community Oriented Policing Services, U.S. Department of Justice.
http://www.theiacp.org/portals/0/pdfs/BuildingPrivateSecurity.pdf
In a more recent study titled, "The United States Security Industry: Size and Scope, Insights, Trends, and Data," by ASIS International the Institute of Finance and Management (IOFM) find that private security in the U.S. is a $350 billion market and that there is estimated to be between 1.9 and 2.1 million full-time security workers.

curity that proudly claims to employ more than 230,000 individuals;[19] and the Department of Justice that employs 116,512 individuals.[20] The problem with these figures is that they do not distinguish between direct (i.e., sworn) members and indirect members (i.e., unsworn) members. As we will discuss below, distinctions of sworn or unsworn really do not capture the importance of an individual's authority and role in the particular organization's hierarchy. However, adding these two figures together we have a total of 346,512 and then by subtracting the 120,000 estimated sworn federal law enforcement members and minus 60,000 for TSA, we arrive at the figure of 166,512, which we categorized as indirect federal personnel. In addition, as stated above, using the CNBC[(See footnote 14◀)] report, there are approximately 350,000 employees in various positions throughout corrections. We then calculate that there are 591,458 indirect employees working in the policing sectors; 424,946 in the city and state, 166,512 in the federal, and 350,000 in corrections (see Table 2).

While accounting for members of coercive forces in policing we estimate that there are approximately 4,514,158 million in direct and indirect occupations performing various supportive personnel roles in upholding the social order. This estimation is a mere glimpse into the policing matrix of employment. The coercive matrix

[18] U.S. Census Bureau, Statistical Abstract of the United States: 2012. Section 5: Law Enforcement, Courts, and Prisons, p. 216.

[19] Figures obtained from Department of Homeland Security website: http://www.dhs.gov/

[20] U.S. Dept. of Justice. FY 2014 Budget Request at a Glance Discretionary Budget Authority.

increases when factoring in the military members and personnel.

Table 2: Police Coercive Forces

City and State Law Enforcement Officers (full and part-time)[21]	809,000
Federal Law Enforcement Officers (full-time)[22]	120,000
Prison Guards (city, state, federal, and private) [23]	493,100
TSA[24]	60,000
Probation and Parole Agents[25]	90,600
Private Security Guards [26 (on following page▶)]	2,000,000
Supportive Personnel (known)	
City and State Policing Personnel[27 (▶)]	424,946
Federal Policing Personnel[28 (▶)]	166,512
Prison Supportive Personnel [29 (▶▶)] (city, state, federal, private)	350,000
Total	4,514,158

[21] Reaves, Brian A. 2011. *Census of State and Local Law Enforcement Agencies, 2008.* U.S. Dept. of Justice. Office of Justice Programs, Bureau of Justice Statistics, July. http://www.bjs.gov/content/pub/pdf/csllea08.pdf

[22] Reaves, Brian A. 2012. "Federal Law Enforcement Officers, 2008." U.S. Department of Justice Office of Justice Programs, *Bureau of Justice Statistics,* June, NCJ 238250. http://www.bjs.gov/content/pub/pdf/csllea08.pdf

[23] U.S. Bureau of Labor Statistics. *Correctional Officers: Occupational Outlook Handbook,* Jan/2014. http://www.bls.gov/ooh/Protective-Service/Correctional-officers.htm

[24] See Transportation Security Agency details at the Department of Homeland Security website: https://www.dhs.gov/

[25] U.S. Dept. of Labor Statistics. Bureau of Labor Statistics. *Probation Officers and Correctional Treatment Specialists,* January 8, 2014

⇐ Sources for chart on previous page:26, 27, 28, 29 (& following page notes ▼ ►)

MILITARY COERCIVE FORCES

In 2010, the U.S. Armed Forces reported having had a total of 1,138,044 soldiers stationed in nearly 150 countries around the world for,

---

[26] See "Building Private Security/Public Policing Partnerships to Prevent and Respond to Terrorism and Public Disorder" (2004), Office of Community Oriented Policing Services, U.S. Department of Justice. This report list 90,000 private security organizations and approximately 2 million provide security guards (p. 6) http://www.theiacp.org/portals/0/pdfs/BuildingPrivateSecurity.pdf

A more recent study titled, "The United States Security Industry: Size and Scope, Insights, Trends, and Data" (2013) by ASIS International and the Institute of Finance and Management (IOFM) found that private security in the U.S. is a $350 billion booming market and that at the time of their study there were between 1.75 and 1.93 million full-time workers employed in operational security in the U.S. and with projected numbers of over 2 million by 2015. "Operational security" is defined as traditional protection activities undertaken to keep an organization from harm and which are typically carried out by a security department; this includes physical security and also protection functions such as threat management, investigations, fraud detection, and intelligence. As noted, this figure does not include part-time security guards or the 1 million employed in IT security. https://www.asisonline.org/Documents/ASIS%20IOFM %20Executive%20Summary%208.23.13.%20final.pdf

[27] U.S. Census Bureau, Statistical Abstract of the United States: 2012. Section 5: Law Enforcement, Courts, and Prisons, p. 216.

[28] According to a 2012 U.S. Census Bureau report for the year 2006, there were 424,946 (368,668 full-time and 56,278 part-time) civilian employees (i.e., nonsworn) in city and state policing organizations (see Census Bureau, Statistical Abstract of the United States: 2012. Section 5: Law Enforcement, Courts, and Prisons, p. 216.). In adding the 230,000 in the DHS (Department of Homeland Security website: https://www.dhs.gov/) and the 116,512 in the DOJ (U.S. Department of Justice. FY 2014 Budget Request at a Glance Discretionary Budget Authority) we arrive at a total of 346,512 of individuals employed at these two federal law enforcement ☛

which did not include the Navy or Marine Corps soldiers at sea.[30] Along with conflicting reports on the actual figures of soldiers, there are conflicting reports in the calculations of the actual number of military bases worldwide. Nick Turse states that

> In the grand scheme of things, the actual numbers aren't all that important. Whether the most accurate total is 900 bases, 1,000 bases or 1,100 posts in foreign lands, it's un-deniable that the US military maintains, in Johnson's famous phrase, an empire of bases so large and shadowy that no one—not even at the Pentagon—really knows its full size and scope. (2010)

For the historian, David M. Kennedy, today's military

> wield unprecedented firepower and hold in their hands an almost incalculable capacity for focused violence. Not since the time of the Roman Empire have a single country's arms weighed so heavily in the global scales. (2013, 2)

According to Andrew J. Bacevich, "Ameri-cans... have fallen prey to militarism, manifest-ing itself in a romanticized view of soldiers, a tendency to see military power as the truest measure of national greatness, and outsized ex-pectations regarding the efficacy of force" (2013,

---

☞ branches. Then by subtracting the 120,000 estimated sworn federal law enforcement members and the 60,000 at the TSA, we arrive at the figure of 166,512, which we categorized as indirect federal personnel.

[29] See "Billions Behind Bars—Inside America's Prison Industry." CNBC. NBC Universal. 2013.

[30] See "U.S. Military Personnel by Country" CNN.

2). As a result of a militarized foreign policy, the U.S. military consumes a large part of the national budget. Lindorff provides a more comprehensive account of the U.S. military budget:

> The US, in fiscal year 2012, budgeted a total of $673 billion for the military, plus another $166 billion for military activities of other government departments, such as the nuclear weapons program, much of which is handled by the Department of Energy, or the Veterans Program, which pays for the care and benefits of former military personnel. There's also another roughly $440 billion in interest paid on the debt from prior wars and military expenditures. Altogether, that comes to $1.3 trillion, which represents close to 50% of the general budget of the United States—the highest percentage of a government budget devoted to the military of any modern nation in the world—and perhaps of any government of any nation in the world (2012).

What this also means is that there are not only millions of soldiers who are connected to the coercive military employment matrix, but millions more civilians and industries which require a large budget to keep the empire afloat.

As Michael Parenti reminds us, imperialism is what empires do, because they "bring to bear military and financial power upon another country in order to expropriate the land, labor, capital, natural resources, commerce, and markets of that other country" (2011, 7). The actual number of individuals required in maintaining an empire, and the extensiveness of its employment matrix is what will be examined here. As of 2010, there were 1,458,697 million people in active service and another 857,261 in the various reserve branches, totaling 2,315,958.[31] When including this figure with private contractors, the overall figure increases. According to a recent quarterly contractor census report (2012) issued by the U.S. Central Command that included Iraq and Afghanistan, as well as 18 other countries, there were approximately 137,000 contractors working for the Pentagon (Isemberg 2012).[32]

In a recent attempt to capture the actual number of people employed directly and indirectly by the military, a CNN report stated in 2012 that the military employed 3.1 million military personnel and civilians, with another 3 million who work for the defense industry, making weapons and operating various other businesses (Rizzo 2012). According to Robert Reich, the military is the biggest jobs program in the U.S. and any reduction to it would significantly affect unemployment (2010). Yet, this is only part of the story because the U.S. military or more specifically, the U.S. Defense Department is the world's largest employer with 3.2 million employees (the Chinese military is second with 2.3 million; followed by Walmart with 2.1 million employers) (Ruth 2012). The total number is actually larger than Reich reports. By subtracting the numbers in Table 3, active and reserve armed forces from 3,100,000 million of

---

[31] U.S. Department of Defense. 2010. "Population Representation in Military Services."

[32] There were 113,376 in Afghanistan and 7,336 in Iraq. Of that total, 40,110 were U.S. citizens, 50,560 were local hires, and 46,231 were from neither the U.S. nor the country in which they were working (Isemberg 2012).

military and civilian forces in the CNN report, we arrive at approximately 784,040 civilians directly on the payroll of the armed forces. Furthermore, within the Department of Defense is the National Intelligence Program, which has 16 intelligence agencies (e.g., the CIA, Army Intelligence, Department of State, and NSA) that make up the U.S. intelligence

Table: 3: The U.S. Military Jobs Program

Military and Civilian [33]	3,100,000
Defense Contractors [34]	3,000,000
National Intelligence Program [35]	107,035
Total	6,207,033

Sources: Author's compilations. See footnotes.

community, with 107,035 employees and a budget of $52.6 billion of dollars in 2013 (Gellman and Miller 2013). As the result of recent revelations, a more accurate description is emerging of the real budget and number of employees attached to these agencies.

The figures in Table 3 provide a more accurate picture of how many individuals are integrated into the military coercive occupations. If we were to concern ourselves with conventional figures and official interpretations we would merely derive at a total of 914,300 thousand city, state, and federal law-enforcement officers (LEOs) and calculate a total of 2,315,958 million for members in all branches of the armed

[33] See Rizzo 2012.

[34] See Rizzo 2012.

[35] See Gellman and Miller 2013.

forces (see Table 3); these figures would undoubtedly present a distorted view of actual
numbers involved in the coercive employment
matrix, which is approximately 10,667,193 million in various sectors of U.S. coercive forces
such as direct coercive members, direct coercive auxiliary, indirect coercive members and
greater society. This makes the U.S. coercive
forces the world's largest employer, without exception. Of course, one also has to include all
the millions of families and, in some cases, entire communities (such as military communities), military veterans and ex-LEOs who continue to be attached to the military and policing
services long after retirement, and all the military and police funded academic program and
research that all rely on coercive forces for their
living, careers, and esteem and identities. [36,37]

---

[36] By subtracting the 2,315,958 million individuals in active and
reserve military branches (U.S. Department of Defense. 2010.
"Population Representation in Military Services.") from the
3,100,000 million of military and civilian individuals (CNN report),
we arrive at approximately 784,040 civilians directly on the payroll
of the armed forces.

[37] Refer to Table 2: Police Coercive Forces, we calculate that there
are 591,458 indirect employees working in the policing sectors:
424,946 individuals as City and State Policing Personnel and
166,512 individuals as Federal Policing Personnel.

CHART 2: U.S. COERCIVE EMPLOYMENT MATRIX[38]

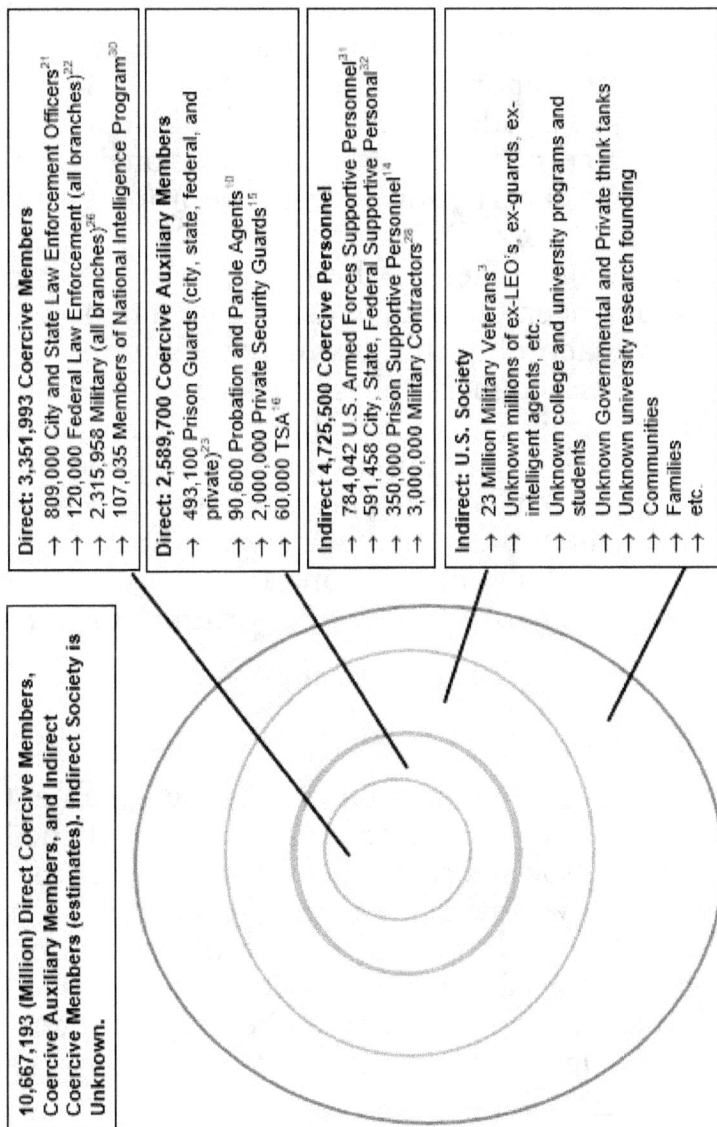

Direct: 3,351,993 Coercive Members

↑ 809,000 City and State Law Enforcement Officers[21]
↑ 120,000 Federal Law Enforcement (all branches)[22]
↑ 2,315,958 Military (all branches)[26]
↑ 107,035 Members of National Intelligence Program[30]

Direct: 2,589,700 Coercive Auxiliary Members

↑ 493,100 Prison Guards (city, state, federal, and private)[23]
↑ 90,600 Probation and Parole Agents[10]
↑ 2,000,000 Private Security Guards[15]
↑ 60,000 TSA[16]

Indirect 4,725,500 Coercive Personnel

↑ 784,042 U.S. Armed Forces Supportive Personnel[31]
↑ 591,458 City, State, Federal Supportive Personal[32]
↑ 350,000 Prison Supportive Personnel[14]
↑ 3,000,000 Military Contractors[28]

Indirect: U.S. Society

↑ 23 Million Military Veterans[3]
↑ Unknown millions of ex-LEO's, ex-guards, ex-intelligent agents, etc.
↑ Unknown college and university programs and students
↑ Unknown Governmental and Private think tanks
↑ Unknown university research founding
↑ Communities
↑ Families
↑ etc.

10,667,193 (Million) Direct Coercive Members, Coercive Auxiliary Members, and Indirect Coercive Members (estimates). Indirect Society is Unknown.

Source: Author's compilations

The above sketches are preliminary at best, but will serve as an outline for this inquiry into the pervasive nature of the coercive forces, and their role in the continuation of the structure of inequalities. There has been a growth in non-productive labor, which is what Samuel Bowles and Arjun Jayadev refer to as "guard labor:" the percentage of the labor force associated "with providing security for people and property and imposing work discipline" (2007, 1).[39] For reasons discussed herein, the system of capitalism has long been dependent on so-called non-productive labor, but this has increased during the rise of its neoliberal phase and should be considered a major form of state facilitation. This topic is extremely important if we hope to understand the vital mechanisms that the coercive employment matrix plays in sustaining inequality by making oppression and repression a problem for some and an opportunity for others.

State Coercion, Legitimacy, and Facilitation

At the core of this inquiry is the argument that coercive forces are more firmly aligned with the social order than the other occupations. As we have seen these coercive forces range from the policing, corrections, national security, to military service. They are conjoined in their various tasks in upholding domestic and foreign policies designed to maintain the

---

[39] Since 1890, according to Bowles and Jayadev, guard labor (police, corrections officers, and private security guards) has increased four-fold, and today police outnumber those working directly or indirectly for the Pentagon (2007, 1-20).

status quo in the U.S. and U.S. hegemony around the globe. It is important that we first understand why so many people, including some of the most oppressed and repressed, would participate, some very willingly, in coercive forces. Although the answer to this question cannot be reduced to individual economic self-interest or careerism, the economic factors are nonetheless important to consider. As we shall see, the best way to view this enigma is from the perspective that focuses on the capability of the hegemonic bureaucratic state's ability to develop identities that are ideologically sanctioned and operate like master statuses because they defy class and ethno-racial identities and solidarities.

Jobs in coercive forces tend to be more secured than other jobs in other industries. This is one of the reasons why they appear detached and insulated from the general public because they are largely shielded from the economic harsh conditions and in many cases have honorific positions. With all the many reports of a shrinking middle class and serious problems with upward mobility, the various occupations in coercive forces appear more secure and promising than others.

The idea that the capitalist system is maintained and reproduced because the capitalists solicit and entice classes into the system is not unique. Marx and Engels stated that the upper middle class (e.g., bankers, financiers, and lawyers) played a "supplementary part" in the functioning and managing of capitalism (1985, 108).[40] It is the

---

[40] According to Karl Marx, although this group does not produce surplus like workers, their role is to assist the capitalists to manage and realize the surplus produced (Suchting 1983, 115).

upper strata that is thought to be the most conservative because of their direct relationship to the capitalist system while the rest of the middle class, depending on the historical context, conditions, and place, have generated much debate, as either being reactionary or revolutionary (i.e., having the potential to radicalize and side with workers and other oppressed people) (Burris 1995). In addition, one can also argue that various other segments of the population such as the working class also play an equally important role in maintaining the social order by following the rules of the game (e.g., respect for laws that protect private property and to work endlessly and obediently to maximize their own self-interests). In this reasoning, it is those outside the workforce, the surplus population who have the greatest potential for mobilization because of their distance from the benefits of capitalism and because they experience the full force of the misery that the system produces.

Understanding class structures and class interests is important because it moves us away from simple dichotomies such as between the 1% versus the 99% and exposes the complex nature of how the social order is maintained and reproduced. It would be extremely difficult to conceptualize members of coercive forces as being members of the so-called 1% or as members of the 99%. What appears to be a more accurate statement is that these occupations draw from a cross-section of the population. Military generals, directors, chiefs of police, and other high level officials may largely be from the upper and middle classes, but many of the rank and files have historically come from the working class and the poor. Military service and, for that matter, employment in law enforcement and corrections is often seen by many from the disadvantaged classes as the only viable option for upward mobility, especially in times of economic insecurity. However, certain branches in the above occupations as well as for many positions in national security are reserved for middle and upper middle classes because of their higher requirements such as college education. In any case, coercive forces appear to be disconnected from some sense of class identity and solidarity, at least in the traditional sense, such as in the expression of a working class consciousness. Yet, they do appear to have a strong sense of solidarity and an alliance, but to themselves, the organizations they are embedded in, and the system that sustains them materially and ideologically.

The various organizations within coercive forces have lobbies, unions, and other organizations that operate like a "class-in-itself," pursuing their own narrow occupational interests as opposed to broader "class-for-itself" interests. For example, their unions and associations are clear examples of how their organizations pursue narrow interests. Organizations such as The Fraternal Order of Police, Patrolmen's Benevolent Associations, California Correctional Peace Officers Association, and the American Legion fight for job security, better wages, benefits, and they stand against legislation that will either reduce police sizes or prison populations. Many of these unions and associations also tend to circle the wagons and close ranks when a fellow officer or department is scrutinized by the public or media. Their organized power promotes their vested interests and appears to be firmly grounded in the continuation of the status quo rather than in a particular class, in the classical sense. After all, there have been very rare occurrences in which members in policing, corrections, or military organizations have joined or acted in solidarity with other workers or participated in social movements with other sectors of society.

Yet, economic interests do not guarantee acquiesce. As a result, some organizations have developed such as the American Legion, established in 1919, in order to keep the sense of U.S. patriotism alive in veterans long after military service. The Legion currently has 2.4 million members.[41] The Legion developed as an anti-communist organization to prevent the radicalization of former soldiers by keeping them connected to the military (Campbell 1997). In addition, organizations such as the Legion were established to "build a cross class alliance dedicated to nationalism—Americanism in the language of the Legion—as a bulwark against an increasingly organized and radical working class" (Campbell 1997). Veterans have long been selected for special privileges such as pensions, loans, and medical treatment in order to keep this large segment of the population connected to the U.S. state long after their military service ends (Rodriguez-Beruff 1983, 25).

Nevertheless, there has been a history of contentious veterans and veterans' organizations. For example, in 1932 during the Great Depression, some 15,000 WWI veterans and their families marched and occupied Washington, DC demanding payment promised to them. Contentious veteran actions ultimately lead to the passing of the G.I. Bill of Rights in 1944. Not all the actions of veterans were driven by narrow interests. There is also a history of veterans and active military soldiers working in common cause with others out-

---

[41] See American Legion website: http://www.legion.org/history

side the military against U.S. foreign policies—
e.g., during the Vietnam War and to a lesser extent
presently against the Iraq and Afghanistan wars.
This history includes anti-war organizations, con-
scientious objectors, and whistle blowers.[42]

There have been moments in which the police
and correctional guards have gone on strike or engaged in other forms of contentious action, but
much of their actions were restricted to the improvements of their working conditions and not
the overall conditions of all workers or oppressed
peoples. Ever since the Boston Police Strikes of
1919 laws were enacted to prevent law enforcement from striking. However, police now have the
right to join unions; these unions are usually exclusively made up of police and excluded from
broader labor coalitions. The police and correctional officers tend to be paid on average more
and receive more benefits than other public employees and in many cases this includes the private sector and its millions of low-wage service
sector employees. The state has enacted other
mechanisms to prevent those in coercive occupations from sympathizing and identifying with the
conditions of the exploited and oppressed by reducing discontent by raising wages and increasing
pensions, which appears to have done much to increase separation not only from other occupations, but the general plight that many outside the
employment matrix experience. Yet, there are
rank and file police officers at city, state, and federal levels who have exposed corruption, racism,
violations to the U.S. Constitution within their de-

---

[42] A possible explanation for higher levels of veterans' opposition to
the Vietnam War than the more permanent wars in Iraq and
Afghanistan and beyond is due in part to the military draft that
was present during the war in Vietnam (among other factors).

partments and as a result, many of these have suffered severe consequences.

In fact, rather than joining in solidarity with labor movements and social movements, the historical record actually illustrates the opposite. The various organizations within the coercive forces have historically followed orders and policed, surveilled, incarcerated, contained, killed, or otherwise neutralized contentious (or combatant) individuals and oppositional organizations. The separation that divides the individuals in coercive occupations from a large part of the general public can be attributed to salaries, benefits, and job security, which all point to economic motive and interests. However, it would be a mistake to underestimate the degree of institutional socialization that individuals within these paramilitary and military bureaucratic organizations are subjected to. Many of these organizations are designed to instill discipline, loyalty, and to a large extent a particular sense of patriotism. According to Knottnerus, these organizations utilize ritualized symbolic practices such as trainings, drillings, parades, and other ceremonies that impact the cognitions or symbolic thoughts of actors and generate ritual experiences that heighten group and wider system allegiance (2005). For Weber, "The discipline of the army gives birth to all discipline" (Gerth and Mills 1946, 261). Bureaucratic organizations are capable of producing efficiency, but this is largely dependent on the development of hierarchical lockstep discipline. For example, bureaucratic structures in the military and police forces are designed to make obedient self-sacrificing soldiers and police officers, who have, by design, been socialized into being disciplined individuals that "go along" and comply with command hierarchical structures, and above all do not disrupt the system but defend it.

According to Chappell and Lanza-Kaduce's extensive research on police paramilitary-bureaucratic organizations, police departments are "highly specialized, with complex divisions of labor, vertical authority structures, and extensive rule systems" (2010, 2). Even in the era of community policing, all the characteristics of highly bureaucratic structures, which are often associated with the production of individuals into cogs are seen in police departments. The paramilitary-bureaucratic structures in police forces move police officers away from "problem solving, community involvement, organizational decentralization, and prevention of crime" (Chappell and Lanza-Kaduce 2010, 2) and into top-down types of soldiers, who are removed from community involvement.

Unlike other types of occupations, coercive occupations draw significant numbers from the lower middle class, working class, and even from the poor, and since the passage of the Civil Rights Acts of 1964 there has been in many respects the racial integration of many coercive occupations. In examining the all-volunteer armed forces since 1973, Blacks and Latinos, which are the two largest racial minority groups in the U.S., have been heavily recruited into the armed forces. For example, in 2006, 12.6% of the civilian workforce aged 18 to 45 were Black, compared to 19.3% of active-duty enlistments and although Latinos had a civilian labor force participation of 17.1%, they only accounted for 12.8% of the enlistments (Segal and Korb 2013, 113-114). The above numbers only account for active-duty and not all the reserve branches. Clearly, Blacks were and continue to be overrepresented in active duty enlistments. According to Segal and Korb, Latinos would likely also be overrepresented had it not been for enlistment requirements such as high school/GED and citizenship or permanent resident status (2013, 114).

According to Sklansky, the virtually all-white, all-male, and heterosexual departments of the 1950s and 1960s have given way to departments with large numbers of female and minority officers, which are increasingly commonplace (2006, 1210). A report in 2007 largely illustrates this increased diversity by stating that 1 in 4 full-time local police officers was a member of a racial or ethnic minority (estimated 117,113); this was about a 10% increase from 2003 (Reaves 2007, 14). Even with this increase in diversity "Nearly three-quarters of all police officers are White, while the U.S. population is about 63% White, U.S. Census data show" (Alcindor and Penzenstadler 2015). However, increases in racial and ethnic minorities have not translated into a major breakdown in the separation between the police and the poor and the ethno-racially oppressed.

In fact, Sklansky argues against the well-established argument that the new demographics are merely cosmetic changes because occupational outlook and organizational culture trumps the personal characteristics of new recruits (2006). Ronald Weitzer, an expert on diversity in the police force states that "Even if police officers of whatever race enforce the law in relatively the same way," the problem is an image problem for police departments who do not represent the communities they police (Ashkenas and Park 2015). In other words, "blue is blue" and the job shapes the officer, not the other way around (Sklansky 2006, 1210). However, after extensive research, Sklansky argues against the prevailing argument and states that police efficiency increases as a result of increases in the diversity of police departments. That basically, increased diversity has changed police culture to make it more effective in policing—i.e., more effective in maintaining the social order.

Although poor and racial minorities are considered threats to the social order, they still join coercive forces for a multitude of economic and ideological reasons. The fear of collusion between members of coercive forces with segments of the population appears to be the major motivator in the construction of master statuses that can buttress efforts to prevent class and ethno-racial alliances. It is in this way that the state conducts a dual-strategy of integration and neutralization by facilitating incorporation. In other words, in many cases, the most oppressed are tasked with essentially policing and oppressing themselves. After all, coercive forces are in direct proximity with the marginalized and are tasked with upholding the social order by physically managing and controlling the people who tend to be the most oppressed and exploited by the system. The military offers one of the very few escapes from poverty for many individuals and their families. The military appears to not have problems meeting its quotas in times of economic decline. Its enticements of a stable and secured salary and benefits can be overwhelming when employment is scarce and economic insecurity is pervasive. The military as a source of employment is well known, but the military also has a long tradition of providing career opportunities for the middle and upper classes, which are concentrated in the command structure.[43]

Perhaps the best way to address the supportive personnel's sense of duty and allegiance to the state is to not only consider economic interests, but to understand their proximity to coercive forces and to understand that they too are immersed in the very same bureaucratic paramilitary and military structures as are the more direct members. One might conclude that direct front-line forces and supportive personnel as well as most of the population are embedded in larger bureaucratic structures (Bensman and Vidich 1971; Mills 1951, 1959). The need to connect the larger hegemonic and bureaucratic structures of the U.S. state to the coercive apparatuses and more specifically to the individuals that carry out and support the coercive functions is essential.

Yet it is also assumed that many join coercive forces because they do not view the U.S. state as an imperialist and oppressive power, but believe its power to be legitimate. Some might even subscribe to such interpretations as that of Robert Kagan and others who view the U.S. as the world policeman and the keeper of order based on democracy and freedom (2003). The emphasis on belief is important, because of the ability of the state to socialize individuals, who in many cases have internalized the values and norms of the state. In addition, people may not simply submit

---

[43] According to Robert L. Goldich, "Most first-term enlistees (like most people in the U.S.) certainly do not come from the more affluent sectors of American society," but the popular belief that the military is the last resort for the "substandard" was never accurate based on enlistees having higher standardized test results, higher physical aptitudes, higher family income, and less criminal involvement than their civilian counterparts (2013, 93).

to the social order because they believe it is just, but they may believe that there is no acceptable alternative to it and thus align themselves with it. Some may even be operating with the idea that they will reform it from within. Although reasons for becoming a member in coercive forces vary, one cannot deny the power and influence that a highly bureaucratic and hegemonic state has over individual motives and actions. According to David Held, the state "appears to be everywhere, regulating the conditions of our lives from birth registration to death certifications" (1989, 11); this power certainly includes the shaping of educational institutions, the media, and the validation and promotion of particular ideas that reinforce the legitimacy of social order. When it comes to the U.S. state, the most dominant institution in the world, its hegemonic tentacles reach not only into the public and private spheres of U.S. society, but reach around the world.

In evaluating the success of the U.S. state's ability to utilize coercive forces as a means to facilitate the integration of segments of the population into the social order, we need to address the notion of legitimacy, more specifically how the state is able to legitimize its actions. The result has been that there is no short supply of new recruits and all the millions who aspire to be members. Legitimacy is based on the acceptance of a citizenry to state authority. In the context of legal-rational authority, the state exercises its power in accordance with some general notion of consent; this is usually accomplished with a politico-legal system. Of course, a belief in the legitimacy of a social order is not the only means in which a state ensures it continuation. Weber's definition of the nation state centers on the monopoly of the legitimate means of violence within a given territory (Gerth and Mills 1946, 78). For him the coercive apparatus of the state is fundamental to the formation of the state and its ability to maintain its right to dominate/rule. In other words, authority appears to be largely predicated on a (nation) state's monopoly of the legitimate use of violence to enforce its order. In this context, the military and police forces play key roles in this conception of the modern nation state.

Charles Tilly's research identified a link between coercion and legitimacy and wrote that whatever else nation states do, and however they go about legitimizing their power (e.g., the idea of social contract, etc.), "they organize and, wherever possible, monopolize violence" (1996, 171). For Tilly, state legitimacy is obtained over time because eventually "the personnel of states purveyed violence on a larger scale, more effectively, more efficiently, with wider assent from their subject populations, and with readier collaboration from neighboring authorities than did the personnel of other organizations" (1996, 173). Consequently, nation states, in part, maintain power through legitimizing themselves by creating ideologies, which socializes individuals to the norms and values of the state. As Tilly makes clear, control over the physical forces of violence is fundamental to nation states' authority and the fact that legitimacy depends on the conformity to abstract principles such as the consent of the governed only helps to rationalize the monopoly of force (1996, 171). After all, for Tilly it is through the concentration and accumulation of capital and coercion and interstate war waging that the present nation state emerged (1992).

Kent and Jacobs counter assertions that a society based only on coercion could not survive by stating that no social order, not even the most authoritarian, employs coercion by itself; it is often mixed with other means (2004). Kent and Jacobs nevertheless provide historical examples that illustrate what occurs when police suddenly become paralyzed (e.g., on strike) and don't respond; their research suggests that the social order is reliant on coercive force, because without it poor people would not accept the conditions of inequality and would engage in redistribution of wealth endeavors. Robert Cover provides a good example of the state's reliance on force by illustrating how "a convicted defendant may walk to a prolonged confinement, but this seemly voluntary walk is influenced by the use of force. In other words if he does not walk on his own he will most certainly be dragged or beaten" (in Green and Ward 2004, 3). As pointed out above, coercion is aptly referred to as a crucial component to the establishment and continuation of the social order. The amount of force necessary to maintain order in the U.S. is often underestimated. According to many critical theorists, stability is problematic even in the most "democratic" societies because resource distribution is so skewed that only a few reap excessive rewards, freedom, rights, and security. In order to maintain unequal relations there are over 12 million members of coercive forces maintaining this status quo. As a result, there are approximately 7 million individuals under supervision in the U.S. alone and countless populations around the world that live in wretched conditions so that the U.S. state can maintain its global dominance.

State power is complex and possesses a multitude of means by which to repress and/or incorporate and integrate many individuals and groups into its social order. As Weber made clear, the modern rational-legal state was similar to traditional domination because both provide social stability and are "rooted in [their] ability to supply the normal, constantly recurring needs of everyday life and thus has its basis in the economy—the supplier of everyday requirements" (Runciman 1978, 226). The U.S. state fits this description on many levels, two of which stand out: (1) it serves to guarantee the status quo—i.e., stability; and (2) it is the major supplier of everyday requirements such as the material means—e.g., a major provider of employment. Social order, or to be more accurate, state power, functions to reproduce itself, not merely through coercion but by the use of economic means and ideology.

Similar to other imperialist powers, systems of slavery, or authoritarian regimes, the U.S. has managed to legitimize its power. All these regimes were made legitimate by those in power because they possessed and controlled the means of violence, and controlled the distribution of wealth, resources, and employment. Those regimes also had systems of law and order. In addition, those societies also had a large degree of citizen participation; this occurred with the exclusion of others. And those regimes certainly had the ability to integrate various segments of the oppressed population into their social order. It was not unusual to find colonial subjects fighting alongside their European masters. Nor is it incredibly unusual to see the poor or oppressed ethno-racial minorities such as Native Americans, African Americans, and Puerto Ricans in the Armed Forces or in policing agencies managing marginalized communities and countries. One could make the claim that these groups are acting against their own self and collective interests, but perhaps, self and collective interests are too narrowly defined and one needs to re-contextualize them within the larger context of the state's ability to define these. Understanding why so many have a vested interest in the continuation of the status quo seems to be a pressing issue if real change is the objective.

The legitimacy of the social orders presented above did not have invisible coercive apparatuses. The injustice and violence employed by them was/is easily identified by the victims and by those whose interests were undermined. Yet, those employed in coercive forces and those who collaborate with the unjust, violent, and repressive systems are more likely driven to comply out of economic motivation and material interest as well as the desire to carry out their duties. States have the ability to normalize and institutionalize their coercion and violence by the use of various ideologies to justify their actions such as the use of nationalism, patriotism, ethno-racial supremacy, "humanitarianism," or national security, and the upholding of the thin-blue-line that separates civilization from mayhem and disorder.

CONCLUSION

The above inquiry is an attempt to address how the U.S. state uses coercive forces to facilitate the integration of millions into its social order. This inquiry contributes to our understanding of how structured inequalities are maintained and reproduced, and how coercive occupations are the byproducts of unequal relations. There appears to be enough substantial evidence to be skeptical about a legitimacy that is dependent on millions of people who are tasked with upholding it through their participation in various coercive occupations. As seen above, large segments of the population, which cut across class and ethno-racial lines, feed off the current unequal arrangement of power within the U.S. and between the U.S. and a large part of the world by their active participation in the coercive employment matrix. This particular state strategy alone is indeed helpful in the development of an explanation of how organized contentious action is hindered when large segments of the population are either directly or indirectly dependent on its continuation.

By examining the coercive forces beyond their functions in maintaining the status quo, we can begin to understand these occupations in terms of their ability to integrate individuals firmly to the state. These occupations have organizational bureaucratic structures and cultures that integrate individuals more methodically into the social order. Further analysis is needed in order to explain the specific mechanisms that produce behaviors and mindsets of the individuals in coercive forces that appear largely detached and shielded from the realities faced by other segments of society because of their insulation from economic harsh conditions.

Ideology, economic reward, and elevated status are some of the ways in which the U.S. state hides and eases the burden for individuals employed in coercive occupations. One need not use the colonial social order or Nazi Germany to illustrate how problematic the concept of legitimacy is, especially the manner in which it is used to justify unjust authorities. What we know is that it is not only the 1% or even the 5% who benefit the most and who extract the greatest privileges from the continuation of the existing status quo. Clearly, the millions of non-elite (or the 99%) derive benefit as well and thus are also culpable. Although this inquiry is specific to understanding the role that coercive forces play in integrating individuals into the social order, it can be argued that large segments of the population in the U.S. as well as in other rich (or core) nations benefit from unequal global relations (see dependency theory, world systems theory, and theories of underdevelopment). As a result of these unequal relations, rich nations have higher standards of living and have more democratic rights because their core nation state in the capitalist world economy affords them the opportunity to appease its workers and alleviate poverty within the core nations (Wallerstein 1983).

It has always been difficult to question an enduring social order because it provides much reward and ideological justifications to many, including the academic scholar, while the needs of the rest are undermined. Analyzing the culpability and compliance of those involved in upholding unjust and violent social orders is no simple matter. Social orders are typically well camouflaged in deception and ideological justification. In fact, the U.S. state is no exception to the rule; it operates at a greater level of sophistication, which provides it the opportunity to better mask its coercion. It is in the tradition of sociology and its critical capacity, which has been largely reserved for authoritarian and non-western nation states, where we now hope to further our analysis on the U.S. state's use of coercive forces in order to facilitate integration and assess the larger implications this has for mobilizations for social change.

References

Alcindor, Yamiche and Nick Penzenstadler. 2015. "Police redouble efforts to recruit diverse officers." *USA Today*, 21 January. http://www.usatoday.com/story/news/2015/01/21/police-redoubling-efforts-to-recruit-diverse-officers/21574081/

Alexander, Michelle. 2010. *The New Jim Crow: Mass Incarceration in the Age of Colorblindness.* New York, NY: The New Press.

Ashkenas, Jeremy and Haeyoun Park. 2015. "The Race Gap in America's Police Departments." *New York Times,* 8 April. http://www.nytimes.com/interactive/2014/09/03/us/the-race-gap-in-americas-police-departments.html?_r=0

Bacevich, Andrew J. 2005 [2013]. *The New American Militarism: How Americans are Seduced by War.* New York, NY: Oxford University Press.

Bensman, Joseph, and Arthur J. Vidich. 1971. *The New American Society.* Chicago, IL: Quadrangle Books.

"Billions Behind Bars - Inside America's Prison Industry." CNBC. NBC Universal. 2013.

Blackstock, Nelson. 1975 [1988]. *COINTELPRO: The FBI's Secret War on Political Freedom.* New York, NY: Pathfinder Press.

Bobo, Lawrence D. and Victor Thompson. 2012. "Racialized Mass Incarceration: Rounding Up the Usual Suspects." Charles A. Gallagher, *Rethinking the Color Line: Readings in Race and Ethnicity.* New York, NY: McGraw Hill: 225-229.

Bowles, Samuel and Arjun Jayadev. 2007. "Garrison America." *Economists' Voice,* March.

"Building Private Security/Public Policing Partnerships to Prevent and Respond to Terrorism and Public Disorder." 2004. Office of Community Oriented Policing Services, U.S. Department of Justice. http://www.theiacp.org/portals/0/pdfs/Building PrivateSecurity.pdf

Burris, Val. 1995. "The Discovery of the New Middle Class." In Arthur J. Vidich (ed.), *The New Middle Classes*, London, UK: Macmillan Press: 15-54.

Campbell, Alec. 1997. "American Veterans and Class Conflict after World War I." Unpublished paper presented at the New School for Social Research, December 9.

Carson, E. Ann. and Golinelli, Daniela. 2013. "Prisoners in 2012: Prisoners in 2012 Trends In Admissions and Releases, 1991–2012." Washington, D.C.: Bureau of Justice Statistics, NCJ 243920

Chappell, Allison T. and Lonn Lanza-Kaduce. 2010. "Police Academy Socialization: Understanding the Lessons Learned in a Paramilitary-Bureaucratic Organization." *Journal of Contemporary Ethnography,* vol. 39 no. 2: 187-214.

Churchill, Ward and Jim Vander Wall. 1988. *Agents of Repression.* Boston, MA: South End Press.

_____. 1990. *The COINTELPRO Papers.* Boston, MA: South End Press.

Christie, Nils. 1993. *Crime Control as Industry.* New York, NY: Routledge.

Cohn, Scott. 2011. "Private Prison Industry Grows Despite Critics." CNBC, 18 October. http://www.nbcnews.com/id/44936562/ns/business-cnbc_tv/t/private-prison-industry-grows-despite-critics/#.VSwabvnF-So\

Cole, David. 1998. *No Equal Justice: Race and Class in American Criminal Justice System.* New York, NY: The New Press.

Corrections Corporations of American website: www.cca.com

Davenport, Christian. 2005. "Understanding Covert Repressive Action." *Journal of Conflict Resolution* 49: 120-140.

Davenport, Christian, Hank Johnston, and Carol Mueller. (eds.) 2005. *Repression and Mobilization.* Minneapolis, MN: University of Minnesota Press.

della Porta, Donatella and Herbert Reiter. 1998. *Policing Protest.* Minneapolis, MN: University of Minnesota Press.

Department of Homeland Security website: http://www.dhs.gov/

Deutsch, Michael R. 1984. "The Improper Use of the Federal Grand Jury: An Instrument for the Internment of Political Activists." *Journal of Criminal Law & Criminality,* Vol. 75, No. 4, 1159-1196.

Garland, David. 2001. *The Culture of Control. Chicago: IL:* University of Chicago Press.

Green, Penny and Tony Ward. 2004. *State crime: Governments, Violence and Corruption.* Sterling, VA: Pluto Press, 2004

Gellman, Barton and Greg Miller. 2013."'Black budget' summary details U.S. spy network's successes, failures and objectives." *The Washington Post,* 29 August. http://www.washingtonpost.com/world/nationa l-security/black-budget-summary-details-us-spy-networks-successes-failures-and-objectives/2013/08/29/7e57bb78-10ab-11e3-8cdd-bcdc09410972_story.html

Geo Group, Inc. 2012 Annual Report. http://www.geogroup.com/documents/GEO_2 012_Annual_Report.pdf

Gerth, Hans and C. Wright Mills. 1946. *From Max Weber: Essays in Sociology.* New York, NY: Oxford University Press.

Glaze, Lauren E. and Thomas P. Bonczar. 2006. "Probation and Parole in the United States." *Bureau of Justice Statistics Bulletin,* December 2007, NCJ 220218.

_____. *Probation and Parole in the United States, 2010,* Office of Justice Programs, Bureau Of Justice Statistics. http://www.bjs.gov/content/pub/pdf/ppus10.pdf

Glaze, Lauren E. and Erinn J. Herberman. 2012. "Correctional Population in the U.S., 2012." United States Department of Justice. Office of Justice Programs. Bureau of Justice Statistics, December 2013, NCJ 243936

Goldich, Robert L. 2013. "American Military Culture from Colony to Empire." In David M. Kennedy (ed.), *The Modern American Military.* New York, NY: Oxford University Press: 79-110.

Greenwald, Glenn. "Petraeus Scandal in Reported with Compelled Veneration of All Things Military." *Guardian, 12 Nov. 2012.* http://www.theguardian.com/commentisfree/2012/nov/10/petraeus-scandal-media-military

Hagan, John. 1994. *Crime and Disrepute.* Thousand Oaks, CA: Pine Forge.

Held, David. 1989. *Political Theory and the Modern State.* Stanford, CA: Stanford University Press.

Isemberg, David. 2012. "Contractors in War Zones: Not Exactly 'Contracting.'" TIME.com, 9 October. http://nation.time.com/2012/10/09/contractors-in-war-zones-not-exactly-contracting/#ixzz2pmEGGyuC

Katz, Michael. 2007. "Why Aren't U.S. Cities Burning?" *Dissent,* Summer.

Kent, Stephanie and David Jacobs. 2004. "Social Divisions and Coercive Control in Advanced Societies: Law Enforcement Strength in Eleven Nations from 1975 to 1994." Social Problems, Vol. 51, No. 3: 343–361.

Kennedy, David M. 2013. *The Modern American Military.* New York, NY: Oxford University Press.

Knottnerus, David. 2005. "Structural Ritualization Theory: Current Research and Future Developments." Presented at the Sociological Imagination Group Conference, Philadelphia, 13 August.

Linebaugh, Peter. 1976. "Karl Marx, The Thief of Wood, and the Working Class Composition: A Contribution to the Current Debate." *Crime and Social Justice*, No. 6, Fall-Winter, 5-16.

Lindorff, David. 2012. "The US is the World's Biggest War-Monger: American Militarism." *Counterpunch*, September 24. http://www.counterpunch.org/2012/09/24/ame rican-militarism/print

Loury, Glenn C. 2008. *Race, Incarceration, and American Values*. Boston: Boston Review Books, MIT Press.

Lovell, Jarret S. 2010. *Good Cop / Bad Cop: Mass Media and the Cycle of Police Reform*. Boulder, CO: Lynne Rienner Publishers, Inc.

Marx, Gary T. 1970a. "Civil Disorder and the Agents of Social Control." *Journal of Social Issues* 26: 19-57.

_____. 1970b. "Thoughts on a Neglected Category of Social Movement Participant: The Agent Provocateur and the Informant." In Mayer N. Zald and John D. McCarthy (eds.), *The Dynamics of Social Movements*. Cambridge: Winthrop: 94-125.

_____.1979 "External Efforts to Damage or Facilitate Social Movements: Some Patterns, Explanations, Outcomes, and Complications." In *The Dynamics of Social Movements*, M. Zald and J. McCarthy, New York, NY: Cambridge University Press.

Marx, K. and Engels, F. 1985. *The Communist Manifesto*. Melbourne: Penguin Books.

Mills, C. Wright. 1951. *White Collar*. New York, NY: Oxford University Press.

_____. 1956. *The Power Elite*. New York, NY: Oxford University Press.

Montes, Vince. 2009. "The Web Approach to the State Strategy in Puerto Rico." David

Knottnerus and Bernard Phillips (eds.), *Bureaucratic Culture and Escalating Problems: Advancing the Sociological Imagination*. Boulder, Colorado: Paradigm Publishers.

National Advisory Commission on Civil Disorders. 1968. New York, NY; Bantam.

Oliver, Pamela. 2008. "Repression and Crime Control." *Mobilization: The International Quarterly* 13,1: 1-24.

Parenti, Christian. 2008 (1999). *Lockdown America: Police and Prisons in the Age of Crisis*. New York, NY: Verso.

Parenti, Michael. 2011. *The Face of Imperialism*. Boulder, CO: Paradigm Publishers.

Pelaez, Vicky. 2014. "The Prison Industry in the United States: Big Business or a New Form of Slavery?" El Diario-La Prensa and Global Research, 10 March. http://www.globalresearch.ca/the-prison-industry-in-the-united-states-big-business-or-a-new-form-of-slavery/8289

Piven, Frances Fox and Richard A. Cloward. 1977. *Poor People's Movements*. New York, NY: Vintage Books.

_____. 1971 [1993]. *Regulating the Poor: The Functions of Public Welfare*. New York, NY: Vintage Books.

"Projected Veteran Population 2013 to 2043," Prepared by the National Center for Veterans Analysis and Statistics October 13, 2014. http://www.va.gov/vetdata/docs/quickfacts/population_slideshow.pdf

Public Interest website:
http://www.inthepublicinterest.org/ (Search:
Corrections Corporation America)

Quigley, Bill. 2010. "Corporations Profit from
Permanent War." *Huffington Post, 25 May* 2010.
http://www.huffingtonpost.com/bill-
quigley/corporations-profit-
from_b_586896.html?

Quinney, Richard. 1977. *Class, State, and Crime: On
the Theory and Practice of Criminal Justice.* New
York, NY: Longman.

Reich, Robert. 2010. "America's biggest jobs
program: The US military," *The Christian Science
Monitor*, 13 August.
http://www.csmonitor.com/Business/Robert-
Reich/2010/0813/America-s-biggest-jobs-
program-The-US-military

Reiner, R. 1985. *The Politics of the Police.* New York,
NY: St. Martins Press.

*Report of the National Advisory Commission on Civil
Disorders.* 1968. New York, NY: Bantam Books.

Rizzo, Jennifer. 2012. "Defense cuts: The jobs
numbers games." *CNN*, 22 Sept.
http://security.blogs.cnn.com/2011/09/22/defen
se-cuts-the-jobs-numbers-game/

Robb, David L. 2004. *Operation Hollywood: How the
Pentagon Shapes and Censors the Movies.* New
York, NY: Prometheus Books, 2004.

Rodriguez-Beruff, Jorge. 1983. "Imperialism and
Militarism: An Analysis of the Puerto Rican
Case." *Proyecto Caribeno de Justicia y Paz,* Rio
Pedras: Puerto Rico.

Rubenstein, Edwin S. 2012. "The High Cost of
Cheap Detentions." *The Social Contract,* Volume

22, Number 3, Spring. http://www.thesocial contract.com/artman2/publish/tsc_22_3/tsc-22-3-rubenstein-detentions.shtml

Runciman, W.G. 1978 [1998]. *Max Weber: Selections in Translation.* New York, NY: Cambridge University Press.

Ruth, Alexander. 2012. "Which is the world's biggest employer?" BBC News Magazine, 19 March. http://www.bbc.co.uk/news/magazine-17429786

Sabol, William J., Heather C. West and Matthew Cooper. 2009. "Prisoners in 2008." United States Dept. of Justice. Office of Justice Programs. Bureau of Justice Statistics Bulletin. June 30, 2010, NCJ 228417.

Segal, David R. and Lawrence J. Korb. 2013. "Manning and Financing the Twenty-First-Century-All-Volunteer Force." David M. Kennedy (ed.), *The Modern American Military.* New York, NY: Oxford University Press: 111-134.

Sklansky, David Alan. 2006. "Your Father's Police Department: Making Sense of the New Demographics of Law Enforcement." *Journal of Criminal Law and Criminology,* Vol. 96 Issue 3 Spring, Article 9.

Suchting, W.A. 1983. *Marx: An Introduction.* Sussex, UK: Wheatsheaf Books.

Surette, R. 1998. *Media, Crime, and Criminal Justice: Images and Realities* 2nd Edition, New York, NY: Wadsworth Publishing.

Tarrow, Sidney. 1998. *Power in Movement.* New York, NY: Cambridge University Press. "The United States Security Industry: Size and Scope, Insights, Trends, and Data," by ASIS

International the Institute of Finance and
Management (IOFM)

Tilly, Charles. 1978. *From Mobilization to Revolution.*
Boston, MA: Addison-Wesley.

_____. 1996. "State Making and War Making as
Organized Crime." Peter Evens, Dietrich
Ruechemeyer, and Theda Skocpol, *Bringing the
State Back In, New York, NY:* Cambridge
University Press.

_____. 1992. *Coercion, Capital, and European
States, AD 990-1992.* Maiden, MA: Blackwell
Publishing Ltd.

Turse, Nick. 2010. "Empire of Bases 2.0." *Asian
Times.*
http://www.atimes.com/atimes/South_Asia/MA
12Df01.html

United Nations Office on Crime and Drugs. "The
Tenth United Nations Survey of Crime Trends
and Operations of Criminal Justice Systems"
(Tenth CTS, 2005-2006).
https://www.unodc.org/unodc/en/data-and-
analysis/Tenth-CTS-full.html

U.S. Bureau of Labor Statistics. Correctional
Officers: Occupational Outlook Handbook,
Jan/2014. http://www.bls.gov/ooh/Protective-
Service/Correctional-officers.htm

U.S. Census Bureau, Statistical Abstract of the
United States: 2012. Section 5: Law
Enforcement, Courts, and Prisons, p. 216.
http://www.census.gov/prod/2011pubs/12statab
/law.pdf

U.S. Department of Defense. 2010. "Population
Representation in Military Services."
http://prhome.defense.gov/portals/52/Document

s/POPREP/poprep2010/summary/PopRep10Sum
m.pdf

U.S. Dept. of Justice. 2011. "Census of State and
Local Law Enforcement Agencies, 2008." Office
of Justice Programs, Bureau of Justice Statistics,
July, NCJ 233982.
http://www.bjs.gov/content/pub/pdf/csllea08.p
df

_____2012. "Federal Law Enforcement Officers,
2008." U.S. Department of Justice Office of
Justice Programs, Bureau of Justice Statistics,
June, NCJ 238250.
http://www.bjs.gov/content/pub/pdf/fleo08.pdf

U.S. Dept. of Justice. FY 2014 Budget Request at a
Glance Discretionary Budget Authority.
http://www.justice.gov/sites/default/files/jmd/le
gacy/2013/11/11/fy14-bud-sum.pdf

U.S. Dept. of Labor Statistics. Bureau of Labor
Statistics. Probation Officers and Correctional
Treatment Specialists, January 8, 2014.
http://www.bls.gov/ooh/Community-and-
Social-Service/Probation-officers-and-
correctional-treatment-specialists.htm#tab-1

U.S. Department of Labor, Bureau of Labor
Statistics. Occupational Employment and
Wages, May 2014, 33-9032 Security Guards.
http://www.bls.gov/oes/current/oes339032.htm
#ind

"U.S. Military Personnel by Country" CNN.
http://www.cnn.com/interactive/2012/04/us/ta
ble.military.troops/

Wacquant, Loic. 2008a. *Urban Outcast: A
Comparative Sociology of Advanced Marginality*.
Cambridge, UK: Polity Press.

_____. 2008b. Forum on "Race, Incarceration, and American Values." In Glenn C. Loury, ed., *Race, Incarceration, and American Values.* Cambridge, MA: Boston Review.

Wallerstein, Immanuel. 1983. "The Three Instances of Hegemony in the History of the Capitalist World-Economy." *Journal of Comparative Sociology* XXIV, 1-2, January-April, 100-08.

Walmsley, Roy. 2011. World Population List, 9th Ed. Essex: International Centre for Prison Studies.

Western, Bruce. 2006. *Punishment and Inequality in America.* New York, NY: Russell Sage Foundation.

Squatting in Racialized Berlin 1975-2015: Vietnamese Transnational Subjectivity in a Climactic Double Division

Trangđài Glassey-Trầnguyễn

Diasporic communities and transnational discourses have become important research topics of late, though they have existed for centuries and their studies have remained uneven. I have argued elsewhere that the Vietnamese diasporas have emerged much earlier than the year 1975, but this historic year marks the greatest exodus out of Vietnam and the subsequent formations of Vietnamese diasporic communities around the world. In this paper, I look at the Vietnamese populations in the German capital Berlin(s). During my four fieldwork trips in Berlin (and other parts of Germany, in March 2005, June 2005, August 2005, and March 2008[1]), I encountered Vietnamese from

[1] Mr. Olivier Glassey-Tranguyen underwrote the bulk of my research and travel expenses during the March 2008 trip to Berlin. I received partial support for my March 2008 fieldwork in Berlin from the UCSD Dean's Social Sciences (International) Research Grant and the UCSD Ethnic Studies Research & Travel Grants. I thank Dr. & Ms. Nguyễn Văn Thanh for airport rides; and Dr. Markus Stauff, and Drs. Asta & Patrick Vonderau for

both East and West Germany, and heeded their expressions on the challenges of the historical 1954 North-South partition of Vietnam and the present East-West division in Berlin. I paid particular attention to how Vietnamese Berliners' perception that the North-South division, which is felt across the Vietnamese diasporas worldwide, is at its climax in Berlin.

Weaving together excerpts from field notes and oral history interviews, I show that the Vietnamese immigration experiences in Germany —which continue today—are much more complex and diverse than the perceived East-North/West-South double division. I argue that Vietnam's colonial history, the Vietnam War, the Cold War, and Germany's history of division have all contributed to the continued North-South opposition found among the Vietnamese Berliners. As such, I argue that Vietnamese are squatting in racialized Berlin(s), forging a borderland-motherland diasporic subjectivity within a climactic double division. Squatting—both physically and metaphorically —is a form of resistance that enables the Vietnamese Berliners to carve out a space for themselves in an exclusionary Berlin, evoking how human bodies are simultaneously sites of transnational racialization as well as sites of transformation.

accommodating me during this trip. I thank the U.S. Department of State, Fulbright Program; and the Swedish Fulbright Commission for according me with the opportunity to encounter Berlin as a research site for the first time in March 2005.

FIELDWORK: OVERVIEW & MOMENTS OF ENCOUNTER

My interest in Berlin as a research site came under the auspice of attending the 52nd annual Fulbright Berlin Seminar in March 2005, hosted by the German Fulbright Commission. I was a Fulbright scholar in Sweden at the time, and received support from the Swedish Fulbright Commission to attend the event. My paper proposal "Viet Birds, World Sky" was selected for the research panel at the Seminar. I obtained permission from the Swedish Fulbright Commission[2] to stay in Berlin after the Seminar, and conducted fieldwork and oral history interviews with Vietnamese living there. I returned to Germany in June and August 2005, and in March 2008.

During my fieldwork in March 2005, I visited the Vietnamese homes and community facilities across Berlin, talking to both Buddhist and Catholic groups, conducting interviews with workers from various fields, experiencing lunches at Vietnamese imbiss[3], meeting with Vietnamese originally from both the North and South Vietnam, and identifying with Berlin's history of division when I visited the remnants of the wall[4]. Be-

---

[2] I thank Ms. Jeannette Lindstrom, Executive Director of the Swedish Fulbright Commission, for permission to extend my stay in Berlin and helping me make needed air travel arrangements.

[3] Imbiss (German) is a small food stand or food-to-go store, usually located on the street, near a train or Ubahn metro station or in a corner shop. Convenient for an on-the-go meal or quick snack, the several thousands imbiss across Berlin serve either the basics such as currywurst, pizza, döner kebab, or the ethnic varieties such as Asian and Turkish food.

[4] I shared my initial thoughts about Berlin and the Vietnamese communities there in an interview by Mr. Phan Đăng Hiển, anchor for the Vietnamese section, for two consecutive sessions

fore all of these encounters, at the town hall organized for Fulbrighters as part of the Fulbright Seminar, I asked André Schmitz, the Berlin Mayor's representative, about strategies that the Berlin government had attempted to process the East-West division and its effects[5]. My question stemmed from my perspectives as an ethnic Vietnamese with two decades of lived experiences in Vietnam and one decade in the U.S. (at the time of this encounter). More importantly, the question was part of my engagement in transnational conversations about division and healing, particularly in the context of Vietnam and its diasporas.

My first contact in Berlin was Dr. Phạm Văn Thanh (penname Phạm Việt Vinh) through the introduction of Mr. Nguyễn Gia Kiểng[6], a writer and founder of Tập Hợp Dân Chủ Đa Nguyên[7]. Dr. Phạm came to Alexanderplatz, where the Berlin Seminar was hosted, to meet with me.

on Radio Multikulti in March 2005, "A Vietnamese-American Fulbrighter's Initial Observations about Vietnamese in Berlin."

[5] 2005, Summer. *The Funnel*, a newsmagazine of the German American Fulbright Commission. Number 2, Volume 41. Pg 15 ("Trangdai Tranguyen, Fulbrighter in Sweden, discusses the continuing psychological division of Berlin with André Schmitz during the reception at city hall.")

[6] I thank Mr. Đinh Quang Anh Thái, the then anchor of Little Saigon Radio in Orange County, CA, for introducing me to Mr. Nguyễn Gia Kiểng, and Mr. Nguyễn Gia Kiểng for connecting me with Dr. Phạm Văn Thanh.

[7] Tập Hợp Dân Chủ Đa Nguyên (Rally for Democracy and Pluralism, or Rassemblement pour la Démocratie Pluraliste, RDP) was founded in 1982 by a group of Vietnamese intellects from the pre-1975 Republic of South Vietnam. Headquartered in Paris, the RDP has active chapters in the U.S., Canada, Western and Eastern Europe. The RDP aims at peaceful non-violent multi-party democratization of Vietnam. I had the pleasure of meeting the core group in Paris in February 2005. For information on the group, see http://www.ethongluan.org/.

Upon learning about my research interest, his family offered to host my post-Seminar stay. Dr. Phạm introduced me to several Vietnamese Berliners, including the Multi-Kulti Radio[8] host Mr. Phan Đăng Hiển and his family, the political activist and community leader Ms. Thuý Nonnemann[9], Mr. Lê Lương Cẩn the owner of Thuỷ Tiên Vietnam (Cultural and Wholesale) Center[10], and several others. The Phạm family also took me to the abandoned apartment complexes in which Vietnamese guest workers had once lived and pointed out the shattered glass windows from the

---

[8] Radiomultikulti (September 18, 1994-December 31, 2008), or RM, was a multilingual radio station of the seven stations in the Rundfunk Berlin Brandenburg (RBB). After 14 years, the RM was closed due to budget cuts (alongside the TV program Polylux) despite its being the only radio station for several ethnic groups in Berlin. A poll in March 2008 with Germans showed that the RM audience had the least audience at 37,000 listeners per day, versus the Radio Antenne Brandenburg with 218,000. These results failed to account for the non-German listeners that the RM served. A video clip of the last day of the RM can be viewed here: http://www.youtube.com/watch?v=DT8HzbboHkY.

[9] On October 1, 2013, Ms. Nonnemann was accorded "The Order of Merit of Berlin" (German: Verdienstorden des Landes Berlin) for her services to the Vietnamese refugees since the 1970s and the former guest workers since the 1990s in Berlin and Germany. This is the highest honor by the German State of Berlin and awarded in the name of the Senate of Berlin. Recognizing oustanding contributions to the State of Berlin since July 21, 1987, the Order is awarded each year on October 1, the anniversary of the Berlin Constitution. The Order is limited to no more than 400 living recipients, and has only been awarded 359 times as of 2011. Further information can be found at: http://www.berlin.de/rbmskzl/regierender-buergermeister/auszeichnungen-und-ehrungen/verdienstorden-des-landes-berlin/artikel.6759.php.

[10] Dr. Phạm gave me a ride to the Thuỷ Tiên Vietnam Center and participated in my interview with Mr. Lê Lương Cẩn. The Center is listed as "Asiatische Lebensmittei * Im-& Export * GroB-& Einzelhandel." It was located at Meeraner Straße 9, 1268 Berlin.

gangs' rivalries, recounting how in that small apartment complex, there were up to tens of thousands of people living during the transitional years of *Wende*. We also spent a long evening at the refugee camp in East Berlin where I met Mr. Lê Thắng Lợi and his family.

I met Mr. Phan Đăng Hiển at the Vietnam Haus (1975-2005)[11], an agency under the Berlin government set up to help Vietnamese refugees and immigrants adjust to German life. Though I intended to interview him, Mr. Phan asked for a rain check and interviewed me instead for two sessions about my studies and work in Orange County and Stockholm, as well as my perspectives about Berlin and the Vietnamese populations there. Both sessions of the interview were aired on Radio Multikulti while I was in Berlin. Mr. Phan also brought me to visit a Vietnamese Buddhist family living in Berlin after the interview. I also had an extended unrecorded oral history interview with Mr. Trường Sơn (pseudonym) at Dr. Phạm's residence, who spoke in great length about how the Vietnamese North-South division is at its climax in Berlin. Dr. Phạm and his wife

---

[11] In the late 1970s, the Berlin government created Vietnam Haus to help Vietnamese boat people integrate into German life. In 2005, the Berlin government deemed that after 30 years, their needs were met and the Vietnamese boat people have established themselves in the German society. As a result, Vietnam Haus was closed. The Vietnamese community in West Berlin has established a new organization to facilitate communal, cultural, and support programs, see http://danke-deutschland.org. I thank Mr. Hồ Văn Phước for bringing my attention to this new establishment and the website. On the other hand, in 1992, the Association of Vietnamese in Berlin and Brandenburg (Vereinigung der Vietnamesen in Berlin & Brandenburg) located at Sewanstr. 43, 10319 Berlin, was founded to meet the needs of former Vietnamese guest workers who fought to remain in Germany. See http://vietnam-bb.de/.

were surprised about the length of the interview when they came home that day, since Mr. Trường Sơn was a very quiet and private person.

In retrospect, I believe that my knowledge of the practice of tomb relocation in Northern Vietnam had catalyzed our rapport. When he first arrived at Dr. Phạm's home, Mr. Trường Sơn was very quiet and melancholic. He said, "I just came back from Vietnam where I took care of some matters for my deceased mother, who passed away a few years ago." I asked, "You meant *sang cát?*" He said, "Yes, but we call it *thay áo*[12]." And from that moment on, he poured out his heart without me asking too many questions. I wish to point out how my different encounters with Vietnamese in Berlin have been shaped—and even made possible—by my Vietnamese cultural knowledge and language facility. Because of his personal background and to protect his loved ones in Vietnam, Mr. Trường Sơn asked that I not record the oral history interview with him and that he remain anonymous, and I honored both of his requests. During this trip, I conducted the first fifteen Berlin oral history interviews, some were unrecorded per the narrator's preference.

In June and August 2005, I visited various Vietnamese-owned small businesses as well as florist stands at metro stations in Berlin and talked to the workers, who were eager to tell me about "my hometown" Orange County[13] even though they

---

[12] Both words refer to the practice of exhuming the tomb after a certain number of years after the burial, retrieving and cleaning the bones of the deceased, and reburying them in a new smaller tomb.

[13] Orange County, California, USA, is home to the largest Vietnamese population outside of Vietnam and probably the most desired location in the diaspora. Ethnic Vietnamese around the

had never been to California. At a Vietnamese takeout store in East Berlin, the workers even told me about the owner of the store, Cô Vân, an industrious worker. However, her husband allegedly slacked off in Northern Vietnam and squandered her remittances, which were meant for their daughter's college education. The workers admired her endurance, and said that they enjoyed working for her.

The sensitive information that the workers openly shared with me during such a chance encounter might be puzzling to any observer, given the North-South division between Vietnamese in Berlin. However, such openness was probably due to my coming from Orange County and my being a native Vietnamese speaker. Though I spoke with a Southern accent and the workers used a Northern dialect, the regional language distinction was nullified by the two workers' aspiration for Little Saigon. Orange County's Little Saigon came across as a common point of reference, as the workers enthusiastically told me about how they perceived it as a "dreamland" and their hope to be able to come visit one day. This instantaneous forging of ethnic connection between me and the imbiss workers contrasts deeply with the distance between East and West Berlin Vietnamese that my various informants expressed. While I was able to chat with the workers on all sorts of topics, the conversation was refrained and avoided between Vietnamese in East and West Berlin. This double division, in the word of Mr. Trường Sơn, is at its climax in Berlin.

---

world know about this place through videos, personal stories, or visits. During my Fulbright year in Sweden, the Vietnamese there told me that to them, California means Orange County's Little Saigon and Hollywood.

In March 2008, I made a fourth visit to Germany and conducted fieldwork in Berlin[14] where I interviewed twenty Vietnamese and participated in various community meetings and organization events. Dr. Markus Stauff and Drs. Patrick and Asta Vonderau kindly accommodated me during my fieldwork stay. Dr. Phạm and his wife gave me airport rides. Toward the end of this sojourn, I witnessed the "first encounter" between the Vietnamese Catholics in East and West Berlins at the Lent Retreat at Canisius Kolleg in Berlin—an event that I view as a symbolic beginning for reconciliation between the South and North Vietnamese communities. I visited community organization offices, Radio Multi-Kulti Vietnamese section at the RBB building, community archives, and churches. I relied on Dr. Phạm Văn Thanh and his wife for introductions to organizations of my interests, and took the initiative to contact other people by phone and requested to meet in person. Ms. Bình Nguyễn, Dr. Phạm's wife, went with me to visit Hội Láng Giềng Phục Vụ, an NGO serving former guest workers and recent arrivals in the East.

I also asked my new contacts to introduce me to their networks. Through Ms. Mai Hà Phượng, Mr. Phan's wife, I met a few more informants, including Ms. Yến Bùi, who helped me schedule an interview with her brother, Rev. Antôn Đỗ Ngọc Hà. From a bulletin I received from Ms. Bùi, I contacted the Vietnamese Catholic Community in Berlin, and interviewed several members including the chairman Mr. Dương Văn Đá, both in their

---

[14] Dr. Phạm Văn Thanh had kindly arranged a ride for my fieldwork in Leipzig, but I was unable to pursue due to time shortage and health reasons. I did get to meet with Vietnamese living in Leipzig at Dr. Pham's home during a group gathering and discussion.

homes and at the Lent retreat at Canisius Kolleg. Through Mr. Dương's introduction, I met with and interviewed Vietnamese business owners in West Berlin. I contacted Father Lê Phan (Stefan Taeubner) several times by phone without success, but did get to talk to him at the retreat. During this visit, I met Dr. Nguyễn Văn Hương through Dr. Phạm, and interviewed him at his office at the Berlin's Bureau of Immigration and Integration. On the last day of my trip, after a group dinner at Dr. Phạm's, Mr. Phan surprised me with a two-session interview about my Berlin project in front of everyone. It was a challenging interview because I did not anticipate it, nor did I have the private space to think about the answers given the room full of attentive people.

The most significant event for me during my last fieldwork visit was the three-day Lent retreat "Tam Nhật Tĩnh Tâm" at Canisius Kolleg, that brought together—for the very first time—Vietnamese Catholics in both East and West Berlins. Though I first became aware of the North-South division through my conversation with Mr. Trường Sơn in March 2005, it was only until March 2008 that I witnessed this climax played out in a group setting at the retreat. While the priests, Father Lê Phan and Father Hà, intended to forge unity through this retreat, the distance between the two groups were obvious. The emotional and social distance expressed at the retreat helped me fathom what a former guest worker whose several family members were boat people told me in an interview the week before, "I go buy food at the [Vietnamese] markets [in East Berlin], but I never talk to anyone. I just make the purchase and leave."

One striking moment during the retreat was when I witnessed an elderly lady talk to a teenage boy who had just arrived in Berlin via underground migration networks. She said, "I was a boat person. I did not have any choice but to leave my homeland. It was painful. I lost everything. You don't have to leave your parents like that. Do what is right: go to school, learn German, stay out of illegal acts. You are young. You have many opportunities." Her words did not connect with the teenager, whose family had taken out a hefty loan to send him to Germany underground. He was there not to learn German and lead an exemplary life. He was there to make money right away to remit home to pay back the loans and support his family, even if it means to give himself to the black labor market in Berlin. He was there to ensure the economic survival of his entire family in Vietnam. The elderly lady spoke from her positionality, and saw in the teenager a criminal in the making, another mark of shame on her community. She neglected to see that this young man, while pursuing a condemned path by the German polity, does not enter Germany on the same terms she did.

In 2005, when I interviewed Mr. Phan, the director of Vietnam Haus and anchor for Radio Multikulti's Vietnamese section, he told me that the Haus was closing. That is because the Berlin government has observed that after thirty-three years of integration into German society, Vietnamese in West Berlin no longer need the services that were originally intended for newly arrived refugees. Yet, in October 2008, I found a news article in *Labor (Lao Động)*, a Vietnam-based electronic newspaper, about the grand opening of a new Viethaus in East Berlin. Several conclusions abound, but one immediate corollary is that the needs that were served in West Berlin thirty three years prior to 2008 are now being serviced to Vietnamese in East Berlin. This shows the diversity that is distinctly Berlin in comparison to other Vietnamese diasporic populations such as Orange County.

Here in Berlin, there are not only boat people as perceived in Little Saigon, but there are those I call "wall people" (climbing over the wall to enter West Berlin before the wall fell) and "woods people" (undocumented immigrants coming to Berlin through Eastern Europe, having to stay in car trunks or walk through the forest for days). And yet, Berlin is very much connected to Orange County because in the midst of those narratives about the last fifty years, the Vietnam War has not yet culminated as we witness the many exoduses that continue on long after the boat people phenomenon in the late 1970s through the early 1990s. At the same time, in Berlin, the Vietnamese diasporic immigration patterns are disrupted and diversified. Not only that there are refugees and established immigrants calling this city their home for over three decades, there are trafficked immigrants who have just arrived yesterday. The paradoxical aspects of Berlin as a site on its own and in relation to Orange County have enticed me to conceptualize Berlin as a comparative site. Nonetheless, while focusing on Germany and referencing the US, this project is in fact encompassing many other sites and integrating all the projects pertaining to the Vietnamese Diasporas that I have conducted. That is, in today's global world, different locations are connected and mutually influential. The excerpted narratives in the third section of this paper provide concrete illustrations of this interconnectedness.

These various encounters shed light on my enculturation into the Vietnamese life in Berlin. As an ethnographer, I am still learning what the different conversations mean and how they play out in the everyday life. As a bilingual oral historian, I listen to how the gaps in experiences and perspectives between Vietnamese in East and West Berlin lead to further distancing and oppositions that are rooted in the historical contexts of the homeland and host land. My ultimate goal is to explore how these texts and contexts can help the two communities build mutual trust, understanding, support, compassion, and respect.

CONTEXTUALIZING THE VIETNAMESE BERLIN EXPERIENCES

While this paper focuses on Berlin, it is necessary to conceptualize how this site is directly linked to and affected by the Vietnamese diasporic experiences since 1975 at large and the Vietnam War context in particular. Additionally, it is important to see how Berlin's context—with the 1989 collapse of the Berlin wall and its lingering effects of division—enters the Vietnamese Berlin discourses. I am also wary of the current debates on fortress Europe, contemporary immigration, and inclusion/exclusion. These contexts and discourses are integral in my analysis of the concepts of refugee/immigrant, political legitimacy, legal rights and self-perceptions.

Following the 1975 Fall of Saigon, Vietnamese refugees primarily from South Vietnam arrived in West Germany as boat people and subsequently through family reunification[15], while Vietnamese guest workers[16] arrived in record-high numbers in the early 1980s in East Germany[17]. There were also Germans' spouses and Vietnamese adoptees in the West, as well as exchange students, undocumented immigrants, and entrepreneurs in the East. In West Germany, the government assigned Vietnamese boat people and their ethnic fellows to locations across the country as part of the integration policy, and provided them with language and vocational training[18]. On the other hand, the GDR kept the Vietnamese guest workers in surveillance and isolation, with the intention of getting rid of them at the end of their contract[19].

---

[15] Trangdai Glassey-Tranguyen. 2009. Bilingual Keynote. *"Thuyền Nhân Việt Nam Toàn Cầu trong Thiên Niên Kỷ Thứ Ba: Tìm Lịch Sử, Giữ Tương Lai. Vietnamese Boat People in the Third Millennium: Seeking History, Growing Legacy."* Year-long Project and Multidisciplinary Program: "Ra Khơi: Tưởng Niệm Thuyền Nhân Vượt Biển. Set Sail: Commemorating the Vietnamese Boat People." Gạch Nối Magazine Association, UC San Diego. Also, 2007. *"The Stateless and the Nameless: Sovereignty in the Liberal World."* 5th Annual Conference of Ethnic Studies at UCSD, "Ghosts, Monsters, and the Dead."

[16] I prefer the term "guest workers" over the term "contract workers" because the former conveys the sense of 'dis-belonging' as a guest, while the latter alludes to a contract—but this contract was not honored to the end.

[17] Dennis, Mike. "Working under Hammer and Sickle: Vietnamese Workers in the German Democratic Republic, 1980-89," *German Politics*, Volume 16, Issue 3, 2007, Pages 339 – 357.

[18] Glassey-Trầnguyễn, Trangđài & Phan Đăng Hiển. Oral History Interview. March 11, 2008. Berlin, Germany.

[19] Dennis, Mike. "Working under Hammer and Sickle: Vietnamese Workers in the German Democratic Republic, 1980-89," *German Politics*, Volume 16, Issue 3, 2007, Pages 339 – 357.

Kept apart by the Berlin Wall, the two groups did not come into contact until the 1989 fall of the Berlin Wall, though there were Vietnamese trying to climb the wall to come to the West unsuccessfully[20]. Like Western Germans, Vietnamese in the West opened their homes and hearts to welcome their ethnic counterparts from the East when the Berlin Wall fell. However, the initial comity was short-lived, quickly challenged by the differences in political orientation and cultural expectations. Several Vietnamese women in West Berlin found their husbands being "taken over" by Vietnamese women from the East that they had taken in and helped[21]. I argue that this family disruption, which some narrators had described as "ingratitude" and "devil-doing," was the impetus for the North-South opposition that manifests till today, two and a half decades later. Here in Berlin, the city's historical East-West division is coupled with as well as superimposed on the Vietnamese immigrants' North-South division, with the post-1989 geographical proximity augmenting the division to its climax.

Upon the loss of their contract caused by the demise of the Berlin Wall, Vietnamese guest workers were forced to return to Vietnam. The majority did leave. About 20,000 guest workers fought to stay, because they were used to the German life and did not wish to go back to Vietnam. Moreover, except for those connected to

---

[20] Field notes, March 2005 and 2008. Also, Trangdai Glassey-Tranguyen 2008. *"Immigration in the Vietnamese Diasporas: 1975-2008,"* Bilingual Keynote. Black April Commemoration, Colina Park, San Diego. VAYA Vietnamese American Youth Alliance.

[21] Field notes, March 2008.

the political elites in Vietnam, all guest workers
and their families incurred great debt to acquire
the work contract. Workers spent the first two
years repaying the fees and interests, and could
only start earning profit from the third year on-
ward. If their contract ended prematurely, they
were left with an exorbitant debt that they
would not be able to repay if they returned to
Vietnam[22]. To earn a living, some former guest
workers engaged in contraband cigarette trade,
a predominantly Polish network. To exacerbate
the opposition between Vietnamese in the East
and the West, the German media portrayed the
Vietnamese former guest workers and new undocumented immigrants as criminals and
brought an ethnic stigma upon the Vietnamese
population in general[23]. This ethnic stigma and
public shame caused not only the Vietnamese
in the West to dis-associate with their counterparts in the East, but even Vietnamese in the
East felt the same way.

In the Berlin government's brochure (1986,
1990, and 1997) on migration and integration,
the City's Commissioner Barbara John uses the
Vietnamese boat people as model examples
against the unwanted criminalized Vietnamese
former guest workers[24]. As the spokesperson for
the Berlin Office of Foreigners' Affairs, John has
the power to influence public opinion about

[22] Dennis, Mike. "Working under Hammer and Sickle: Vietnamese
Workers in the German Democratic Republic, 1980-89," *German
Politics*, Volume 16, Issue 3, 2007, Pages 339 – 357.

[23] Chase-Jacobson, Jordan. "Vietnamese in Berlin." Internal Report,
Berlin's Bureau of Immigration and Integration. 2003. Provided by
Chase-Jacobson's Supervisor, Nguyễn Văn Hương, J.D., in 2005.

[24] Ibid.

non-Germans living in the Federal Republic. John's tone of voice, her sense of guiding Germany and its people in dealing with foreigners, and her differentiation between herself and the immigrants show her orientation on the matter. She starts by stating the interconnections between the history of Berlin and that of the Vietnamese immigrants, contextualizing the latter in the German East-West struggle. I argue that the act of fixing the Vietnamese immigrant discourse onto the German history shows the meta-narrative that persists on a German-centric perspective, and excludes the voices of the Vietnamese immigrants by "speaking for them." This is where I believe my project will make an important intervention. With a focus on the narratives and perspectives of the Vietnamese immigrants on both sides of the once-divided Berlin, I am foregrounding the Vietnamese language and experiences in an attempt to study the subject formation of the Vietnamese in both the East and the West. This focus also illuminates the squatting metaphor that I build from Simon Leung's project. The boat people set the first foot down in the West, and the contract workers set the second foot down in the East. The two groups come into the squatting position with the presence of the other group, unlike the exclusionary analysis found in the Berlin brochure. The boat people are no longer used to exclude the contract workers, as they were in the brochure.

In his internal report as an intern at the Berlin Bureau for Immigration and Integration[25], Chase-Jacobson observes that John does not dwell on the history of the boat people, though she does give the contours of their experiences from arrival to what she calls "an example of successful integration" (pg 8). She notes the many self-help Vietnamese groups, suggesting that the Vietnamese boat people have fully integrated into Berlin society. This partially explains the closing of Vietnam Haus in 2005. At the same time, new ethnic-based agencies and organizations continue to emerge in East Berlin around this time, but this emergence might have escaped John's notice because it does not serve the purpose of her argument.

I am wary of how convenient it is for the government of Berlin to use the contexts of the two Vietnamese groups to narrate the meta-narrative of division. Since the Vietnamese guest workers came on a contract basis, they were never considered for integration. These disposable bodies—members of the global assembly line—were supposed to provide short-term labor and return to their country of origin. I ask: does the East German government work, and if so—how—to help the former guest workers adjust and cope with reverse culture shock when they return to Vietnam? At the time of the brochure, the status of the former guest workers who chose to remain in Germany was still uncertain. More than a decade later, that is still the

---

[25] I thank Dr. Nguyễn Văn Hương for providing me with a copy of Chasse-Jacobson's report after my oral history interview with him in March 2008.

case. Nonetheless, John's attention is selectively on the refused asylum seekers and the alleged Vietnamese cigarette sellers, not on the former guest workers who have earned their rights to stay in Germany with hard work and perseverance.

I find this distinction disturbing and ambiguous. Such a distinction erases the fact that many refused asylum seekers were also former guest workers, several of whom applied multiple times for asylum in Germany after they lost their contracted work. The demonstrations and marches of the former guest workers after the *Wende* show that they were as much asylum seekers as anyone else who might have come to Germany undocumented[26]. While John states that the Berlin brochure offers a "differentiated perspective of the Vietnamese Berliners," this differentiation betrays the diverse yet interconnected realities that Vietnamese in Berlin share, whether they have come by boat or via a work visa. According to Chase-Jacobson, "the motivation of Barbara John and the authors of the pamphlet is to isolate the perpetrators of violent trade from the rest of the Vietnamese population in order to *diminish ethnic-stigmatization*" (italics mine, pg 10). Yet, contrary to the authors, the pamphlet in fact can only cause more disruption and division within the Vietnamese immigrant communities, exacerbating

---

[26] Glassey-Trầnguyễn, Trangđài & Nguyễn Sơn Thạch. Oral History Interview. March 19, 2008. Berlin, Germany. During this interview, I also accessed the extensive archive of photos and newspaper clippings of the guest workers' marches and struggles for the right to stay at the office of Hội Phục Vụ Láng Giềng.

the double-division East-West North-South praxis.

The meta-narrative of the Berlin government, through Barbara John as the official spokesperson, reflects a dichotomy-perspective about immigrants: the good/wanted/legal versus the bad/unwanted/illegal. By "legitimizing" the good and condemning the "bad," Barbara John has denied the unwanted immigrants of their "right to a city" as Henri Lefebvre[27] describes,

> The right to the city manifests itself as a superior form of rights: right to freedom, to individualization in socialization, to habitat and to inhabit. The right to the *oeuvre*, to participation and *appropriation* (clearly distinct from the right to property), are implied in the right to the city.

This de/legitimizing of the boat people and the guest workers fails to account for East Germany's interest in and benefits from the guest workers. This act also fails to account for the detrimental disruption in the guest workers' life and their contracts upon the fall of the Berlin wall in 1989. Their de-legitimization renders the guest workers "illegal," while their entry into East Germany was legal and wanted—and wanted urgently. By 'isolating' them as the problematic segment of the Vietnamese immigrant collective in Berlin, Barbara John fails to acknowledge the role of the Berlin government in addressing post-*Wende* issues for the populations already marginalized prior to 1989. While the guest workers were marginalized through surveillance, isolation, and

---

[27] Lefebvre, Henri (trans. Eleonore Kofman and Elizabeth Lebas). *Writings on Cities*, Blackwell Publishing, 1996.

harsh regulations during their contract work, they continued to be treated as "illegitimate" after they unfairly lost their contract beyond their control or desire. As workers, they benefited both the East German and Vietnamese governments, with direct labor that sustained an economy in labor crisis, and direct withdrawals from their salaries respectively[28]. Yet neither government took responsibility to address their needs and rights upon the fall of the Berlin Wall. The guest workers, therefore, are doubly marginalized before (by Vietnam and East Germany) and triply marginalized (as well as by West/United Germany) after the *Wende*.

As such, the Berlin brochure dehumanizes the guest workers, while fitting the boat people into the humanitarian positivistic mold that purports German values and success. By amputating the guest workers from the Vietnamese immigrant body of Berlin, John illustrates what Stuart Hall calls the "internalist narrative" that excludes non-Germans[29]. The de-legitimization of the guest workers also acts as a double negation of their part in the most recent period of German history, and can be very well part of the longitudinal negation of non-European bodies in Germany since medieval times[30]. Here, the Berlin brochure absconds the guest workers' autonomy and agency, speaking for them (i.e. on their behalf) and against them. In this process of denying the guest workers a voice and a place in German society, the

---

[28] Dennis, Mike. "Working under Hammer and Sickle: Vietnamese Workers in the German Democratic Republic, 1980-89," *German Politics*, Volume 16, Issue 3, 2007, Pages 339 – 357.

[29] Cited by El-Tayeb, Fatima. *European Others: Queering Ethnicity in Postnational Europe* (Difference Incorporated). University of Minnesota Press. 2011.

[30] Ibid.

brochure has racialized them as "others" and outside of the German polity. The brochure continues the work of the exclusionary history deep-
rooted in Europe's past that Fatima El-Tayeb has
describes in her works (2004, 2008, 2011).

Furthermore, Barbara John separates the Vietnamese immigrants in four categories: students,
boat people, contract workers, and refused asylum
seekers. This separation further illustrates the
negation of the connectedness and relatedness of
members of this ethnic group. By condemning
the last group, John fails to acknowledge the historical context of division that leads to the immigration of Vietnamese on both sides of the Berlin
Wall. John leaves her own point of departure
hanging when she fails to acknowledge that all
four groups of Vietnamese came to Germany as a
result of the Cold War aftermath, the very root of
the German East-West division which she uses as
the premise of her argument. Additionally, the
model-minority myth and "yellow trash" work
hand in hand, at once elevating some and debas-
ing others of the same ethnicity.

Barbara John uses the term "boat people" and
evokes the historical period of the late 1970s and
1980s when Vietnamese war refugees poured into
the Pacific Ocean in search of freedom. The dona-
tion and creation of the rescue ship Cap Anamur[31]

---

[31] At the plight of the Vietnamese boat people drowning in the high
sea in the late 1970s, concerned West Germans donated money to
build the ship named Cap Anamur to rescue the Vietnamese
escapees. This was one of several worldwide efforts to rescue the
boat people. Cap Anamur operated as an NGO helping the
Vietnamese boat people during its genesis, and has continued to
be an international organization committed to assisting those
living in developing countries with medical aid, healthcare,
building hospitals and schools, and providing relief materials to
communities in crisis. Dr. Ruppert Neudeck (1939-2016) of

conjures an important and proud moment in West Germany's history of immigration and integration. At the plight of the Vietnamese boat people, concerned Germans were able to act out their humanitarian deeds. The Vietnamese boat people have expressed their gratitude in a multitude of ways, including raising funds to erect commemorative monuments in honor of the rescuers and Germany[32]. The *Wende* brings a new light for the boat people, who were not previously viewed as a success. Yet in contrast to their counterparts in the East post-*Wende,* the boat people were seen in much brighter light than they have ever been— when the boat people narrative was used to make a case against the guest workers and argue for social and political exclusion of the latter.

Pipo Bui[33] points out the significant changes in the brochure over its three consecutive editions in 1986, 1990, and 1997. The Vietnam War becomes less important in the latter editions. The criticism of Vietnamese socialist government decreases. The Vietnamese immigrants in the West are perceived as more successfully integrated than their recent counterparts. These changes are used to differentiate the two groups, and widen the existing divisions between them. Bui also notes that:

> In the early part of the decade, Vietnamese migrants barely surfaced in the national

---

Troisdorf was the founder of the Cap Anamur project. See www.cap-anamur.org

[32] See, for instance, Radio Free Asia. "Khánh thành Bia tỵ nạn tưởng niệm thuyền nhân ở nước Đức" (Vietnamese Boat People Commemorative Monument in Germany) by Minh Thuỳ, May 1, 2007.

[33] Bui, Pipo. *Envisioning Vietnamese Migrants in Germany: Ethnic Stigma, Immigrant Origin Narratives and Partial Masking.* LIT Verlag Münster, 2003.

press. This is surprising, because in the interval between 1991 and 1996, Vietnamese were implicated a couple of items of national news and political interest, including the wave of racist violence in 1992 (as victims) and the 1993 right-to-stay policy for people who had been brought to the GDR as laborers as agents in the political process.

I wonder what it takes for the Vietnamese, especially those in the East, to go from "migrants" to "vagrants," from illegal to criminal. As El-Tayeb[34] points out, non-European bodies have always been considered outside of the Republic polity, and as such, have always been 'vagrant' in all senses. How does the process of "de-legitimization" such as the one found in the Berlin brochure create an excluded community, in Simon Leung's vein of community as processual that I will explore in the next section? The 1992 Rostock incident[35] renders Vietnamese as victims, but they are still in the background of right-wing politics and xenophobic violence in the face of limited police and government responses. Nonetheless, the image of background victims was soon replaced by that of contraband cigarette sellers and gangsters only three years later.

When I revisited my Berlin field notes several years after the day I met a Vietnamese family in the refugee camp there in March 2005, the image of a little boy dominated my mind. He was barely three years old, circling the room that had minimal furniture and a "playground" with discarded

[34] El-Tayeb, Fatima. *European Others: Queering Ethnicity in Postnational Europe* (Difference Incorporated). University of Minnesota Press. 2011.

[35] Kinzer, Stephen. "Vietnamese, Easy Target, Fear Outster by Germany." *The New York Times*, December 6, 1992.

toys. He was carefree and spirited. Yet his presence and energy disturbed his bipolar father, Lê Thắng Lợi, who described himself as having turned lunatic after hiding from the police raids so many times and for so many months. I ask: how does this child, barely three years old, figure into the Vietnamese immigration reality and German geo-politics? How does he enter the Vietnamese disaporic communities in Germany and to be more particular, the Vietnamese communities in Berlin? Is he counted? What category does he fit in, if at all? He certainly did not fit in at home—his playful zest angered his father. But to a total stranger like myself on the very first visit to their shelter, the boy's childhood of being in limbo hit home for me. He was with his father, who at times didn't want him. There were also moments when the boy was separated from his parents and siblings, in a strategy to delay the police arrest and immediate deportation. The German government must deport the whole family and not its minor members on their own, hence self-identified stateless refugees like his father would split up the family in order to divert the police actions.

Where does this child fit into the East-West Berlin division, and the North-South climactic oppositions between the two Vietnamese Berlins? Mr. Trường Sơn's words stayed with me across the years, and prompted me to particularly heed the psychological and physical divisions that run deep amongst Vietnamese communities in Berlin during my studies there. The man only spoke of division stemming from the 1954 Rivervine Division in Vietnam, but I have found other lines of division beyond the demarcation zone that once split Vietnam in halves six decades ago. There used to be two Berlins, but there are still two Vietnamese Berlins. Several scholars have recognized the divisive effects of the wall that linger on long after its 1989 demise. Yet I argue that the wall is very much standing for the Vietnamese populations in Berlin. As a West-Berlin Vietnamese told me, even when she went to East Berlin to procure ethnic Vietnamese food, which the Vietnamese there have recently made diversified and abundant, she never talked to anyone. She simply came for the food.

There are divergences in the way immigrant and refugee Vietnamese came to Berlin, and historical underpinnings in both their homeland Vietnam and the host country Germany have contributed to the contemporary divisions and differences. I argue that together with the Vietnamese immigration trajectories, German integration and im/migration policies have shaped the conditions and developments of the two Vietnamese communities in Berlin. I argue that supportive programs at arrival, legal equity, integration opportunities, and other factors have helped Vietnamese in West Berlin participate better in the German society. To reduce the crime rates amongst Vietnamese in East Berlin and to advance their future in the German society as a whole, Vietnamese immigrants in East Berlin should be treated under similar policies that their counterparts in West Berlin have enjoyed since 1975.

Towards an Understanding of Vietnamese Berlins: Contemporary Integration

In the mixing of today's world, it is almost impossible to remain "isolated" in any given context, more so in a cosmopolitan space like Berlin. Yet it is shown that several walls are still standing between the two Vietnamese Berlin communities. I argue that the moment of encounter has taken place, and while clashes and oppositions will continue to drive the interactions, a new sense of understanding and fellowship will emerge if the Vietnamese in East Berlin can attain political equity, legal rights, and social inclusion. The East Berlin Vietnamese have been seen in a negative light by their own ethnic counterparts and the local communities. Their immigration experiences are frowned upon, and their economic and moral practices are not endorsed by the West Berlin Vietnamese. Nonetheless, oppositions must make way for collaborations, and mutual interest will lead to a more open and inclusive dialog.

When I was in Berlin in March 2008, the city court processed the case of a florist who trusted her two infants in the care of a babysitter. The babysitter left the kids at home to go buy yogurt, and one of the two young infants fell from the balcony and died. Such heart-wrenching incident is not rare—cases of domestic mismanagements and/or filial dysfunction amongst Vietnamese in East Berlin often make it into the German media. I ask: what does it take for the Vietnamese in the East to be able to sustain their life better? Legal rights and political equity are the impetus for any improvement in the lives of this community.

Here, I want to take into consideration the social costs endured by the East Berlin Vietnamese —the burden of separation with their immediate family in Vietnam, the challenge to perform Western economic gains, and the oddity of being at the bottom of a labor ladder in one society yet delivering at the higher end of a living survival in yet another society. They experience the absence of a family in Berlin in order to help maintain a family in Vietnam. Many young Vietnamese teens arriving in Berlin today do not come for any other purposes rather than to remit the Euros home. The contradiction of the global currencies—the US dollar and the Euro—works against these worker immigrants.

Excerpted Immigration Narratives

The following excerpted narratives are gleaned from hours-long oral history interviews with Vietnamese in Berlin, Warsaw, and Malmö. They show the various ways in which Vietnamese (im)migrants come to (and through) Germany, and that immigration is multi-directional rather than linear as often perceived. These narratives complicate the discourses of Vietnamese in Germany, and challenge the binary division found in the Berlin brochure.

As is true for all my projects on the Vietnamese diasporas[36], these interviews were biographical instead of topic-oriented, allowing the narrators to

---

[36] In the 1990s, I started the Vietnamese Diasporas Project (VDP), which uses oral history interviews and community participation to document the experiences and perspectives of Vietnamese populations around the world. The first component of the VDP was the Vietnamese American Project, the first and only of its kind to simultaneously conduct ongoing fieldwork alongside community participation, and to gather extensive oral histories of Vietnamese living in Orange County, CA, USA, which is home to the largest Vietnamese community outside of Vietnam. In 2004, I started the Vietnamese Stockholm Project under the auspice of an exceptional-ranking Fulbright full-grant. In 2004-05, while a Fulbrighter, I initiated the Vietnamese Berlin Project and the Vietnamese Warsaw Project as components of the Vietnamese European Project. In 2005, through a doctoral fellowship at Stanford University, I started the Vietnamese Taiwan Project to study the trafficking of Vietnamese women through marriage brokerage.

express themselves freely and fully[37]. I conducted all interviews in Vietnamese, transcribed, and translated them into English. Each transcript is between sixty to one hundred pages. For the purpose of this paper, I extracted the contours that are most relevant to each narrator's immigration history. I recognize the violence in stripping the narratives of their larger contexts and the more nuanced recollections that are omitted. I trust that by acknowledging this risk expressly, I prompt the readers to be more attentive to the details in these excerpted narratives and to keep in mind the larger contexts behind these contours.

I have selected four distinct oral history interviews among the one-hundred plus from my projects on the Vietnamese in Europe for this section, with narrators originating from the North, the Central region, and the South. Only the excerpted narratives for each interview are included here owing to the space constraint. However, the contours of each person's narratives all address themes pertaining to wars, family separation, migration history, adjustment in the new country, and aspirations for the future. These narratives reflect both similarities and differences of how life was for Vietnamese in the three parts of Vietnam during and after the Vietnam War, and their diverse migration trajectories to Germany (and Europe).

Of the four, I would like to privilege the excerpted narratives of Phan Hiển Mạnh conducted in Sweden. Coming to Vietnamese (East) Berlin was a way for me to enter pre-1975 Northern Vietnam and to encounter the unfamiliar narratives of

---

[37] For further details on my approach in oral history methodology, see Tranguyen 2004 and Glassey-Tranguyen 2008.

diasporic Vietnamese coming from the North after 1975. Phan Hiển Mạnh's narratives not only open the portals to how life was in the North in the 1960s-1980s, but also reveal the paths through which Vietnamese bodies have passed in Eastern Europe. His narratives are rich with emotions, complex with multi-directional movements, and powerful with articulations of diasporic subjectivity. His experiences encompass so many facets of Vietnam's modern history and how its people have negotiated with the disruptions in their country's recent past. His recorded stories started with wartime, and remained a search for peace, even though he has lived for several years in the land of 200 years of unbroken peace called Sweden.

It is important to note that Phan Hiển Mạnh's narratives encompass the multiple trajectories that illuminate the experiences of stateless Vietnamese in Europe, and express so profoundly the North-South division in his family across generations, both at home in Vietnam and in the diasporas. His articulation of the difficult instability in the life of a stateless Vietnamese in Berlin and Germany chimes with Lê Thắng Lợi's stories, as well as confirming the challenges facing trafficked Vietnamese migrants in Eastern Europe. Phan Hiển Mạnh, like Lê Thắng Lợi, repeats certain aspects of his experiences with intense emotions that might not be so obvious in a text. I am working on a documentary using video footages of these interviews and my fieldwork in Europe to convey the narrator's immediacy through the screen.

Phan Hiển Mạnh's narratives are also significant in how they point out the North-North division, complicating the familiar North-South binary. While in Vietnam, Phan enjoyed the privileges that his parents had earned through their participation in the Communist army in the North, and as a result, he was able to come to the Czech Republic as an exchange student. When Phan eventually got to Sweden, he realized that despite all of his struggles, he was not treated equally as his fellow Northern Vietnamese, who had escaped by boat to Sweden and who might have been less privileged than Phan in Northern Vietnam. This is where Vietnamese immigrants from the North wished they were received and admitted as refugees like their counterparts from Southern Vietnam. Here, the boat people and the stateless Vietnamese immigrants—all hailed from the North—switched role, occupying a space I call borderland-motherland. In this space, they are simultaneously outside of Vietnam and still very much in it.

I find it violent to extract excerpts from any of the biographical oral history interviews I have conducted across the Vietnamese diasporas around the world, because those hours-long interviews were already a stifling reduction of the narrator's experiences. I face even greater challenges with Phan Hiển Mạnh's narratives because of their richness, interconnectedness, and complexity. Nonetheless, given the interest of space and theme, I have gleaned the passages that are most relevant to this entry and pertain to immigration, Vietnamese history, and diasporic subjectivity. As we traverse the excerpted narratives, we can see that not only are the Vietnamese squatting in Berlin, but other parts of Europe and the world over.

A. Father Võ Thành Khánh, Warsaw, Poland

Roaming the stadium helped me understand the Vietnamese' lives here: the suffering, the difficulties, and the depths of their pain.

They invite me over after work and serve a six-course meal. It feels like a party. Food is much more affordable here than in Vietnam.

The undocumented refugees face the every-day threat of being imprisoned, interrogated by the police, and pushed around. Such pressure prompts them to bond and extend their love to each other.

I listen to their stories, and receive their pain. I was not sure how to process all of that. They let me touch the deepest corners of their lives.

Around seven to eight thousand Vietnamese work at the stadium. They suffer a great deal. They are emotionally deprived because their families live in Vietnam.

They always call me for help. Even when I can't help them, I still come to be with them.

Their primary challenge is the dismantling of the families they have in Vietnam. They came here as single individuals, and just pair up. Women look for men for support.

For some, their wives and husbands in Vietnam are unfaithful. They endure all the hardship and the separation from the family, but the hard money they earned is wasted.

Because of their il/legal status, they often get arrested, strip-searched, abused and harassed.

Everyone keeps fifty or a hundred Zloty as their "passport." They would be lucky to go free if the police search them and take the cash. Otherwise, the police take the money and send the illegal immigrants to the refuge camp for deportation.

I often visit the prisons to talk to them, and help them make phone calls to the outside world. My cell phone enables their families to connect with them and to provide them with basic necessities. I have to cheer them up, reminding the prisoners that they are the hope of their family.

Very few know Polish that well, only about five percent are fluent. Those are the exchange students who stayed behind after graduation. They lead a much easier life than the rest.

The Vietnamese undocumented immigrants do not have a social life. They cannot even take a walk. The poorest in Poland could always take a walk. But the Vietnamese immigrants would be so afraid to walk outside of their homes.

The immigrants live in a Vietnamese cultural food environment, with many ethnic restaurants and grocery stores. Food is transferred on five daily flights between Vietnam and Poland. The flights go through different routes, such as Paris, part of the Asian food chains.

Fifty to one hundred Vietnamese come to Poland illegally everyday. They fly from Vietnam to Moscow, and stay in car trunks from Moscow to Ukraine. They go through the forest from Ukraine to Poland. Each person pays 5500 to 6000 Zloty.

It is very expensive to immigrate this way. Everyone hopes to work and earn enough to repay the trafficking fee, and to provide for their family. Both the rich and the poor go through this channel.

Some spend up to seven months trying to immigrate illegally. They are caught, imprisoned, and trying again once released. Some try for an entire year.

Trafficked men face less problems than women. They all endure the lack of food and strenuous walking between sites. People walk around 200 kilometers in the forest. Women, especially young beautiful girls, run the risk of being raped. All of the girls are sexually abused.

The second problem is the fee increase en route. Between sites, the fee jumps up. If the people are unable to pay extra, the traffickers beat them up and force the families to send more money.

The trafficked people have to pay many prices throughout the journey. Many young girls

jump off from the high buildings to commit suicide when forced into sexual activities. Word gets out. People are frightened when they go through those sites.

The trafficked people are afraid of many things. They are afraid of the police. They are afraid of the traffickers. They are afraid that they can't pay the extra fee." (End of excerpted narrative.)

B. LÊ THẮNG LỢI, BERLIN, GERMANY

I was born in 1974 in Hanoi. Life was difficult, from the everyday conditions to issues such as freedom of speech. Albeit the great injustice, we had to accept it or else risked persecution.

I first sought asylum because of faith. In 1993, the Christian ministers here in Berlin had baptized me. I came back to Vietnam in 1995 and returned to Germany in 1999.

In the Vietnamese constitution, the government said that freedom of religion is granted but it is the opposite in reality.

In 1996, we had our first child. I planned to escape again because of harassment from the local authority. We split up and hid. Our firstborn soon asked, "Where is Daddy?" My wife could not tell my daughter where I was.

In 1998, we had our second baby and life became too difficult. We either died there in Vietnam, or escaped.

In 1999, we went to Russia and then Germany. The German government asked us where we had been. I said that we went back to Vietnam. But they did not believe us.

No one left with efficient luggage. We did not have the right documentation. Each family quickly escapes, running way from the Vietnamese government.

If you succeed, you are very lucky. An escape is a matter of life and death, but you escape regardless. We only hope to have a decent life.

After my second arrival in Germany, I joined groups demonstrating against the Vietnamese government. On October 10, 2001, I attacked the Vietnamese Prime Minister Phan Văn Khải, who came to Germany to urge our repatriation.

We tried to bring awareness to the German public that if they want to invest in a country, such country should be politically established and stable. If you invest in an unstable government like Vietnam, you are giving money to a robber.

The Vietnamese government is a mafia with a Communist label. They claim to serve the people, but in fact the common people suffer a great deal.

The worst came, and we left. But what about those who could not afford to escape? This is our people's greatest dilemma. If we keep leaving Vietnam, what will become of it?

I have never experienced a moment of peace here in Germany. The court had just processed my refugee application, and turned it down again. I reapplied right away.

Back then, the police had caught me and wanted to deport me. I got crazy. I just went nuts. Imagine living eighty days in a space that is 40x7 meters. My only friend was the watch. My only food was instant noodle, three packs a day.

When I ate, it was only to stay alive. I had no feelings, no taste. I had insomnia. I was too shocked by the persecution and fearful for my condition. At midnight, I was soaked in sweat. I was scared and I was screaming loudly.

Then the court agreed not to deport me. They forced me to report to them which church had hidden me. When I came to this refugee camp, they punished me by not giving me any food stamps for three months. I just came out of six starving months in hiding, and was confronted with three months without food.

I had to rely on my wife and children's aids. For three months, I left during the day and I could only come back to sleep during the night. The police and government had pushed us to our dead end.

Because of my mental disorder, I had requested a quiet facility but was turned down. This room is very small and it echoes. My children are small, and their noise disturbs me. When the children play and shout, it gives me migraines.

I want to work, but am not allowed. I do not want to be burden to the German society. Had it not been for my wife and my children, to live like this is suicide for me.

There's no return for me in Vietnam. But to stay here is barely an option. The door to freedom has shut closed.

I am the father of three children and a husband. I must do my part regardless of the suffering. If I collapse, my wife and children will be in trouble.

During my six years in Germany, the government had turned me from a healthy young man to a sick person. The German political system is a complete legal system. Once it pushes the Vietnamese refugees out, we have no way to go.

I am one of the strong activist voices in this community. I had stood in front of the Vietnamese embassy in Berlin and burned the Vietnamese flag. In Vietnam, I would have been sentenced to death. But it's the free world here in Germany. Therefore, they do not understand the price that dissidents pay in Vietnam.

In this so-called Free World, they do not understand how it is like in unfree places. When a person from an oppressive society talks to someone from a free society, they do not understand each other. Neither of them understands the other. (End of excerpted narratives)

c. Phan Hiền Mạnh

...I was born in 1964 into a worker family. It was wartime. My family lived on the campus of the Economy and Chemistry University in Thừa Sơn, Bắc Ninh. Since the time that I was born, I lived in Vietnam. In 1982, after I graduated from high school in Vietnam, I left for the Czech Republic.

We were impoverished. We were poor to the extent that my father had to take a loan for me to go to school. The awareness and consciousness that you had to help your parents was very clear.

My parents were very hardworking and they dedicated their lives to us their children. That was my most astounding impression. It is also my lasting impression of Vietnam, the parents' love for their children. Although I have left Vietnam since 1982, it has been twenty-two years, but that love has never faded in me.

There were occasions to meet with my extended family in the countryside. My father's older sister and younger brother left for the South in 1954. For those individuals, I have never met them until today, even so with my cousins. I do know that some of them live in America, but I have no way of contacting them or tracing them.

When I left Vietnam in 1982, my father's older sister did come back to visit from America, and she did come back for a few times, and after that, they lost touch. My father lived under the Communist regime, but his older sister had already left in 1954, so maybe they do not see eye to eye on certain things. In spite of that, they still visit each other and go to the countryside together in order to commemorate the ancestors, or they would come back to pay homage at the family commemoration houses.

My father had joined the Vietnamese Communist Guerrilla [Army] before. He said that after many years in the Guerrillas, there wasn't anything special there. So he was hoping that his children would become educated and have a better life, to improve their life and to have something better than their parents.

I arrived in the Czech Republic in October of the year 1982. I was almost 18 years old when I left. I was very sad when I left my family.

When my mother took me to the airport to go to the Czech Republic, I was still crying very hard. From the time I was born until that time, I never left my family and I never traveled away from my family for over two hundred kilometers.

When we first arrived, we started with language training. Later on we started vocational training and focused more on technology. I was trained from 1982 to 1986. Since I was younger, I had the advantage of acquiring and mastering language skills faster than my seniors in the delegation.

Back then in 1989, Vietnam sent quite many students to the Czech Republic, and they also sent exchange workers. Vietnam sent exchange workers to work at factories and manufacturers. Those exchange workers ran into several different problems. They only got to have language training for three months. After that, they had to work continuously. After I graduated from the program, I applied to work as an interpreter for the Vietnamese in the Czech Republic who had difficulties with the Czech language in the city that I lived in.

I remember arriving in the Czech Republic in the morning. It was very cold and it was October. Their airport was huge and ours was just very tiny, and we only had old airplanes. When I was in Prague, their airport was huge. So I was surprised and I said, "Wow, how come their country is so beautiful?" During the time that I lived in Vietnam, there was no information flow, especially in the North.

When we arrived, even the Czech people were very friendly and helpful. Everything was different. So I was thinking, "Wow, that was my chance to change my star." We received the same benefits as other local students. The school provided everything and we only focused on studying. Although I had a scholarship, it wasn't enough. Many times I wanted to send something home, but I wasn't able to and that made me very sad.

But I do have to say that the time that I went to school there was a lot of fun. For instance, we went to school in the morning and in the afternoon, we played sports together. There were people of my age and we were of different ethnicities. That diversity really excited me at that time.

I worked as an interpreter until 1989, having lived in the Czech Republic for 7 years. That's when changes started to take place in the Eastern European countries in political structures and regimes. It started out in Germany and then in the Czech Republic, in Poland, in Hungary, then my perception started to shift. Back then, information about the West was very scarce, but in 1989, I started to see things clearly.

I was prompted to leave and I became curious about other places. I was not pushed around or oppressed in any way in the Czech Republic, but I only wanted to pursue what deemed better.

After 1990, I also followed my friends. After I finished my studies, I did go back to Vietnam once in 1986 and again in 1990. People often say that after a period of time living and studying abroad, you will change a lot, but I didn't see that much change in me, not in me. I did not see much change in Vietnam during that time.

In 1990, I would like to stay with my parents as much as possible, but I had to earn my living so I came back to the Czech Republic to continue working as an interpreter. Of course, when I talked with my friends in 1989, I already had that idea of leaving my family for good.

I met my current wife when we were on the plane in 1990. So we started dating then. In 1990, there was an ordinance from the embassy that forced us to come back to Vietnam. So I thought, well, I have heard about life elsewhere. It would be a pity if I did not get to see what it's really like. So I decided to go to Germany. At first, I went to East Germany and I saw a friend. There, some Vietnamese had established small businesses and I already started to see that life was much better than what it was in the Czech Republic or in Vietnam. Of course, everything was strange to me and I was a new fish in a strange pond, but because I had heard stories from friends before, I remained curious and continued to explore. Then I went to West Germany and, wow, they had changed so much. So I looked between East and West Germany and I saw huge differences, not to mention Vietnam. It was very different in West Germany. How could that be?

At that time, I decided not to come back to Vietnam or to return to the Czech Republic. I decided to disobey the ordinance from the Vietnamese embassy. So I remember that in 1990 after I met with a friend in East Germany, he said that I should stay with him if I did not wish to return to Vietnam. He said that we could stay together and collaborate to earn a living.

At first, we also ran a small business like any other Vietnamese, but I was more fortunate than the rest because I spoke Slovakian. There were many Poles coming to Germany for trades. So it was fortunate that there were many Poles coming to West Germany and I was able to connect different niches and developed my marketing network. So I, of course, could communicate much more efficiently with the Polish business people than the Vietnamese in Germany. Of all the goods and merchandises that they had, I was able to acquire them.

So I started to establish a small business for myself. I worked together with my friend, and we purchased a car. I'm not sure why I was that adventurous at that time. I did not have any kind of legal documentation, and to buy a car like that was very risky. And, in my mind, I thought that in Western European countries, even when they caught you, they would not abuse you physically like in Eastern European countries. It was a thought that I had in mind and I kept believing in it. And because of that very simple belief, I was convinced to stay in Germany.

Although I had my business, I kept sneaking back and forth through the border, because for all the time that I lived in the Czech Republic, there were many memories. Those memories still remain fresh in me. I would never be able to forget them. And although at that time in Germany I was a stateless person, I kept going back and forth between the two countries to visit my girlfriend.

When I first came to Germany, I had thought that if the police were to arrest me, they wouldn't beat me up. Of course it was very difficult. Quite frankly, at that time, the retail business like that was rather normal. We worked out the paperwork together. I had no other choice. I wanted to leave the Czech Republic. I had no choice, so of course I was worried, but I couldn't do anything else. Although through my friend, I was able to acquire some kind of document, but it was all an illusion. It was only something to hold on to.

After a time, I realized that such a life was not stable. I then ran into a friend who also worked in the translation services with me in the Czech Republic. He was the one who later on came to Sweden with me. He had family members in Sweden, so he came to me and said, "Listen, why don't we go to Sweden?" We had known each other through the time in the Czech Republic, and we were very close. So I decided, "All right, let us go to Sweden." Through visual images of Sweden, I felt that the country was very peaceful, very beautiful. I looked at the houses and they looked very peaceful and quiet.

The time that I was running a small business with my friend in Germany was extremely chaotic. That was not my purpose for living. That was not my purpose in life. I did not see a bright future in that particular living condition.

At that time, I did not think that there was any future in coming back to Vietnam. All my siblings advised me to return to Vietnam. My parents requested that I return home, but because I had gone on and seen a different country... So for me to come back, I thought I could not get used to the lifestyle there during the times I visited.

Therefore, I decided to go to Germany, and it was only because I connected with a friend that I stayed and collaborated with him in the business. But at that time, I did not establish a clear direction for my life. I did not have a clear purpose in life like I do right now living in Sweden. So after a time running that business, life became too chaotic. Of course we had to work for survival.

I remember that very night. I just sat down and smoked a whole pack of cigarettes, and my girlfriend at that time wondered why I was smoking so much. I needed to decide whether I would leave Germany to go live in Sweden. The next morning I told my friend that I decided to go to Sweden. I decided so only because through the postcards and pictures I found that life in Sweden was very peaceful. Up to that point, I had followed the news, and I gathered some information. I learned that Sweden, for a long time, did not have any wars, and I looked at the houses on the mountain and they were beautiful.

Life in Sweden seemed very carefree. I didn't think that I would have to work as much as I do now. So after a long night, without sleeping, the same way when I was little and my father promised to bring me to Hà Nội, I would not sleep... Of course that night I was much stronger, and I decided the next morning... So we purchased documents. We bought visas because we were to cross the borders.

As soon as I set foot on the Swedish soil, I confirmed my impression that this is a very peaceful place and the people are really gentle. They are very calm. So immediately, I felt a great connection with the people and the place. We had the people who have lived here before help take us to the refugee camps for those who would like to seek refuge in Sweden.

After a few months in the refugee camp, I asked a few friends in Germany to help bring my girlfriend to Sweden. When she got here, we both lived in the refugee camp. My wife gave birth to my first daughter in 1993. I remember the night that my wife went into labor. I took her. It was in the middle of the night. They called a Slovakian-speaking interpreter because I spoke the language of the Czech Republic. There were no Vietnamese interpreters at the time.

All the way until 1997, Sweden issued a humanitarian policy for refugees to let those who had come to Sweden by 1995 and have had children stay in Sweden. We were very fortunate that we met the requirements. But because of my legal documents in the Czech Republic, they did not let us enter Sweden right away.

My family lived in the refugee camp for seven years. At that time, I already had my own family, and I had decided for myself that we would live in Sweden, and I did not want to go anywhere else. It was a final decision. Everyone in the refugee camp was approved to stay in Sweden, but we kept waiting.

There was a time that my paperwork was so messed up and even if I recount my situation, I do not think that people could imagine such complications. So when my documents did not go through, I did all kinds of odd jobs. I worked on the farm, I picked berries.

I did anything I could to earn a living. I had some complications with the paperwork, so my wife and my children remained in the refugee camp. For me, I had to leave the refugee camp for instance, so that the police would not catch me. I was afraid that they would remove me from Sweden, but now that I think about it, I do not think that they would send me anywhere because I was a stateless person.

In 1998, we received the approval. And we were allowed to remain in Sweden as refugees forever. During the time I lived in the refugee camp, I looked at the families living in Sweden and I thought eventually one day my family would have a life like that.

My hope was very high. I never anticipated that I would experience a period of chaos and suffering. In Vietnam, we would say it was the time when you started another cycle of your zodiac reading. It was horrible, it was a very bad time. And now that I have gone through that state, I am very appreciative of whatever I have.

There is a price for everything. There are refugees who were received by the Swedish government all the way from the Hong Kong refugee camps. They felt that it was a breeze, and they took it easy. These individuals found that it was too easy to go to Sweden, so they have lived in this country for decades and they still rely on social benefits.

I was told to learn Swedish first, then I could find a job. When I was hiding from the police here in Sweden, I had taken so many jobs, and I had gained so many experiences.

I came to the job placement office and said I would like to start working, but they did not allow me. But I kept coming back, and there was one time that I got helped by this very friendly person, who said, "You're right. If you could do that, then why not?"

I was in the middle of the language training program, and I quit. I already learned a lot of Swedish in the refugee camp and I also taught myself. I even helped translate for those who had lived in Sweden for more than a decade.

Even though it could be easy to take government handouts, I hated coming to the welfare office every month and file the paperwork. I think it's rather disgusting and boring.

It was six years ago. I received my approval in September 1998, and in June the next year, I established my own business. (End of excerpted narratives)

a. Thúy Nonnemann

My family is from the North. We were from Hà Đông, near Hà Nội. In 1954, we went South. We first went by bus to Hải Phòng and we went by ship to Sài Gòn. My siblings and I continued to go to school in Sài Gòn. We attended French school and graduated from high school. I also studied at the university for three years.

In such a big city like Sài Gòn, I did not know much about the war because there was no bombing, there was no battle in Sài Gòn. I only knew that there were soldiers going to war and family members who were injured in battle. I knew my male cousins and my male friends who went to the battles and never returned. That was how I knew about the war. I did not have to face bombings or impoverishment. Sài Gòn was an international place with delegations from many countries, and we did not lack anything.

In 1966, I met my husband in Vietnam. He went there to work for the German Red Cross. He was a medical doctor. He was sent on a mission, which was part of West Germany's efforts to help South Vietnam. When he returned to West Germany, he took me with him. We got married in 1968.

When I first came to West Germany, I did not know any other Vietnamese. At that time, I heard about Vietnamese students in Germany, but I did not have the chance to meet with them. At that time, I lived entirely in a German society.

When I came, I realized that the Germans were very friendly towards foreigners. I received a great deal of help. My neighbors, and even people on the streets, were very willing to help me. Sometimes when I was standing there on the street getting lost, people would come out of their house and asked me what I needed help with.

I had the advantage of speaking French and English. Most Germans did speak some English, and they asked me in English, and I was able to respond. At that time, I did not know any German yet, so I wasn't able to carry on a conversation in German yet. In a short while, I was able to acquire the German language facility and started working. When I started working, I was able to learn the language

much faster because I was interacting extensively with German speakers. I was forced to
think and speak in German, so I learned very
quickly.

When I arrived in West Germany, it was almost Lunar New Year. When I walked on the
streets, there were many bushes with yellow
flowers that reminded me of the Vietnamese
cherry blossoms, and I was very much home-
sick.

It took a long time for postal mail to arrive
because I came in 1968. At that time, it was
right on the eve of the Tet Offensive. I was extremely worried about the safety of my family. Snail mail took a long time to get there.
Being away from home, I was very concerned
for my family.

During that time, in 1968, students in Germany as well as in America protested against
the Vietnam War. When I walked on the
streets, sometimes there were young people
who asked me where I came from, and I said
Vietnam. So they invited me to come with
them to demonstrate against the war.

At that time I was somewhat disoriented, and
I was not sure what their objectives or underpinnings were, so I declined. During that time
in Vietnam, the communists had bombed
schools and supermarkets, and I could not
endorse them or demonstrate in support of
the communists. I was against the war, but
not with the conditions that the protesters
had in mind. I wanted the war to end but with
other conditions.

I was very fortunate. I worked at a bank. Only
with my language skills in English and

French, I was hired, although my German skills were very limited. The president of the bank said that if I could speak German within a year, he would hire me permanently. So I focused on acquiring the German language skills. I just went to work and went home, I did not go out or I did not take vacation. So they hired me.

In 1973, I had anticipated how the Vietnam War would end because we had updated information flow here in the west. At that time, I had already urged my family to leave Vietnam. As a journalist, my father had a wide network, but he did not want to leave Vietnam. On April 30, 1975, my family was stuck behind. My child was too young at that time for me to leave for Vietnam to bring my family here. After 1975, I filed for application to sponsor my family here, but it was not until 1980 that my parents were able to come. They lived here and passed away a few years ago.

In 1976 and 1977, there was a ship by the name of Cap Anamur. People knew that there were boat people escaping and getting drowned in the high sea. There was a rescue team sent out to rescue the boat people. I joined forces with the Vietnamese student associations to collect donations from German companies to help finance activities for that ship. Since 1979 and '80, West Germany started to receive Vietnamese refugees from Southeast Asian refugee camps and admitted them to West Germany. I also came to the refugee camps here in West Germany to help the refugees and to give them language instructions. I volunteered and helped translate or teach German to them at the camps near my house. There were some camps established by the

Red Cross. At that time, I worked with the different organizations in connection with the Red Cross and church groups to assist the poor or the refugees. After I took care of my husband and daughter, I would volunteer to help the refugees.

I have retired now, but I still continue my activist work, which is rather extensive. (End of excerpted narrative)

SQUATTING AS RESISTANCE AND AGENCY

Simon Leung's "the residual space of the Vietnam War" (1992-1998) was a multi-genre art series that looks at the ways in which identity is forged via bodily practices such as surfing and squatting (129)[38]. The project was displayed in Huntington Beach, Berlin, and Vienna. The second project, which is immediately relevant to this article, is titled, *"Squatting Project/Berlin"* (1994) which "addressed the xenophobic violence manifesting in the newly unified Germany, in the Balkan states upon the collapse of the former Yugoslavia, and elsewhere in Europe" (132). Leung pasted one thousand posters across the city of Berlin, half of which included German text inviting the readers to imagine a city of squatters—to participate in squatting, and to observe the city from the squatting position. "In these squatting projects, Leung depicts the displaced body as one whose posture is removed from a context in which it is common practice and

---

[38] Leung, Simon and Sturken, Marita. "Displaced Bodies in Residual Spaces," *Public Culture* 17(1): 129-152.

inserted into a context in which it is strange, out of place, alien" (133).

While his theoretical and conceptual approach in the series is apt, Leung's focus on the informal underground economy chimes with the mainstream German media's one-sided portrait of the Vietnamese there, a "mis-recognition" (137) in the Lacanian sense. Using the concept of "residual space" (133, without claiming original authority) and practicing "a politics of difference" (139), Leung "was thinking of the way in which the trauma of this historical event returns in fragments, in innocuous, slight, but emotionally undigested forms," alluding to "a psychic border between fiction and history" (135). Following Zizek's "the indivisible remainder" (138), he reframed subjectivity in the city. Leung considers "community as a kind of procedure" (139). In looking at the effect of a particular historical event, Leung thinks of "the discourse of history as a social space where the meaning and unity of the social (events, relationships, legacies, memory) are at once constituted and questioned" (151).

While Leung's focus is on the underground economy (132) and its coupling with mainstream German media's portrayal of Vietnamese in East Berlin, I find the visuality of his project productive to the analysis of the two Vietnamese Berlins. To Leung's credit, I will assert that this coupling has its own productive violence given the objective of his project and "thinking of the way in which the trauma of this historical event returns in fragments, in innocuous, slight, but emotionally undigested forms" (135). But let me return to my point of visual acuity. First, the act of squatting is an apt metaphor to think about the two Vietnamese populations as being connected through one single body (ethnic minority) but located in two distinct spaces (East versus West).

Here, I want to advance the connectedness of the two Vietnamese groups by calling forth Vietnam as the country of origin and the Vietnam War (in tandem with Western colonization in the world, World War II, and the Cold War) as the one common event that eventually leads to the immigration of both groups. This is where I argue for, alongside other points, a negation of the politics of difference —that in fact, these two groups are as much connected as they are different. In other words, both groups are in a shared contested "residual space." Second, I find Leung's take on "community as a kind of procedure" a useful concept in understanding the way in which the two Vietnamese groups came to occupy their places in Berlin. That is, while the Berlin brochure had rendered the histories of the two groups with single events such as boat people's arrival and guest workers' overstay, looking at the communities they have formed as a "procedure" will illuminate the larger processes that have brought them into being.

Besides these two stances, I wish to elaborate on one point that I feel crucial to Leung's project and my article. As I alluded to earlier, Leung's focus on the underground economy is, on the surface, a stereotype and a confluence with the German mainstream media's representation of the Vietnamese in East Berlin. Additionally, squatting as the theme of the poster project blatantly makes use of a stereotypical image of people of Asian background. This ostensibly double-stereotype is in fact used to get at the exclusion that Vietnamese Berliners face in both the East and the West. I ask, then, how can the use of the squatting image either or simultaneously dispel the stereotype and reinforce such stereotyping in the mainstream society and the ethnic population it speaks of? How many Germans actually followed Leung's invitation to squat, whether physically or mentally, in order to view Berlin from the positionality of the immigrants?

Though the effects of the squatting project are worth looking into, I did not find the related literature to comment on this except the interview cited. However, I do think that whether Leung was successful or not with his proposition to have Berliners squat and look at the city from the ground, the metaphor is crucial. In squatting, the Vietnamese immigrants bring their own habituation and queer Berlin's public scene together, and by so doing, make themselves hyper-visible beyond their legal status or lack thereof. After all, I deem that with one thousand posters, Leung had visually forced Berliners into squatting—even for the mere instant in which they viewed the posters. By using the "out-of-place" image to engage with thinking about the place of Vietnamese immigrants—particularly those in East Berlin engaging in informal economy—Leung lets us in on how "difference" can be mediated by the simple act of changing one's position.

Borderland-Motherland Diasporic Subjectivity

The various excerpted immigration narratives above show that the Vietnamese populations in Berlin are far more diverse than the boat-people-and-guest-worker binary. I argue that the two Vietnamese groups in East and West Berlin are mutually constitutive. In particular, this squatting augments the fact that Vietnamese Berliners are highly visible—both physically and discursively. This heightened visibility is owed to their non-white physical appearance and East-Berlin criminalized discourses, neither of which fit into the definition of Germanness. Together with other racialized minorities in Berlin and Europe, Vietnamese refugees and immigrants serve to define what is *not German or not European*. I concur with El-Tayeb (2008) that exclusionary treatments of "European others" are in fact continent-wide—a political racelessness that is omnipresent in Europe at the disadvantage of racialized ethnic Europeans.

While acknowledging the continent-wide practices of exclusion in Europe, I argue that the nation-states are still playing a dominant role in controlling people's lives through policies and regulations[39]. This stance is clearly indicative in the discourses of Vietnamese guest workers, who were closely regulated and monitored both in Vietnam and in the GDR (Mike Dennis 2007). These workers' bodies become sites of power control, the micro-level where "the nation-state manages transnationalism"—to use Roberto Alvarez' phrase (2005). Likewise, the boat people were managed by both the Vietnamese government, who persecuted them, and the West German government, who rescued and resettled them. More importantly, West Germany assigned Vietnamese boat people to various locations as part of the integration policy. This spatial management of people of color restricts their transnational experiences by severing their ability to concentrate in an area. Nonetheless, over the years, Vietnamese populations in both the East and the West gravitate toward Berlin, where they have been squatting. I argue that it is in Berlin that the experiences of the guest workers and the boat people synchronize in their squatting, despite the inherent divisions.

Squatting, then, in every sense of the word, is an act of resistance. I argue that seemingly

---

[39] See, for instance, Alvarez Jr., Roberto. *Mangos, Chiles, And Truckers: The Business Of Transnationalism.* University of Minnesota Press, 2005.

powerless people—such as the Vietnamese guest workers upon the loss of contract following the 1989 fall of the Berlin Wall, as well as the Vietnamese boat people who newly arrived in the FRG in the late 1970s—do find ways to manage their own fate through resistance and self-definition. The boat people's autonomous relocation to West Berlin[40] and the guest workers' starting of small ethnic businesses both in the hostels and in the post-*Wende* Berlin are different forms of similar resistance against social, spatial, and legal subjugation. In like manner, in Pun Ngai's critical class analysis on migrant women workers from rural China, the dagongmei's conscious decision to participate in the global circuit of production and consumption—albeit its exploitation—shows how agency is at work on the ground[41]. As Luis Alvarez[42] puts it, forms of resistance such as zoot suiting are "fundamentally about self-valorization," and "also part of an outlook on and approach to life

---

[40] Housing is an important factor in spatial in/exclusion. In Sweden, for instance, Vietnamese immigrants who are unable to find housing in Stockholm after several years would give up and resettle in the remote areas, telling themselves that they would not be in the "light of civilization" (Stockholm living) in this lifetime. I argue that by keeping immigrants out of cosmopolitan centers such as Berlin and Stockholm, European nations successfully exclude them from "contaminating" the public scene and culture. Yet immigrants resist and some succeed in finding their place in these exclusionary spaces.

[41] Ngai, Pun. "Subsumption or Consumption? The Phantom of Consumer Revolution in 'Globalizing' China." *Cultural Anthropology*, pp 469-492, Nov 2003.

[42] Alvarez, Luis. *The Power of the Zoot: Youth Culture and Resistance During World War II*. University of California Press, 2008.

that helped them claim dignity in a society that routinely dehumanized them." Through their resistance and establishment of an ethnic economy, Vietnamese guest workers make it possible for new waves of (undocumented) immigrants to come from Vietnam via Eastern European countries, such as Ukraine and Poland (Julia Schweizer 2004 & 2005, Claire Wallace 2002). Personal decisions and family migration trends can lead to hemispheric changes, as Roberto Alvarez argues in *Familia* (1987), a study of his own family's migration history.

Given the interconnectedness between nation-specific and Europe-wide practices of racial exclusion, I tack back and forth between Berlin as my site and the larger European continent. Vietnamese Berlin is a site where the corporeal and cultural realities of race are augmented. I use Natalie Molina's (2005 & 2006) concept of "unfit citizens" and Mae Ngai's "impossible subjects" (2005) to argue that the Berlin government has formulated the discourses of Vietnamese former guestworkers as undesirable, and consequently not legitimate for citizenship. This point connects with Simon Leung's image of squatting—a visual rendition of the physicality of race—that these bodies are squatting between the spaces of il/legitimacy. At the same time, Leung's act of squatting also highlights Molina and Mae Ngai's articulation of how human bodies are being racialized and excluded. That is, in their very act of squatting, Vietnamese Berliners are interpolated as "others" and "unfit," or "criminalized."

Furthermore, the fatal coupling—to use Ruthie Gilmore's phrase (2002)—of race/class/gender exacerbates the lot of racialized Europeans. I appreciate Pun Ngai's (2003) class analysis of the assembly workers at an amusement park in China. In a stratified society, the working class is treated as inferior and ought to confine themselves to the factories where they supposedly belong. There are parallels in the way the first-class visitors interpolated the dagongmei at the amusement park in China, and the way Vietnamese guest workers are surveilled in Germany. In both cases, the workers are under a strict watch, supposed to confine themselves to their space as workers, and should not intrude into the larger social scapes.

This spatial exclusion is but one of the various forms of discrimination that racialized Europeans confront. For most Vietnamese in East Berlin, legal exclusion renders them vulnerable in multiple ways. As Heidi Castenada (2009) argues, "illegality as risk" conveys the challenges and barriers that undocumented migrants face in Berlin, confirming what El-Tayeb (2011) calls the "precarious living conditions" of ethnic minorities in Europe. "Illegality as risk" speaks of health risks that are not addressed beyond the lack of basic health care and the burden of being legally excluded. In this sense, race is again a very "bodily" phenomenon, both in how ethnic bodies are racialized, as well as in how these bodies are excluded from the realm of normal standard health care and become more prone to health issues because of their very living conditions. Along this line, Natalie Molina's (2005) analysis of the process of "medicalizing" the Mexicans in Los Angeles shows how ethnic bodies were at once neglected and pathologized.

Yet against this racialization is the emergence of a thriving ethnic community—albeit doubly divided—that rises from the 1989 demise of the Berlin Wall and all exclusionary policies targeting Vietnamese guest workers that follow. I choose the year 1989 as the beginning point instead of 1975 to reflect the moment of contact between the two Vietnamese populations in the East and West, both of which have emerged in the late 1970s or early 1980s separately but not entirely independent of each other. Here, I work with the duality of one-but-two, two-yet-one Vietnamese Berlin(s). The two communities have divergent historical backgrounds, but they do have similarities such as country of origin, mother tongue, and culture. On the other hand, each Vietnamese population on the two sides of Berlin begins and develops in such distinct ways, with a mutual sense of dissociation, that they behave as two separate entities. Nonetheless, organic interactions such as inter-group marriages and religious membership—besides exchanges in the trade activities and service industry—sustain this duality with all of its tensions and uneven congruence. In this sense, the Vietnamese Berlin population exemplifies what Simon Leung (2005) calls "community as procedural" and purports El-Tayeb's (2003) recognition of grassroots movements as a way to forge a space for racialized European others.

However, it is important to recognize that tensions and divergence are part of every resistance movement. Luis Alvarez (2008) argues that the politics of dignity is in fact complex and diverse, "a complicated and sometimes contradictory cultural politics" beyond the obvious binaries. The nuanced complexity of dignity and/or self-determination in the zoot suite culture is also apparent in the discourses of the Vietnamese guest workers (Dennis 2007), or dagongmei (Ngai 2003), or U.S./Mexican truckers and produce traders (Alvarez 2005). It is only with a grounded approach from the bottom up that we can understand how everyday people participate in transnationalism across the social spectrum. Pun Ngai (2003), like Roberto Alvarez (2005), emphasizes the materiality of economic disparities in her studies and warns against "a nostalgic search for symbolic exchange of a 'general economy of expenditure.'"

Furthermore, Leung's (2005) concept of space as 'residual' reflects El-Tayeb's discussion of how even with an internalist narrative (Stuart Hall's term) that erases the contributions and participation of people of color in the continent's past and present, the "residual" aspects of the presence of people of color play an important role in the making and sustenance of Europe and "the West." As El-Tayeb (2008) puts it, there is no modern world without people of color, and no queer theory without queer people of color. In residual Vietnamese Berlin(s), the internalist narrative insists on pushing racial minorities out of the public discourses through ethnic stigma. But people of color have learned to belong to everywhere and nowhere. In the words of Gloria Anzaldúa (1995), they are the new race that embraces all. In this spirit, I argue that squatting Vietnamese have transformed Berlin into a new space, a borderland-motherland that sustains the transnational connections with Vietnam (and its diasporas) while combating the racialized exclusion of white Europe.

By way of conclusion, I would like to argue that despite the climactic division between Vietnamese in East and West Berlins, there are already several "moments of encounter" and ongoing interactions between the two groups. I assert that both formal and informal processes of coming together have been taking place in an organic and productive fashion. As I have described at the beginning of this entry, the 2008 Lenten retreat in Berlin had brought together members from both communities, and while resentment continued to be part of such an encounter, the desire to connect and collaborate was also there.

Activist groups, such as the Berlin chapter of Tập Hợp Dân Chủ Đa Nguyên, bring together Vietnamese from both East and West Germany who are concerned with democratization and multi-party governance in Vietnam. During the gatherings and discussions at Dr. Phạm's residence that I participated in across the years, there were boat people, former guest workers, undocumented immigrants, exchange students coming to pre-1989 GDR, post-1975 Vietnamese diplomats who left the Vietnamese Communist Party after experiencing what they uphold as the free world, activists, and professionals who have worked with Vietnamese from both the East and the West. These discussions put me in direct contact with what it looks like for the North/South East/West division to be bridged.

Beyond formal engagements are the natural ways in which people come together, which I phrase "meet, greet, and breed." Phan Đăng Hiển was a boat person, and Mai Hà Phương was a former guest worker whose family has close ties with the Vietnamese government in Hà Nội. Yet they have been happily married with grown children, and while their political orientations continue to differ, they accept one another for who the other person is. Several other couples with similarly divided backgrounds can be found across Berlin and Germany. Moreover, Vietnamese people often form surrogate families to support each other, as the Vietnamese proverb goes, "To trade your blood relatives in the distant land for your nearby neighbors" (translation mine, original: Bán bà con xa, mua láng giềng gần). This social fabric has played a key role in helping Vietnamese create new communities and economic niches. I argue that this social practice of adopting each other as secondary family also helps alleviate the division so vividly felt. Mai Hà Phương and "Surrogate Grandma"—while clashing in political views because the latter condemns the current Vietnamese regime—take each other as daughter and mother to look out for each other. Mai shares her food with Grandma, and Grandma provides much-needed postpartum care to Mai for both of her births since her mother still lives in Vietnam. These two people each has her own opinions and orientations, but that does not stop them from coming together. It is this form of informal social mutual assistantship that is salient in the Vietnamese culture that has been at work in helping Vietnamese in Berlin and in the diasporas negotiate the lines of demarcation they inherit from Vietnam's long history of wars.

Selected Oral History Interviews in Vietnamese in Chronological Order

These are oral history interviews I conducted across the years since 2004 in Sweden, Poland, and Germany. All interviews were conducted in Vietnamese, and the narrators occasionally used

German, Polish, or Swedish words. All English translations in this entry are mine.

<u>Note:</u> *Names in quotation marks (Kay, Uncle Stateless, Mr. Trường Sơn, Sister Autonomy) are pseudonyms for narrators who wish for their stories to be anonymous and without tape recording. The names are based on self-identification characteristics of the narrators. Kay is a name I came up with for a lady who split her time between Germany and Sweden. Uncle Stateless is an undocumented immigrant living in Bandaghen, Stockholm, who calls himself a stateless and had come to Sweden from Eastern Germany. Mr. Trường Sơn speaks about the Vietnam War and posits that the Trường Sơn route (during the Vietnam War) is not justifiable in the face of human loss. Sister Autonomy invokes the difficulty of straddling a Vietnamese-oriented family environment and a German individualistic society. Those names are only mnemonic cues to help me keep track of the narratives and field notes.*

From the Vietnamese Stockholm Project, 2004:

Glassey-Trầnguyễn, Trangđài & "Kay." Oral History Interview. September 30, 2004. Stockholm, Sweden.

Glassey-Trầnguyễn, Trangđài & Phan Hiển Mạnh. Oral History Interview. November 6, 2004. Malmo, Sweden.

Glassey-Trầnguyễn, Trangđài & "Uncle Stateless." Oral History Interview. December 2004. Stockholm, Sweden.

From the Vietnamese Berlin Project, 2005:

Glassey-Trầnguyễn, Trangđài & "Mr. Trường Sơn." Oral History Interview. March 6, 2005. Berlin, Germany.

Glassey-Trânguyễn, Trangđài & Lê Thắng Lợi. Oral History Interview. March 2005. Berlin, Germany.

Glassey-Trânguyễn, Trangđài & Lê Lương Cẩn, Owner of Thủy Tiên Wholesale & Cultural Center (non-recorded, with video footage of the Center). Berlin, Germany. March 6, 2005.

Glassey-Trânguyễn, Trangđài & Ms. Đào (cloth stand at Ost Bahnhof Station). Oral History Interview (at open air market, non-recorded). March 6, 2005. Berlin, Germany.

Glassey-Trânguyễn, Trangđài & Mr. Dũng & Spouse (China Pan food stand owner). Oral History Interview (at open air market, non-recorded). March 6, 2005. Berlin, Germany.

Glassey-Trânguyễn, Trangđài & H.P. Oral History Interview (at residence, non-recorded). March 6, 2005. Berlin, Germany.

Glassey-Trânguyễn, Trangđài & Thúy Nonnemann. Oral History Interview. March 7, 2005. Berlin, Germany.

Glassey-Trânguyễn, Trangđài & Phạm Đặng Hiển. Oral History Interview. March 7, 2005. Berlin, Germany.

Glassey-Trânguyễn, Trangđài & Trần Thị Hồng Sương. Oral History Interview. March 7, 2005. Berlin, Germany.

Glassey-Trânguyễn, Trangđài & Nguyễn Đình Tam. Oral History Interview. March 7, 2005. Berlin, Germany.

Glassey-Trânguyễn, Trangđài & Dr. Phạm Việt Vinh. Oral History Interview. March 8, 2005. Berlin, Germany.

From the Vietnamese Warsaw Project, 2005:

Glassey-Trầnguyễn, Trangđài & Võ Thành Khánh. Oral History Interview. September 1, 2005. Warsaw, Poland.

Glassey-Trầnguyễn, Trangđài & Nguyễn Văn Khanh. Oral History Interview (non-recorded). August 26, 2008. Warsaw, Poland.

From the Vietnamese Berlin Project, 2008:

Glassey-Trầnguyễn, Trangđài & Phan Đăng Hiển. Oral History Interview. March 11, 2008. Berlin, Germany.

Glassey-Trầnguyễn, Trangđài & Bùi Ngọc Yến. Oral History Interview. March 11, 2008. Berlin, Germany.

Glassey-Trầnguyễn, Trangđài & "Surrogate Grandma." Oral History Interview. March 14, 2008. Berlin, Germany.

Glassey-Trầnguyễn, Trangđài & "Sister Autonomy." Oral History Interview. March 14, 2008. Berlin, Germany.

Glassey-Trầnguyễn, Trangđài & Mai Hà Phượng. Oral History Interview. March 15, 2008. Berlin, Germany.

Glassey-Trầnguyễn, Trangđài & Dương Văn Đá. Oral History Interview. March 15, 2008. Berlin, Germany.

Glassey-Trầnguyễn, Trangđài & Rev. Anton Đỗ Ngọc. Oral History Interview. March 17, 2008. Berlin, Germany.

Glassey-Trầnguyễn, Trangđài & Phạm Thị Hà Thu. Oral History Interview. March 18, 2008. Berlin, Germany.

Glassey-Trầnguyễn, Trangđài & Mr. & Mrs. Hà Minh Châu. Oral History Interview. March 18, 2008. Berlin, Germany.

Glassey-Trầnguyễn, Trangđài & Ms. Bình Phạm. Oral History Interview. March 19, 2008. Berlin, Germany.

Glassey-Trầnguyễn, Trangđài & Ms. "Guest Worker" (at flower shop, Ost Bahnhof). Oral History Interview. March 19, 2008. Berlin, Germany.

Glassey-Trầnguyễn, Trangđài & Nguyễn Sơn Thạch. Oral History Interview. March 19, 2008. Berlin, Germany.

Glassey-Trầnguyễn, Trangđài & Dr. Nguyễn Văn Hương. Oral History Interview. March 20, 2008. Berlin, Germany.

Glassey-Trầnguyễn, Trangđài & Đỗ Thế Hoàng. Oral History Interview. March 21, 2008. Berlin, Germany.

Glassey-Trầnguyễn, Trangđài & Hồ Văn Phước. Oral History Interview. March 21, 2008. Berlin, Germany.

Glassey-Trầnguyễn, Trangđài & Nguyễn Văn Hưng. Oral History Interview. March 21, 2008. Berlin, Germany.

Author's Publications on Vietnamese Berlin

2012. Guest lecture. *"Cyber Exclusion in the Global Information Age: Stateless Vietnamese in Tonle Sap, Berlin, and Warsaw."* Women's Studies 795/ International Studies 795/895: Gender and International Migration. Spring 2012. (Invited by Ms. Erika Frydenlund and Dr. Jennifer N. Fish, Associate Professor and Chair of Women's Studies, Old Dominion University, Virginia, USA).

2012. *"Cyber Exclusion in the Global Information Age: Stateless Vietnamese in Tonle Sap, Berlin, and Warsaw."* Internationals Studies Association, Annual Convention.

2009-2010. "Viet Birds, World Sky," a commissioned bilingual weekly column, *Việt Herald Daily.* Orange County, CA, USA.

2009. Bilingual Keynote. *"Thuyền Nhân Việt Nam Toàn Cầu trong Thiên Niên Kỷ Thứ Ba: Tìm Lịch Sử, Giữ Tương Lai. Vietnamese Boat People in the Third Millennium: Seeking History, Growing Legacy."* Year-long Project and Multidisciplinary Program: "Ra Khơi: Tưởng Niệm Thuyền Nhân Vượt Biển. Set Sail: Commemorating the Vietnamese Boat People." Gạch Nối Magazine and Association, UC San Diego.

2009. *"Vietnamese Berlins 1975-2010: Historical Inequalities, Contemporary Diversities."* All-Grad Research Symposium, UC San Diego.

2009. *"Vietnamese Berlins 1975-2008: Historical Divergence, Contemporary Integration."* Crossing Borders Conference, "Serve the People? Ethnic Studies Between Theory and Practice." University of Southern California.

2008. *"Immigration in the Vietnamese Diasporas: 1975-2008,"* Bilingual Keynote. Black April Commemoration, Colina Park, San Diego. VAYA Vietnamese American Youth Alliance.

2008. Radio Multikulti. "Vietnamese Berlin Project." Interviewed by Mr. Phan Đăng Hiển for the Vietnamese section. (2 consecutive sessions).

2007. "In Their Own Spaces: Children En Route." Enthnographic Documentary, ftsmj Productions. Premier screening at Anthropology Conference, UC Davis.

2007. Issue's Feature. "Which Route? Vietnamese Communities around the Globe." Nhà Magazine, a San Jose-based monthly publication focusing on Life Style, Culture, and Identity.

2007. *"The Stateless and the Nameless: Sovereignty in the Liberal World."* 5th Annual Conference of Ethnic Studies in California. "Ghosts, Monsters, and the Dead." UC San Diego.

2007. *"The Subtexts of Conjurals and Construals: Children En Route."* A Documentary, Premiere. Symposium "Midnight University." University Club, UC Davis.

2005, Summer. *The Funnel*, a newsmagazine of the German American Fulbright Commission. Number 2, Volume 41. Pg 15 (Trangdai Tranguyen, Fulbrighter in Sweden, discusses the continuing psychological division of Berlin with André Schmitz during the reception at city hall.)

2005. Interview by Ms. Nguyễn Huỳnh Mai for the New Horizon Radio. "Trangđài Trầnguyễn: Her Fulbright Project in Sweden and Perspectives about Vietnamese in Europe."

2005. *"Contemporary Childhood in the Vietnamese Diasporas."* 37th World Congress of the International Institute of Sociology. Stockholm, Sweden.

2005. Radio Multikulti. "A Vietnamese American Fulbrighter's Initial Observations about Vietnamese in Berlin." Interviewed by Mr. Phan Đăng Hiển for the Vietnamese section. (2 consecutive weekly sessions).

Bibliography

2005. *The Funnel, a newsmagazine of the German American Fulbright Commission.* Volume 41(2, Summer): 15.

Algan, Yann and Christian Dustmann, Albrecht Glitz, Alan Manning. 2010. "The Economic Situation of First and Second-Generation Immigrants in France, Germany and the United Kingdom," *The Economic Journal,* Volume 120(542, February): F4–F30.

Alvarez, Luis. 2008. *The Power of the Zoot: Youth Culture and Resistance During World War II.* University of California Press.

Alvarez, Robert R., Jr. 1987. *Familia: Migration and Adaptation in Baja and Alta California, 1880-1975.* Berkeley: University of California Press.

Alvarez Jr., Roberto. 2005. *Mangos, Chiles, And Truckers: The Business Of Transnationalism.* University of Minnesota Press.

Aly, Götz. 2008. *Hitler's Beneficiaries: Plunder, Racial War, and the Nazi Welfare State* (Hitlers Volkstaat). (January 8). New York: Holt Paperbacks.

Anzaldúa, Gloria. 1999. *Borderlands/La Frontera: the New Mestiza.* 1987, second ed., San Francisco, Annt Lute Books.

Article 116 of the Basic Law for the Federal Republic of Germany (German law allows persons of German descent living anywhere in the world the right to return to Germany and claim German citizenship).

Bui, Pipo. 2003. *Envisioning Vietnamese Migrants in Germany: Ethnic Stigma, Immigrant Origin Narratives and Partial Masking.* LIT Verlag Münster.

Castañeda, Heide. 2009. Illegality as Risk Factor: A Survey of Unauthorized Migrant Patients in a

Berlin Clinic. *Social Science & Medicine* 68(8):1552–1560.

Chase-Jacobson, Jordan. 2003. "Vietnamese in Berlin." Internal Report, Berlin's Bureau of Immigration and Integration. Provided by Chase-Jacobson's Supervisor, Nguyễn Văn Hương, J.D., in 2005.

Cohen, David. 1994. *The Combing of History*. Chicago: University of Chicago Press.

Cooke, Kieran. 2001. "Trapped in no-man's land." BBC News, *"From Our Own Correspondent."* Monday 29 January.

Cap Anamur, German emergency doctors e.V.(nonprofit): http://www.cap-anamur.org

Danke Deutschland, e.V. (Intercultural project): http://danke-deutschland.org

Dennis, Mike. 2007. "Working under Hammer and Sickle: Vietnamese Workers in the German Democratic Republic, 1980-89," *German Politics*, 16(3): 339–357.

El-Tayeb, Fatima. 2003. "'If You Can't Pronounce My Name, You Can Just Call Me Pride:' Afro-German Activism, Gender and Hip Hop." *Gender & History*, 15(3, November): 460–486.

El-Tayeb, Fatima. 2004. "The Archive, the Activist, and the Audience, or Black European Studies: A Comparative Interdisciplinary Study of Identities, Positionalities, and Differences." *TRANSIT,*, UC Berkeley: Department of German. http://escholarship.org/uc/item/4tc204x4.

El-Tayeb, Fatima. 2008. "The Birth of a European Public:" Migration, Postnationality, and Race in the Uniting of Europe. *American Quarterly*, Special Issue Nation and Migration: Past and Future,60(3, Sept.): 649-670.

El-Tayeb, Fatima. 2011. *European Others: Queering Ethnicity in Postnational Europe (Difference Incorporated)*. Minneapolis: University of Minnesota Press.

Ellerman, Antje. 2008. "The Limits of Unilateral Migration Control: Deportation and Inter-state Cooperation." *Government and Opposition*, 43(2): 168-189.

Ellermann, Antje. 2005. "Coercive Capacity and the Politics of Implementation: Deportation in Germany and the United States." *Comparative Political Studies*, 38(10): 1219-1244.

Groenendijk, Kees. 2005. "Chapter 10: The legal integration of potential citizens: Denizens in the EU in the final years before the implementation of the 2003 Directive on long-term resident third country nationals." *Acquisition and Loss of Nationality: Policies and Trends in 15 European Countries*, ed. by Rainer Bauböck, Eva Ersboll, Kees Groenendijk, & Harald Waldrauch. Amsterdam University Press.

Gutinger, Erich. 1998. "Chapter 8: A Sketch of Chinese Community in Germany: Past and Present," in *The Chinese in Europe,* edited by Gregor Benton and Frank N. Pieke, (January: 197-208). London: Macmillan Press LTD.

Hanf, Theodor. 2001. "Education in a cultural lag: the case of Germany," *International Journal of Educational Research,* 35(3): 255-268.

Hillmann, Felicitas and Rudolph, Hedwig. 1997. "Redistributing the Cake? Ethnicisation Processes in the Berlin Food Sector." *Social Science Research Center Berlin [WZB Wissenschaftszentrum Berlin für Sozialforschung],* (March).

Huwelmeier, Gertrud. 2011. "Socialist cosmopolitanism meets global Pentecostalism:

charismatic Christianity among Vietnamese migrants after the fall of the Berlin Wall." *Ethnic and Racial Studies,* 34(3)(March): 436-453(18).

International Migration, Integration, and Social Cohesion. Rotterdam: Department of Social Sciences, Erasmus University. http://www.imiscoe.org/

Kaplan, Sara Clarke. 2008. "A Response to Maurice Wallace." *American Literary History, 20 (4): 807-813.* Oxford University Press. doi: 10.1093/alh/ajn059

Kemper, Franz-Josef. 1998. "Restructuring of Housing and Ethnic Segregation: Recent

Developments in Berlin," *Urban Studies, 35*(10) (October): 1765-1789.

Kim, Suzy L. 2006. "Black Enterprise in Berlin: Labor Market Integration of Black Immigrants Through Entrepreneurship." *NEURUS - Network of European and US Regional and Urban Studies,* June. Berlin: University of California, Irvine and Humboldt.

Kinzer, Stephen. 1992. "Vietnamese, Easy Target, Fear Ouster by Germany." *The New York Times,* December 6.

Landau, Saul. 1993. "Borders: The New Berlin Walls." *Socialist Register: Real Problems False Solutions (*29).

Lefebvre, Henri . 1996. *Writings on Cities,* translated by Eleonore Kofman and Elizabeth Lebas. Hoboken, NJ: Wiley-Blackwell Publishing.

Leung, Simon and Marita Sturken. 2005. "Displaced Bodies in Residual Spaces," *Public Culture* 17(1): 129-152. Duke University Press. doi: 10.1215/08992363-17-1-129

Migration News. 1995. "Germany Returns Vietnamese, Discusses Legalization." UC Davis, 1 (4)(May).

https://migration.ucdavis.edu/mn/more.php?id=641

Migration News. 1995. "Germany: Asylum, Construction, Voting, and Vietnamese." UC Davis. December), Volume 1, Number 4. https://migration.ucdavis.edu/mn/more.php?id=822

Migration Policy Institute. "Vietnamese in Germany 1995-2002." Statistisches Bundesamt (Federal Statistical Office).

Molina, Natalia. 2006. *Fit to be Citizens? Public Health and Race in Los Angeles, 1879-1939.* Berkeley: University of California Press.

Molina, Natalia. 2006. "Medicalizing the Mexican: Immigration, Race, and Disability in the Early-Twentieth-Century United States." *Radical History Review*, Winter 2006: 22-37.

Ngai, Mae. 2004. *Impossible Subjects: Illegal Aliens and the making of modern America.* Princeton, NJ: Princeton University Press.

Ngai, Pun. 2003. "Subsumption or Consumption? The Phantom of Consumer Revolution in 'Globalizing' China." *Cultural Anthropology*, (November): 469-492.

Radio Free Asia. 2007. "Khánh thành Bia tỵ nạn tưởng niệm thuyền nhân ở nước Đức" (Vietnamese Boat People Commemorative Monument in Germany) by Minh Thuỳ, (May 1).

Saberschinski, Hagen. 1995. "Berlin: theatre of East-West organized crime," *European Journal on Criminal Policy and Research*, 3(4)(December): 26-33.

Schweizer, Julia. 2004. "The Informal Behind the Formal: The Unofficial Workers Supporting Vietnamese-Owned Retail Businesses in Berlin,"

Praktiken informeller Okonomie: 54-70. uni-franfurt.de

Schweizer, Julia. 2005. "The Vietnamese Ethnic Economy in Berlin: Actors, Niches, and Spatial Dimensions." *Magisterarbeit* (MA Thesis in Geography). University of Berlin-Humboldt, Geography Institute (February 26).

Schengen Accord.[43] 1985. "Agreement between the Governments of the States of the Benelux Economic Union, the Federal Republic of Germany and the French Republic on the gradual abolition of checks at their common borders." European Union Law: http://eur-lex.europa.eu/legal-content/EN/ALL/?uri=CELEX:42000A0922(01)

Senatskanzlei (Berlin Mayoral Office). http://www.berlin.de/rbmskzl/regierender-buergermeister/auszeichnungen-und-ehrungen/verdienstorden-des-landes-berlin/artikel.6759.php

Siemon-Netto, Uwe. 2011. "Germany's up-and-comer—an Asian Christian in liberalism's 'post-secular' era." *World Tribune* (April 6).

Sutherland, Claire. 2007. "Digesting Diasporas: Vietnamese Migrants and German Multiculturalism" in *Rethinking Diasporas: Hidden Narratives and Imagined Borders* Edited by Aoileann Ní Éigeartaigh, Kevin Howard and David Getty. Newcastle, UK: Cambridge Scholars.

Thông Luận. http://www.ethongluan.org/

von Lampe, Klaus. 2005. "Explaining the emergence of the cigarette black market in Germany" in *The Organised Crime Economy: Managing Crime Markets*

---

[43] The 1985 Schengen Agreement created a borderless area across some 26 European nations, covering a population of over 400 million people and an area of 4,312,099 square kilometers.

Europe (209-229). Nijmegen, The Netherlands: Wolf Legal Publishers.

Vereinigung der Vietnamesen in Berlin & Brandenburg e.V. (Association of Vietnamese in Berlin & Brandenburg, non-profit): http://vietnam-bb.de

Vertovec, Steven. 2006. "Fostering cosmopolitanisms: A conceptual survey and a media experiment in Berlin," in *Toward a New Metropolitanism: Reconstituting Public Culture, Urban Citizenship, and the Multicultural Imaginary in New York and Berlin*, edited by Guenter H. Lenz, Friedrich Ulfers, Antje Dallmann (277-98). Heidelberg: Universitätsverlag.

Wallace, Claire. 2002. "Opening and closing borders: Migration and mobility in East-Central Europe," *Journal of Ethnic and Migration Studies,* 28(4): 603–625.

Whitehall, Geoffrey and Rachel Brickner. 2009. "Opening Global Politics: A New Introduction?" *International Studies Perspectives* (10): 216-223.

SOCIAL CONTROL AND SECURITY IN TIMES OF CRISIS: THE CRIMINALIZATION OF THE SEROPOSITIVE WOMEN IN GREECE

MARIA GKRESTA AND MANUEL MIREANU

In recent years, Greece has experienced an unprecedented economic crisis, with severe political and social implications. The intervention of three international organizations—the European Commission, the European Central Bank and the International Monetary Fund—brought about structural changes and the introduction of policies that continue to considerably lower living standards and produce societal divides. Unsurprisingly, the crisis creates conditions conducive for right-wing political groups to flourish (Mireanu and Gkresta 2013). Consequently, the political discourse has shifted and new paradigms of governance have emerged. Issues such as irregular immigration and public health have become prominent in Greek politics and public debates, and are subject of daily media attention.

Irregular immigration was a major preoccupation for the government before the May 2012

national elections, whilst crackdowns on illegalized migrants living in the center of Athens
were and continue to be common practice. In
spite of data suggesting that the numbers of undocumented migrants are much lower than
usually believed,[1] controversial police operations, such as Xenios Zeus,[2] continue to enjoy
public approval and are presented as highly
successful by the government and the media at
large.

The imposed austerity programs made inequalities sharper for the people living in
Greece. The country currently has one of the
highest unemployment rates in the EU (24.4% in
June 2012, a 7.2% increase compared to the previous year). Youth unemployment figures were
at 55.4% in June 2012, with women more likely
to be unemployed than men[3]. According to a
recent survey, sex trade in Greece increased by
1.500%.[4] For the sex workers, the economic cri-

---

[1] According to a recent report of the Human Rights Watch, almost
85,000 foreigners were forcibly brought in to police stations to
verify their immigration status between August 2012 (when
Operation Xenios Zeus began) and February 2013. Out of them,
fewer than 6 percent were found to be in Greece unlawfully.
Human Rights Watch, Unwelcome Guests, June 12th 2013,
http://www.hrw.org/node/116082 , last accessed on 29 February
2016.

[2] *Xenios Zeus* is the name of an ongoing law enforcement program
with the purpose to sweep off the streets irregular immigrants.

[3] Eurostat, Unemployment statistics (data up to August 2012),
http://epp.eurostat.ec.europa.eu/statistics_explained/index.php/Un
employment_statistics

[4] The data are the result of a research conducted by the National
Centre for Social Research in collaboration with the Department
of Criminology of the PanteionUnivrsity of Athens and the
Ombudsman. "Η κρίση απογειώνει την πορνεία," 03/10/2012,

sis has resulted in a shrinking client base. On the one hand, people have less money to spend on sexual services. On the other hand, in order to attract more clients, sex workers are pushed to take higher risks and have unprotected sex.

As part of the structural reforms imposed by the politics of austerity, the already over stretched social welfare programs are being crippled. Budget cuts greatly impacted outreach programs designed to counsel and treat the most vulnerable, which provide services such as needle exchange and condom distribution, along with spreading information on HIV prevention. The resources allocated to social welfare and the healthcare system have been reduced dramatically. To give a few examples a 40% cut in hospital budgets (Kentikelenis et al. 2011) that translates into shortages in personnel and supplies, the suspension of the needle exchange program in Athens, the suspension of payment of benefits to people with disabilities, and the introduction of a 5 euro fee per hospital visit, and so on. In other words, the access to services and preventive care is severely compromised. The impact of the crisis on health is reflected in the number of reported HIV cases, which in 2011 increased by 57% compared to 2010[5], and also the growing numbers of drug

---

http://archive-gr-2013.com/gr/l/2013-01-08_1091660_128/Left-gr/ (see also http://www.tovima.gr/vimagazino/views/article/? aid=618417) (both links last accessed on 29 February 2016)

[5] See "Global AIDS Response Progress Report 2012, Greece," Reporting period: January – December 2011, pg.4, http://www.unaids.org/sites/default/files/en/dataanalysis/knowyo urresponse/countryprogressreports/2012countries/ce_GR_Narrativ e_Report.pdf (last accessed: 29 February 2016)

users—in 2010 the number of heroin users grew by 20% compared to the previous year (Kentikelenis et al. 2011). As it happened with all vulnerable groups, the crisis increased the precariousness of persons using drugs, who might turn to sex work in order to sustain themselves.

In the mainstream political agenda, the cuts are presented as unavoidable, the only way to "save the country." This has proven to be an efficient strategy to guarantee the approval of the society (loosely defined), since it capitalizes on xenophobia and nationalism. Since the urban environment is more vulnerable, the effects of the crisis are mostly felt and manifested in cities. The center of Athens has been significantly affected, and the transformations of the urban landscape are glaringly noticeable. Public spaces are being neglected, sanitation services have deteriorated, and commercial spaces in the city's most expensive areas are now vacant. The only business that seems to be flourishing is that of pawnshops. Evictions have become regular, and the numbers of homeless people are on the rise. Although the "war against criminality" is part of the dominant political discourse, it has become hard to conceal activities such as drug trafficking and sex work. These activities and the rise in HIV cases are being linked by the authorities to undocumented immigration.

This article will describe how a government project that was initially targeting undocumented immigrants evolved into the castigation of a group of twenty-seven seropositive women. The women were detained by the Greek police and forcibly tested for HIV, shortly before 2012's national elections. Their personal data were disclosed, their mug shots were published by the media, and they were charged with felony offences and imprisoned. Less than a year later, the initial charges against them collapsed and all of them were set free. We will look at this case through the lens of the literature on the securitization of HIV and we argue that the Greek authorities did not just present the seropositive women as a security threat, but, further to this, the women were framed and criminalized as sex workers, migrants, and non-citizens. In contrast to what the literature on risk and security suggests, we will then argue that there is *always* an exceptional moment that triggers the generalized panic.

Our methodology is a combination of interviews and discourse analysis. Maria conducted a series of interviews in the summer of 2013 in Athens: with doctor Chrysa Botsi from the NGO "Act Up Hellas," with Sissy Vovou from the "Solidarity Initiative for the Persecuted HIV-positive Women" and with a volunteer who wished to remain anonymous. Maria has also read the Greek press literature and has put together the timeline of the events, while Manuel helped with the overall analysis of the Greek authorities' discourse.

The case of the persecuted seropositive women in Greece can function as a vantage viewpoint to look at the way in which a perceived risk is used as a vehicle for social control and can shed light on the performative uses of a state of emergency. Social groups that are perceived as somehow hostile or deviant (migrants, homeless, people who use intravenous drugs, transgender persons, sex workers, and even anarchists) exist in the margins of society, in what is presented as a state of disorder beyond legality. This logic legitimizes intervention and justifies the intensification of violent repression in the eyes of the public. This case is also an opportunity to show how debating crises can be a prelude to repressive state policies.

A Chronicle of Castigation

The 2012 parliamentary elections were due to be held in late April or early May. Already in early March, the Greek government had launched a crackdown on illegalized migrants living in the center of Athens. In the first days of April, the government announced (and, subsequently introduced) amendments[6] according to which the law assumes the right to detain indefinitely third-country nationals, if they *pose a risk to public health*. For this to happen, it is enough to suspect that a person "belongs to groups vulnerable to infectious diseases, particularly because of the country of origin, or of the use of intravenous illegal substances or because a person is involved in prostitution [...] or a person resides in conditions that do not comply with minimum standards of hygiene."[7]According to the law, the illegalized migrants[8] would

---

[6] The amendments were made to the law 4075/2012 (Government Gazette Issue 89/A, 11-04-2012), article 59.

[7] Ibid, pg. 2714.

[8] It should be noted that the law extends also to a third-country national that 'resides in conditions that do not comply with

be held in custody,[9] whether they have applied for political asylum or not, for compulsory health checks, including tests for contagious diseases, such as HIV.

The law does not determine who can define which are the countries of origin whose nationals may pose a risk to public health. Neither are the criteria for selecting them stated. Needless to say, the law is discriminatory; it is just as likely that Greek nationals could "satisfy" criteria such as undertaking sex work and drug use or through living in unsanitary conditions. The text of the law reproduces wider racist discourses against migrants. It is worth noting at this point that the crisis years are characterized by an explosion in the intensity of legislative acts. Some were part of the reforms that Greece agreed to in order to receive financial aid, while others did not seem to cover any pressing social needs. Often these changes in the legal framework were met with protests, and the procedures followed were far from democratic.

The decision to introduce the above mentioned amendments was preceded by alarming statements of government officials regarding the imminence of a public health disaster caused by the presence of migrants in the city center. The Minister of Citizen Protection, Michalis Chrisochoidis, stated that the great

---

minimum standards of hygiene', meaning that a person that resides lawfully in Greece can be detained as well.

[9] Paragraph 3 of the article 59 (law 4075/2012, pg. 2715) reads: 'The subjects [...] will be submitted to compulsory health examination and corresponding treatment. For the treatment areas detention regulations apply for the period that the reasons for the subjects' detention apply.'

concentration of migrants at the center of Athens and other big cities creates severe threats for the public health, arguing that their unacceptable living standards cannot guarantee elementary hygiene standards[10.] He called the ensuing public issues "a time bomb with immeasurable consequences, if it explodes."

The Minister for Health and Social Solidarity, Andreas Loverdos, sounded a note of warning on the consequences of contagious ailments for public health. He said that there has been a rise of more than 1000% in AIDS cases and talked about the reappearance of long forsaken diseases,[11] such as malaria and tuberculosis.[12] In the

---

[10] "Λοβέρδος - Χρυσοχοΐδης: Υποχρεωτικόπιστοποιητικόυγείαςγιαμετανάστες", *To Vima*, 01/04/2012, http://www.tovima.gr/society/article/?aid=451357 (last accessed: 29 February 2016).

[11] Ibid.

[12] Note here that human-to-human transmission of malaria only occurs in the cases of congenital transmission and through unscreened blood transfusions. According to the Hellenic Center for Disease Control & Prevention (KEELPNO), during 2011 there have been recorded 27 cases in Greeks, 25 in migrants and 6 unconfirmed cases in Evrotas, a municipality in the Laconia regional unit (source: Ενεργητική αναζήτηση και θεραπεία κρουσμάτωνελονοσίας στη Λακωνία, 2011, http://www.keelpno.gr/el-gr/δράσειςκεελπνο/γενικέςδράσειςκεελπνο/ενεργητικήαναζήτηση κρουσμάτων.aspx). As for tuberculosis, KEELPNO reports that during the period 2004-2010 the cases have gradually decreased from 761 to 490 (source: ΕΠΙΔΗΜΙΟΛΟΓΙΚΑ ΔΕΔΟΜΕΝΑ ΦΥΜΑΤΙΩΣΗΣ ΣΤΗΝ ΕΛΛΑΔΑ, 2004-2010, http://www.keelpno.gr/Portals/0/Αρχεία/Αναπνευστικού/Φυματίω ση/Φυματίωση%202004-2010.pdf). With regards to the HIV cases, there has indeed been recorded an increase of 1500% in the number of cases from 2010 to 2011 in the intravenous drug users (source:, "HIV/AIDS Surveillance in Greece", no 26, December 2011, pg. 15 http://www.keelpno.gr/Portals/0/%CE%91%CF%81%CF

same announcement, Loverdos said that out of the 600 brothels in Athens only seven had a permit and that it is not possible to perform health checks for the women working at undocumented brothels.[13] The amendments gave the authorities the legal support to do so. On the 27th of April, just a few days after the healthcare provisions regarding the migrants were introduced, the Hellenic Centre for Disease Control & Prevention (KEELPNO) started performing controls in undocumented brothels.[14] The first results appeared in the news one day later: the results of the HIV rapid tests ran by the experts had revealed one positive case. It was a 22 year old woman from Russia. The day after the police made public all her personal data: not just her full name, her place of birth and age, but also the date of birth, the names of her parents, the name of the neighbourhood where the woman was living in Athens, the address of the brothel she was working at the time, and of the one she

%87%CE%B5%CE%AF%CE%B1/HIV/EPIDIMIOLOGIKO %20HIV_2011.pdf

[13] Loverdos had already pointed out back in December 2011 that undocumented, unregistered prostitution was a big problem, closely related to the AIDS problem which is now a problem of the Greek family, since it is being transmitted "from the illegal immigrant to the Greek client to the Greek family." See Aris Chatzigeorgiou and DaniVergou, "Να απελαθούν οι ιερόδουλες φορείς του AIDS" (Expel the AIDS-carrier prostitutes), Eleutherotypia, 11/12/2011, http://www.enet.gr/? i=news.el.article&id=332267 (last accessed: 29 February 2016)

[14] "Υγειονομικοι Ελεγχοι Κε.Ελ.Π.Νο - Οροθετικη Σε Παρανομο Οικο Ανοχησ", n/d, http://www.eumedline.eu/post/YGEIONOMIKOI-ELEGXOI-KEELPNO-OROTHETIKH-SE-PARANOMO-OIKO-ANOXHS (last accessed: 29 February 2016)

had worked before. The information was accompanied by two pictures of her that went instantly viral. The woman has been prosecuted for "intentional gross bodily harm," among other charges.[15] According to the data given to the press, she was aware of her medical condition and continued nonetheless to have unprotected sex with clients. However, during her court testimony, the woman said that she did not know she was a carrier.[16] The police, in its announcement, justified the disclosure of the woman's data and pictures and the severe charges against her as a way of protecting society, and as means to legitimize the state's further claims for the criminal punishment of such offences.[17] The public exposure of the data aimed to persuade the men who had intercourse with her to get tested for HIV and to prevent men that have had intercourse with a woman with similar description from panicking. The police invited men who wished to get tested or receive instructions on HIV to contact the Hellenic Centre for Disease Control & Prevention (KEELPNO).

---

[15] The brothel where she was working had been sealed three times in the past and had always resumed function illegally. The woman was charged for violating the sealing, for facilitating debauchery and other infringements of the legislation on sex workers.

[16] Her statement is reproduced in this video: http://www.youtube.com/watch?v=24lwt_POjFQ&feature=related

[17] The police announcement has been reproduced by all media. See "Στη δημοσιότητα φωτογραφίες και στοιχεία της οροθετικής ιερόδουλης", 29/04/2012, http://www.skai.gr/news/greece/article/201653/elas-sti-dimosiotita-fotografies-kai-stoiheia-tis-orothetikis-ierodoulis/ (last accessed: 29 February 2016)

During the following days the Greek media went on reproducing the story and presenting reports on the sex trade that was happening in the city center. This was done under telling titles, such as "This is the Russian prostitute who's an AIDS carrier,"[18] "Horror for hundreds of men who had sexual intercourse with the Russian,"[19] "Panic in Athens because of the prostitute with HIV,"[20]"This is how the Russian prostitute- AIDS carrier advertised [her services] on the internet (images),"[21] "Women-public menace."[22] The woman's personal data and face were plastered all over not only domestic, but also in-

---

[18] Title of the article published at the news website *newsbeast.gr*, "Αυτήείναι η ρωσίδα ιερόδουληφορέας του AIDS", 29/04/2012, http://www.newsbeast.gr/society/arthro/342666/auti-einai-i-rosida-ierodouli-foreas-tou-aids/ (last accessed: 29 February 2016)

[19] Title of the article published on the newspaper "*Proto Thema*", Τότα Καρλατήρα, "Τρόμος για εκατοντάδες άντρες που είχαν συνευρεθεί με τη Ρωσίδα!, 30/04/2012, http://www.protothema.gr/greece/article/?aid=193777 (last accessed: 29 February 2016)

[20] From the Greek social show "*Mila*" (Speak) with popular presenter Tatiana Stefanidou, running on STAR TV station (30/04/2012). The video can be watched on YouTube and it includes the "shocking testimony of the 21 year old man who had sexual intercourse with the prostitute with AIDS".http://www.youtube.com/watch? feature=player_embedded&v=mZJhVqHTxrU(last accessed: 29 February 2016)

[21] "Έτσι διαφημιζόταν στο Ίντερνετ η Ρωσίδα ιερόδουλη-φορέας του AIDS", 01/05/2012, http://www.iefimerida.gr/news/48440/έτσι-διαφημιζόταν-στο-ίντερνετ-η-ρωσίδα-ιερόδουλη-φορέας-του-aids-εικόνες (last accessed: 29 February 2016)

[22] A video from the news broadcast of Alpha TV, uploaded on 29/03/2012. The reporter is interviewing a Bulgarian sex worker who admits she has "no papers from a doctor in Greece." http://www.youtube.com/watch? v=5GTA3m7tnCM&feature=related

ternational media.[23] The Hellenic Centre for Disease Control & Prevention (KEELPNO) and the AIDS-helpline received more than 600 calls in just a couple of days from men reporting that they had had unprotected sex with the Russian woman. The Minister for Health and Social Solidarity made almost triumphant statements:[24] "I've been saying these things for a long time and no one would listen, now unfortunately I was shown to be right. I had given fair warning that AIDS is increasing dramatically in our country and that part of the problem stems from illegal immigration and unregistered prostitution."[25] He went on to stress the danger for Greek families: "I had said that the problem is entering Greek families since family guys are going to brothels and this way they carry the illness into their homes."

Minister Loverdos reassured the citizens that he had instructed the employees of KEELPNO to continue implementing the health provisions with more intensive controls in undocumented

---

[23] See, for example "Active prostitute with AIDS was discovered in Athens", *GRReporter* 30/04/2012, http://www.grreporter.info/en/active_prostitute_aids_was_discovered_athens/6678 (last accessed: 29 February 2016)

[24] The interview was initially given to a website dealing with health related topics and can be found in this link: http://www.iatropedia.gr/articles/read/1738 (last accessed: 29 February 2016). It was, however, reproduced by all mainstream media.

[25] Loverdos went so far as to propose the deportation of foreign sex workers with HIV. See: Fragkiska Megaloudi, "Gay People Living in Fear in Greece," *Huffington Post*, 25/11/2012, http://www.huffingtonpost.co.uk/fragkiska-megaloudi/greece-gay-people-living-in-fear_b_2175056.html, last accessed on 29 February 2016

brothels[26] all around the country: "In the following days, no brothel will go unchecked." Faced with criticisms that the controls were just election populism substituting for the settlement of growing social and economic problems, the minister replied that the controls are not a pre-electoral fad. "Now that we receive a positive response from the Ministry of Public Order, we have all the tools [necessary] to protect public health," he stated. One of the "tools" at the disposal of the authorities turned out to be the Hellenic Centre for Disease Control and Prevention (KEELPNO). KEELPNO's control units comprised not only of administrative personnel, but also of health professionals. Although its stated primary concern is to support and protect "special" (vulnerable) populations (immigrant populations and human trafficking),[27] in this case KEELPNO became a regulatory apparatus in the hands of the authorities and was used in a repressive operation. Not only were the women forcibly tested, but also the notion of medical confidentiality was rendered impossible through the collaboration with the police.

---

[26] It is worth mentioning that controls were also being conducted in building at the centre of Athens in search of migrants whose living standards constituted a threat for public health. According to reports, 200 migrants were found in eleven apartments, 39 of them were undocumented. See: Παναγιώτα Καρλατήρα, "Ξεφεύγει η κατάσταση: Άλλες τρεις πόρνες με AIDS στην Αθήνα!" ("The situation is getting out of hand: Three more prostitutes with AIDS in Athens!"), ProtoThema, 30/04/2012, http://www.protothema.gr/greece/article/?aid=193907 (last accessed on 29 February 2016)

[27] From the webpage of KEELPNO, "The purpose of the HCDCP," http://www.keelpno.gr/en-us/hcdcp/purposeofthehcdcpenus.aspx (last accessed on 29 February 2016)

The controls continued and more and more women—all of them unregistered and working on the street—were found to be HIV-positive and were prosecuted for felony. Twelve women, most of them Greek nationals, some of them homeless, were also accused for "intentional gross bodily harm," meaning that the prosecutor had concluded invariably that they were all aware of their condition. The women explained that they were not aware of their illness, but found few sympathetic ears. The police, following the same procedure as in the first case, published their private data, together with a short statement: "The publishing of the data [...] aims at protecting society. Whoever wishes to get tested [...] should call [...]."[28]

The "success" of the controls made Minister Loverdos quite popular; he gave several interviews that were later on reproduced by various

[28]The data were made public on the 01/05/2012 and the pictures can be seen in many different news websites even today. Indicatively, we provide one link from the news website *iefimerida.gr* :"Αυτές είναι οι 12 ιερόδουλες που βρέθηκαν θετικές στον ιό του AIDS", 01.03.2012 (last accessed on 29 February 2016),http://www.iefimerida.gr/news/48456/αυτές-είναι-οι-12-ιερόδουλες-που-βρέθηκαν-θετικές-στον-ιό-του-aids-εικόνες. The images of the 12 women were shown on TV during the main news broadcast. A video from the news in one of the state TV stations can be watched here: http://www.youtube.com/watch?v=Nm6upGbRl4o&feature=related (last accessed on 29 February 2016) and an article on *The Independent*, Charlotte McDonald-Gibson, "The women Greece blames for its HIV crisis" http://www.independent.co.uk/news/world/europe/the-women-greece-blames-for-its-hiv-crisis-7973313.html, 25/07/2012 (last accessed on 29 February 2016)

media. Talking on a radio show of a Hellenic Broadcasting Corporation station[29] the Minister explained that, in the area where the women were arrested, "drugs and prostitution are one. [...] That's why I've been shouting during the last months that you should not go with non-national illegal prostitutes." The minister claimed that the issue with the undocumented sex workers had gotten out of hand in Greece and yet again he referred to the very first case saying that the clients of the Russian woman were "kids" (young men) that would go to the brothel she worked because they knew they could have sex with her without using condoms. "It is 'cool' not to use [protection]. That is, they [the clients] pay a bit more. They go to her because she accepts [to have sex] without [using] protection. And of course she would accept [to have sex] without protection because she knew she is sick. Because she was not afraid"—the Minister stated confidently. Loverdos even called for the penalization of unprotected sex as a way to make the clients act responsibly.

In just a few days, the Hellenic Centre for Disease Control and Prevention had received more than 1600 calls from men that after seeing the images of the women, realized that they had had unprotected sex with one of the HIV carriers. In the days that followed, the data of many more women were published: on the 3rd of May five women,[30] on the 5th of May another

[29] The parts of the interview discussed in this paper can be found in "Άλλες τρεις πόρνες με AIDS στην Αθήνα!", *Protothema* 30/04/2012, http://www.protothema.gr/greece/article/? aid=193907(last accessed on 29 February 2016)

six,[31] on the 10th of May five more.[32]The format
of the police announcements was always the
same, mentioning that the women were prosecuted and that controls would continue and
concluding by encouraging the clients to get
tested for HIV-AIDS. In the meantime, various
organizations were asking for the cessation of
the castigation of HIV-positive women. As was
mentioned before, divulging such sensitive information meant not only violating human
rights and offending the women's dignity, but
also breaking the rules of doctor-patient confidentiality.[33] The Greek League for Human
Rights pointed out that the police action was violating Law 2472/1997 on the protection of personal data[34] and that, in any case, the publica-

---

[30] The names and birthdates of these five women can be seen here:
http://www.fimes.gr/2012/05/ierodoules-aids-3/ (last accessed on
29 February 2016)

[31] The pictures of the six women can be seen here
http://www.tuned.gr/kosmos/kosmos/13049-aids (last accessed on
29 February 2016)

[32] The data of the five women arrested on 10/05/2012 can be seen
here: http://www.newsbeast.gr/society/arthro/349197/sti-
dimosiotita-oi-fotografies-pede-akoma-ierodoulon/ (last accessed
on 29 February 2016)

[33] One of the organizations that reacted to the data disclosure was
KETHEA, the largest rehabilitation and social reintegration
network in Greece. Their press release on the topic was issued on
03/05/2012 and can be read following this link:
http://www.kethea.gr/Νέα/ΔελτίαΤύπου/tabid/141/articleType/Arti
cleView/articleId/206/language/el-GR/Default.aspx (last accessed
on 29 February 2016)

[34] According to the law, the prosecutor could not disclose sensitive
health data without the permission of the competent Authority
for Personal Data Protection (Article 7, Government Gazette Issue
50/A, 10-05-1997. The law can be accessed following this link:
http://www.dpa.gr/pls/portal/docs/PAGE/APDPX/LAW/NOMOTH

tion of pictures and the disclosure of their seropositivity was unreasonable.[35] Even UN-AIDS released a press statement expressing "concerns about the inappropriate application of criminal law, particularly in a context where clients have the social and economic power to insist upon condom use."[36]

Despite all reactions, the Minister for Citizen Protection, Michalis Chrisochoidis, vindicated the decision to make the women's personal data public as "absolutely legal." Ignoring the issue of medical confidentiality, he said the backlash was "exaggerated"; he added that the point of an AIDS epidemic in the country should not be reached, and neither should those who are not at fault have to deal with the consequences.[37] By that point, it was clear that, since most of the women were Greek, the authorities' rhetoric of the "criminal immigrant" was unsustainable, so HIV had become the main focus of the emergency and the object of criminalization.

ESIA%20PROSOPIKA%20DEDOMENA/%CE%9DOMOTHESIA%20PROSOPIKA%20DEDOMENA_GREEK/2472_97_NOV 2011_FINALVERSION.PDF)

[35] The press release of the Hellenic League of Human Rights was issued on 02/05/2012 and can be accessed here http://www.hlhr.gr/index.php?MDL=pages&SiteID=208 (last accessed on 29 February 2016)

[36] "UNAIDS calls on Greece to protect sex workers and their clients through comprehensive and voluntary HIV programmes," 10/05/2012, http://www.unaids.org/en/resources/presscentre/pressreleaseandstatementarchive/2012/may/20120510psgreece/

[37] From an interview on SKAITV, "M. Χρυσοχοΐδης: Την Κυριακή η Ελλάδα πρέπει να έχει κυβέρνηση," 04/05/2012, http://www.skai.gr/news/politics/article/202164/m-hrusohoidis-tin-kuriaki-i-ellada-prepei-na-ehei-kuvernisi/, last accessed on 29 February 2016

After the last round of data disclosure on the 10th of May, the Hellenic Centre for Disease Control and Prevention (KEELPNO) issued an announcement warning that the institute would not make any more controls unless this practice would stop.[38] Eventually, because of the reaction, the Greek police removed from its webpage the images of the women. It is doubtful that the late decision of KEELPNO made a difference. The Solidarity Initiative with the Persecuted Seropositive Women, a group that was formed shortly after the first arrests, had a crucial role in having the mug shots removed from the police website. The group issued calls for protests and petitions and a bank account for donations was opened to help with covering the costs of the legal procedure and other expenses. Members of the group who were visiting the women in prison said that one of their first requests was the removal of their images.

Unfortunately, public shaming is just one of the tragic aspects of this story. The seropositive women were held in prison cells, not in a hospital. As a precaution, they were held separately from the rest of the prisoners, in the basement of the prison, in highly unsanitary conditions. They did not have adequate medical care during this time. Their prosecution for sex work was based on the information given by one police officer, who testified for all the women—190 approximately—were initially brought in to confirm their data. The charges for sex work

---

[38] Martha Kaitanidi, "Οι εργαζόμενοι του ΚΕΕΛΠΝΟ διαμαρτύρονται για τις ιερόδουλες," 11/05/2012 http://ygeia.tanea.gr/default.asp?pid=8&ct=1&articleID= 14794&la=1, last accessed on 29 February 2016

had to be dropped. It could be argued that these women were controlled because of their appearance and their drug addiction and were persecuted and imprisoned for being HIV-positive. By March 2013, all 27 seropositive women were out of prison. Their release, however, enjoyed little or no media coverage and no statements were made on behalf of the authorities.

SECURITY AND HIV

The ways in which the Greek authorities decided to deal with the issue of HIV-positive women in Athens suggests a logic of securitization, whereby a public threat is articulated as an issue of capital importance that deserves immediate treatment. Ole Waever and Barry Buzan have shown how security threats are discursively constructed through a process of verbal articulation that they coined the "security speech act." An issue becomes a security threat when a social actor labels it as an existential danger that requires emergency measures. If such emergency measures are not taken right away, the threatening issue risks annihilating the political and social body of the community (Buzan et. al. 1998). The proponents of this theory suggest that in most cases the community can be the state or the society. If the issue is threatening the integrity and sovereignty of the state, then it is a case of national security, and it is dealt with by way of military interventions. If, on the other hand, the issue threatens the society, matters are slightly more complicated, because of the heterogeneity of what is called "the society" in comparison to the homogeneity of the state, as a social actor (Waever 1995). In other words, if the leaders of a state have the legitimacy to speak for the state and declare a state of emergency, the voices of a society are always competing with one another for prevalence and legitimacy. In the case of societal security, the threat is being posed to the identity of the community, which can be a nation, an ethnic group, or even supranational entities, such as "Europe" or "humanity." If this identity is annihilated, then the entire group would cease to exist as a social actor.

However, it is difficult to see how the events of spring 2012 in Athens could be fully explained through the grid of the theory of securitization. Despite the fact that there is an obvious mechanism of discursively articulating an issue as a threat to the population, the threatened entity has not been the state or the identity of the population (despite the references to the Greek family—more on this issue later), but the health of the men who seem to have used the sexual services of the women living with HIV. The health of these women themselves was of no concern at any point. The measures taken by the Greek authorities do not pertain to a scenario where the gravity of the threat would justify a general mobilization of the population or the state. To put it in the terms of the securitization theory, the measures were *exceptional*, *but not urgent*. The securitization of HIV in Greece pertains to a less dramatic level. This is a securitizing move that aims at restoring and reinforcing a certain social order and the values that it represents.

Quite a few scholars have pointed out the ways in which such securitizing moves work. Bigo (2002) has shown that the state officials and the so-called "professionals of security" create and sustain a climate of "unease," in which daily threats are exacerbated in order to justify a perpetual regime of surveillance and control. In this way, the authorities maintain a generalized feeling of insecurity among the population, by using data and expertise to point out the great degree of risk that a society is facing from certain threats such as immigration or terrorism (Bigo 2002; Aradau and Van Munster 2007 and 2008). Securitization is thus a process that involves as much scientific knowledge as political decision. It is not only a discursive articulation of an emergency, but a continuous mechanism of everyday assessments (Huysmans 2011). Securitization functions through technologies of surveillance, such as biometrics, CCTV cameras, fingerprints databases and so on, as much as through hard military defence. It functions through insidious and mundane objects such as mail correspondence, computers, or liquid recipients. In this way, anything can become a threat, including an invisible virus.

Stephan Elbe has analysed the patterns of HIV and AIDS securitizations in the last few years on a global scale. He shows how "population dynamics"—including levels of "disease"— have now become strategically significant' at the international level (Elbe 2012, 321). The securitization of the HIV and of people living with AIDS is part of a shift in focus from a need to defend the national territory to a need to defend and increase the population at large. Therefore, keeping populations secure from "deadly diseases" such as AIDS becomes a matter of high governmental priority. This results in a form of knowledge and power that targets bodies and behaviours. Elbe shows how this securitization of the HIV functions by articulating the diseased as "deviant," and juxtaposing this category to the healthy norm of the population (Elbe 2005, 413). This deviance is applied especially in the realm of sexuality. The sexual behaviour of individuals is targeted by 'strategic interventions' aimed at eliminating any abnormal conduct (Elbe 2005, 414).

By constituting the category of the deviant, as the bearer of the deadly virus, the mechanism that articulates HIV and the people living with AIDS as security threats establishes a logic of exclusion whereby the diseased needs to be separated and quarantined from the rest of the society (Elbe 2005, 411). This exclusion is necessary for the threat to be contained and eventually destroyed; but it is also a normalizing and disciplining measure that aims at underlining the consequences of deviant (sexual) behaviour. As such, the person living with HIV becomes an outcast; she or he can transgress forcibly the boundaries of the social norm and quotidian life, only to be ostracised in the exterior, in the realm of the untouchables. In political terms, the person living with HIV loses any legitimacy as a human being and a citizen. AIDS becomes a stigma that exhibits characteristics of deviance, danger, and debauchery.

The underlining argument that Elbe puts forward is that the securitization of the HIV and of people living with AIDS constitutes the diseased as a "social and political problem that needs to be addressed, but without specifying" the means of solving it (Elbe 2005, 409). He uses the concept of "risk" to emphasize the long-term character of this problem. As a "security risk," the issue of HIV is treated in a speculative way, as something that "may" cause instability and insecurity (Elbe 2008, 179). As such, it becomes a useful tool for maintaining the climate of "unease" that we have referred to before. Elbe uses Foucault's thoughts on biopolitics to advance the argument that HIV is treated politically through a rationality of risk and security that is "used to analyse and manage a multitude of collective population dynamics at the level of population" (Elbe 2008, 191). The language of risk is used to devise and apply "biopolitical strategies" and securitizing logics in ways that are more dispersed, quotidian and insidious than those of a direct sovereign power.

In the next sections, we propose two arguments that diverge from this view. First, we argue that the events of spring 2012 in Athens point to a specific mode of dealing with HIV-positive people, which is a mode of criminalization. Thus, we suggest that securitizing the HIV is not an open-ended process as Elbe argues, but a concrete mechanism for rendering certain groups as being outside the law, and therefore outside the possibility of claiming citizenship rights. Second, we argue that the Athens case shows that the securitization of HIV and of people living with AIDS cannot be read only through the language of biopolitical risk. Such a vocabulary emphasizes dispersed articulations of threat. Rather, the events of 2012 point to an exceptional moment of action and coercion against the women living with HIV. We argue that the securitization of HIV-positive women in Athens was primarily a way to criminalize them. In this section, we will show the two mechanisms of this criminalization, as well as the ways in which criminalizing sex workers is part of a series of moves from the Greek state against sex workers, immigrants, and asylum seekers in Greece.

Mechanisms of Criminalisation

The first mechanism is the *criminalization of movement*. This is performed primarily through a discourse of perpetual suspicion towards immigrants. As one of our respondents argued, the action against HIV-positive women was devised from the outset as another step in the crackdown of illegalized immigrants in Athens. Immigration as the movement of people across borders was a main target of the Greek authorities. Moreover, this is not just movement of people, but also that of a virus considered to be deadly. Hence, the movement of the carriers is doubly incriminated: first for having illicitly arrived in Greece, and second for having transmitted the virus to Greek citizens.

The criminalization of movement is also transparent in the spatial logic that triggered the actions of the Greek authorities against women who were using drugs and undertaking sex work in Athens. From the outset, these actions were focused in particular areas of the city —such as Omonoia, Vathi square and Athinas street—which were perceived as a focal point of the disease. As one respondent argued, there is a plan to "push" the areas of sex trade and drug use into specific places of the city, in order to have them out of sight, but at the same time close at hand. Loverdos, the Minister of Health, had confirmed this, by saying that HIV was an issue that belonged to "the ghetto of the illegal immigrants in Greece," and that it spread from there because Greek men were using the services of "illegally prostituting outlanders."[39] From there on, once the women who were living with HIV had been identified, a great deal of effort was made in order to contain and quarantine these women, and to block their movement into other areas of the city. Hence, the space where the women lived became at once an integral part of the stigma they were carrying along with the virus. Any attempt to move out, to escape the environment in which these tragic events happened brought again and again this stigma with it.[40] The spatial logic is also evident in the way that the women were treated during their arrest: they were imprisoned in a basement, in dire insanitary conditions and without any proper medical or psychological care.

---

[39] From an interview published on the personal webpage of Andreas Loverdos, http://loverdos.gr/gr/index.php?Mid=68&art=2432 (last accessed: 15 September 2013; at the time of re-submission, this webpage is under reconstruction)

[40] It is telling that, as one respondent argued, this stigma was more powerful in the case of Greek women than for the migrants, since the former were more connected to their families and native places.

The second mechanism is related to the *politics of citizenship* and the discourses of inclusion and exclusion that pertain to them. As Andrijasevic and collaborators (2012, 501) argue, "despite the emphasis on the free movement of workers within the Union and the importance of this to the development of citizenship in the EU, the legitimacy of EU citizens who are sex workers is put under question." This is even more so for those people who are undocumented immigrants. As we have shown in the outset, the Greek government is waging a continuous war on undocumented immigration, and the operation against (alleged) sex workers in Athens has been a part of this war. Not having legal documents, not having a legitimate status within the country, becomes an additional crime and a reason to hunt down the women who were working on the streets of Athens.

Here the issue of the published photographs becomes of capital importance. Biber (2005, 21) argues that "photography has a close and awkward union with crime," since it serves to identify and classify the suspects. Furthermore, suspicion can be turned into conviction with the help of the visual evidence provided by photographs. Photography illustrates deviance and disorder by "producing guilt from innocence" (Banks 2012, 4). This is a function that has been traditionally associated with the mug shot. By publishing their faces photographed frontally, and juxtaposing them to alarmist captions, the police framed the women as guilty before any trial has taken place. The role of the mug shot is to elicit emotions, and in this case what was sought for was generalized panic. In this scenario, whether the women were guilty or not mattered less than the fact that the panic could have a recognizable face.

As Banks points out, the mug shot is "depicted as capturing the very essence of the individual" (Banks 2012, 15). In this case, this "essence" was supposed to illustrate deviance, drug-addiction and recklessness in regards to spreading a deadly disease. The photographs were meant to alarm the general public—the Greek families—about the spreading danger posed by the women. In this way, several lines of exclusion were being drawn: Greeks versus immigrants, healthy versus diseased, clean versus addicted, normal versus deviant and honest versus criminal. To this it should also be added the right of privacy that every individual has, which was completely abandoned in the case of the HIV-positive women. Despite the 'fact' that most of these women turned out not to be illegalised immigrants but Greek citizens, this actual citizenship mattered less and was denied to them on the basis of these exclusions and on their presumed guilt.

The authorities selectively constructed the identity of these women and directed the public's attention to their selected aspects. They built a triple identity for them: woman—sex worker—dangerous patient. In projecting these characterizations through the media to the public, they create the image of these women as individuals deserving the worst treatment. In the words of Elizabeth Grosz, the female body is seen "as a kind of sponge or conduit of other men's 'dirt'" (Grosz 1994, 197).

In this sense, "Emotions become a technology of government to the extent that they can be used to steer citizens' actions" (Aradau 2004, 255).The sex workers are deprived of their individuality, they are categorized as "high risk" (Aradau 2004, 267) and as posing a threat for the society. As a result, they are perceived by the society as responsible/culpable for the ills that have befallen them (Aradau 2004, 258).

Being infected with HIV was only a part of the discourse that criminalized the women who were arrested in the streets of Athens. If we are to focus on the nexus between disease and securitization, as Elbe suggests, we must pay more attention to the intimate mechanisms of criminalization. The fact of carrying the virus is always entangled in several other discourses of guilt and panic. In the case of the seropositive women in Greece, we cannot analyze the securitization of AIDS without paying attention to the ways in which movement, space, citizenship, and the mug shots operated as mechanisms of criminalization.

Risk and the Exception

In this section we take up the argument of the nexus between the securitization of HIV and risk. According to the generalized arguments made by security scholars, risk is a mode of governance that aims at managing the future and preventing certain dangerous scenarios from taking place, through the use of statistical knowledge and technological devices (Aradau and Van Munster 2007; Amoore and de Goede 2008). A strategy of risk is a way of taming the contingent, and thus of predicting the "unknowns" of the future. Thus, risk policies are an integral part of the neoliberal *dispositif* of governmentality (Aradau and van Munster 2008, 29). Governmentality is the art of self-governance in accordance to the principles of the dominant discourse. Therefore, every social relation will be permeated by power (Foucault 2007).

Within this Foucauldian framework, the locus of power is no longer the sovereign, who is situated on top of the social and political hierarchy; instead, power is dissipated through a series of micro-practices and discourses that make decisions hard, if not impossible, to trace back to a single place of sovereignty (Foucault 1997; 2003). This argument has direct implications for how we conceptualize political decisions. Foucault opposes the view that power is exceptional, and therefore does not agree to a Schmittian view of the exception as the ultimate basis of political decision (Schmitt 1996). Instead, for Foucault the dissipation of power implies the dissolution of the sovereign subject, and therefore the dispersal of decision into a multitude of "highly relational and heavily mediated practices" (Huysmans 2008, 179). The landscape of governmentality that emerges is marked with daily routines and technologies of surveillance, control and punishment that operate as a structure of continuous non-acts. In short, the exception becomes normality, and the political becomes a technology of everyday governance.

Turning back to our case, immigration, AIDS and sex work were not novel or exceptional phenomena per se in Greece. The particular conditions of these women (poverty and even homelessness, drug addiction, trafficking) did not interest the authorities. In their case, a fundamental right, the presumption of innocence, was not guaranteed. They are made responsible a priori on the basis not of a "juridical decision for which careful consideration of evidence is necessary," but of "an administrative decision, where the rule of zero-risk takes precedence" (Aradau and Van Munster 2007, 106).

However, we argue that the measures taken were exceptional, in that the government performed a considerable number of serious breaches of human rights that do not occur on a daily basis. Both the articulation of a perceived threat [seropositive undocumented (immigrant) sex workers] as well as the claim of taking precautions to protect society (the risk of AIDS as having the potential of a future epidemic that threatens the family, the core of the Greek society), are, as this case shows, mere means to achieve a greater goal, that of social control. As Foucault suggests, the *dispositifs* of government operate by generating knowledge and using it to discipline the deviance and control the majority. In the case of the Greek sex-workers, knowledge was the first concern of the authorities—not the health of the workers, their vulnerability in front of the law or their traumatic experiences. It was first and foremost an explicit concern to spread out as much as possible all that was known about these women, including their photographs. The pursuit and usage of knowledge, however, is only the first part of the story. We cannot fully begin to interpret the actions of the Greek state merely as raising awareness for the population. Since the threat has been there for a long time, the policymaking in this case cannot be explained convincingly on the basis of the precautionary principle. After all, taking precautionary measures, aimed at risk management, could have been done through less radical, less spectacular measures (by not penalizing patients and respecting their rights and privacy), but through far more efficient means (needle exchange programs, sex education at schools, access to healthcare, etc). Publishing the data and the images of the women was framed as a way for reducing uncertainty—governing the risk for the Greek family (society is being defined by the government in a monolithic way, as consisting primarily of monogamous heterosexual Greeks). However, disclosing the data did not efficiently minimize/contain/repair the (perceived) risk for the Greek society. What it did instead was to provide an opportunity of controlling/surveying not only a small, "deviant" group of the society (undocumented sex workers), but also the entire society (by May 3rd there were 1600 calls from panicked citizens and by May 16th, KEELPNO had received more than 8,000 calls).[41]

---

[41] See: "Φορείς του AIDS εννέα πελάτες ιερόδουλων", *TANEA*, 16/05/2012, http://www.tanea.gr/ellada/article/?aid=4721211, last accessed on 29 February 2016

Our contention is that the proactive practices of the state mechanism were not simply aimed at preventing the occurrence of dangers in the future, as the state officials were claiming. Rather, the authorities articulated a set of rationalities regarding the present endangered state of public health, under the pretext of raising social awareness. The purpose, as stated, was to prevent (Greek) citizens from panicking. The result, however, was precisely to create panic, in the form of desperate phone calls and the inescapable social control.

What the literature on technologies of risk assessment omits is that the continuum of dispersed and routinized practices associated with governmentality does not occur out of the blue. There is always an exceptional moment that triggers the panic. There is always a spectacular event, like the uncovering of the Greek alleged sex-workers, that sets in motion the processes of threat articulation and risk prediction. Within these moments of extreme emergency, one can detect not only the different agencies that are behind such constructions, but also the discursive building mechanisms of the knowledges needed to foresee or prevent such events from occurring in the future. As such, in the Greek case, we can discern the intertwining of discursive topoi such as the foulness of female sex workers with normative narratives about the righteousness of the heterosexual monogamous family, alongside the ever-present imaginary that distinguishes between "us" (the Greeks) the clean ones and "them" (the immigrants) the dirty and unhealthy ones.

As one of the people that we interviewed put it, the

> issue wore off after some time. This thing had "short legs", and they knew that it wouldn't work out in the end, so they used the case, it was projected a lot by the media, and then it was abandoned. And, as I told you earlier, this happened for political reasons, it was not about fighting the issue of infectious diseases, it was about some politicians "playing the field" in that particular political circumstances, Chrysochoidis, Loverdos and so on. If a person would dig in the issue a bit, she would see that it was an unbelievable event, something you would never expect to happen.[42]

CONCLUSION

In this paper we have presented the case of the criminalization of HIV-positive women who were accused of practicing sex work while living with HIV in Athens in 2012. We read this case through the existing literature on the securitization of AIDS, and we argued that the authorities' reaction goes beyond labelling the women as a security threat. Rather, the policies that were enacted by the police and the health institutions pertain to a mode of criminalization that targets the women as immigrants and non-citizens. These policies also go beyond a *dispositif* of managing risk, as they are a serious and exceptional mis-treatment of marginalized individuals.

---

[42] Text translated from Greek by Maria.

To conclude, we would like to point out that these women were not left alone. Several individuals and associations did intervene with assistance. They were provided with medical help and legal advice while they were in prison. One of the people that we interviewed told us that the people from the Solidarity Initiative brought the imprisoned women basic things that they were lacking, such as toilet paper and phone cards. They also found them lawyers that could represent all the imprisoned women as a group and speak for them in court. Moreover, the Solidarity Initiative put the women in touch with rehabilitation organizations. However, most of the women continued to use drugs, and after they had been released from prison, they soon returned to the streets. One of the women committed suicide in November 2014, after having previously (in April 2014) written a letter about her case.[43]

---

[43] 'Άλλη μια διαπομπευμένη οροθετική λιγότερη', *To Μωβ*, 29/11/2014, http://tomov.gr/2014/11/29/άλλη-μια-διαπομπευμένη-οροθετική-λιγ/

REFERENCES

Amoore, Louise and de Goede, Marieke (eds). 2008. *Risk and the War on Terror.* London: Routledge.

Andrijasevic, R., C. Aradau, J. Huysmans, and V. Squire. 2012. "European Citizenship Unbound: Sex Work, Mobility, Mobilisation" in *Environment and Planning D: Society and Space* 30(3): 835-838.

Aradau, Claudia. 2004. "The Perverse Politics of Four-Letter Words: Risk and Pity in the Securitisation of Human Trafficking" in *Millenium: Journal of International Studies* 33(2): 251-277.

Aradau, Claudia and Rens van Munster. 2007. "Governing Terrorism Through Risk: Taking precautions, (un)knowing the future" in *European Journal of International Relations* 13(1): 89–115.

Aradau, Claudia and Rens van Munster. 2008. "Taming the Future: The Dispositif of Risk in the War on Terror" in *Risk and the War on Terror* edited by L. Amoore and M. de Goede, 23-40. London: Routledge.

Banks, James. 2012. "Unmasking Deviance: The Visual Construction of Asylum Seekers and Refugees in English National Newspapers" in *Critical Criminology*, 20, 3: 293-310.

Biber, Katherine. 2005. "Photographs and Labels: Against a Criminology of Innocence" in *Law Text Culture* 10(1): 19-40.

Bigo, Didier. 2002. "Security and Immigration: Toward a Critique of the Governmentality of

Unease" in *Alternatives: Global, Local, Political*
27(1): 63-92.

Buzan, Barry, Ole Wæver and Jaap de Wilde. 1998.
Security. A New Framework For Analysis,
Boulder/London: Lynne Rienner.

Elbe, Stefan. 2005. "AIDS, Security, Biopolitics,
Special Issue on Health" in *International
Relations* 19(4): 403-419.

Elbe, Stefan. 2008. "Risking Lives: AIDS, Security
and Three Concepts of Risk," *Security Dialogue*,
39(2-3): 177-198.

Elbe, Stefan. 2012. *"Bodies as Battlefields: Toward the
Medicalization of Insecurity'*, International
Political Sociology 6(3): 320–322.

Foucault, Michel. 1977 [1975]. *Discipline and Punish:
The Birth of the Prison.* London: Allen Lane.

Foucault, Michel. 2007. *Security, Territory,
Population. Lectures at the College de France, 1977
– 1978.* Basingstoke: Palgrave Macmillan.

Foucault, Michel. 2003[1997]. *Society Must be
Defended.* London: Picador.

Huysmans, Jef. 2008. "The Jargon of Exception—
On Schmitt, Agamben and the Absence of
Political Society," *International Political Sociology*
2(2): 165–183.

Huysmans, Jef. 2011. "What's in an Act? On
Security Speech Acts and Little Security
Nothings," *Security Dialogue* 42(4-5)(August 1):
371–383.

Kentikelenis, Alexander, Marina Karanikolos,
Irene Papanicolas, Sanjay Basu, Martin McKee,
and David Stuckler. 2011. "Health Effects of
Financial Crisis: Omens of a Greek Tragedy" in
The Lancet, 378(9801): 1457–1458.

Schmitt, Carl. 1996. *The concept of the political.* Chicago: University of Chicago Press.

Waever, Ole. 1995. "Securitization and Desecuritization," in *On Security,* edited by Ronnie Lipschutz, Columbia University Press, pp. 46 – 86.

Making Sense of Repression in Police Studies: Whither Theorizing in the Descent Toward Fascism

Tamari Kitossa

The ongoing chatter about the police in terms of their juridic roles as rule enforcers within a criminal "justice" system mystifies, trivializes and distracts from much needed public consciousness and debate (McCormick and Visano 1992, xii).

What does the future hold for policing? In a sense, the past is the present, and the future is now (Forcese 2002, 125).

[I]n an unjust and exploitative society, no matter how "humane" agents of social control are, their actions necessarily result in repression (Liazos 1972, 117).

When the subject population has had enough of being studied, researched, analyzed, and tabulated and actively demands instead to be fed, housed, clothed, schooled, served, alive, and sovereign, then the sponsors of research shift their assets toward the sponsorship of a

247

different science, an alternate profession...the police profession (Nicolaus 1969, 384).

...all these aesthetic expressions of respect for the established order serve to create around the exploited person an atmosphere of submission and inhibitions which lightens the task of the police considerably (Fanon 1963, 38).

"What is the role of the police" is an enduring question. Capably addressed by others (Balko 2013; Gordon 2006; Kelley 2000; K. Williams 2007; Websdale 2001), my concern is not with policing *per se*, but how what is said about police/ing is made possible from varying theoretical orientations. The two are of course related. It seems to me, however, to see policing more clearly for what it is, one must critically assess the framing of experts who constitute knowledge about the policing apparatus in relation to the state and *society*[1] through a counter-colonial (Agozino 2003; Tauri 2012; Kitossa 2012) and Marxist sociology of knowledge. This amounts, in effect, to a culturology of academic epistemologies of police/ing. This combined approach is vital since around the world, as neo-liberal economies descends into the politics of authoritarianism and fascism, the *potential* for repressive violence by the state *qua* the

---

[1] In quite a different way from Margaret Thatcher who argued there is no such thing as society rather only individuals, for Coulson and Riddell (1980) "society" is a rhetorical shorthand for hegemonic *interests* that are constituted as a social totality within a given social formation. Such a view has resonance with Benedict Anderson's (1983) concept of the "imagined community," where literature plays the role of constituting ruling class hegemony.

police is *actual* in the most naked of ways (Harvey 2011; Martinot 2008). Indeed, this fact is being made manifest by the growing awareness if not the actual growth of police extrajudicial murders of civilians. Normally mobilized against society's "social junk" and "social dynamite" (Spitzer 1975) as a way of generating consent against the perceived forces of disorder (Crichlow 2014; Hall 1973; Nunn 2002), repressive force, convergent and sometimes on a parallel track with the surveillance of both mundane and political life (Parenti 2003;Whitaker, Kealey and Parnaby 2013), is being unleashed against a broad spectrum of dissent occurring even within the limits of liberal democratic "tolerance."

Over the past 40 years, the courts and politicians have simultaneously slackened legal constraints against the police, enlarged its authority for force and surveillance, deepened its cult of secrecy and insulated it against the transformative possibilities of meaningful civilian review (Kelley 2000). The results, even by the standards of liberal democratic contractarian social theory of the European Enlightenment philosphes, is bearing poisoned fruit in the flowering of a fascistic social order overseen by its domestic militarized shock troops: the police. There is little governments can or want to do, after all, as Charles Reasons astutely notes: "[t]he state must obviously protect its protectors" (1974, 270). The examples are legion, wide-ranging and not limited to any country or jurisdiction, though of course the extent to which force is a default seems to correlate with histories of colonialism and imperialism and the cultural dimensions of state formation.[2] Yet, the bald exercise of repressive force cannot be separated from the crisis nature of capitalism (Harvey 2011; M. Smith 2010), its devolution toward neo-feudalism (Zafirovski 2007) and the commensurate indications of fascism most evident in militarized and repressive state control (Hedges 2010; Kraska 2007; Martinot 2008; Morrison 1995; Robinson 2009).

What has policing studies to say of all this? Aside from critical analyses advanced by those outside the academy or those marginalized scholars within, it is not that policing studies has nothing to contribute. It is that *what* and *how* it is said are matters of power, and that the embeddedness of an inherently conservative standpoint within the clerisy of social control—criminology—serves both to constrain radical epistemology while throwing up Consensus-Pluralistic obfuscations that, presumably, serve as explanation. The effect is to impoverish the

---

[2] Examples include: gunning down Native Canadian, Dudley George at the Ipperwash reclamation of Stoney Point; corralling, mass arresting, blasting with sound canons and using agents provocateur at the neoliberal summits—"Battle of Seattle," Montebello (Quebec), Toronto and Philadelphia; gunning down 38 striking miners in South Africa (CBC News 2012); forcing pepper spray into eyes of peaceful student demonstrators in California (CBC News 2011); brutalizing "Occupy protesters" in the US; killing an unarmed African American senior, who did not need their "help," in his home in White Plains New York (Democracy Now 2012a); to beating and killing Latinos, Mexican-Americans and Mexican-American migrants (Democracy Now 2012b); wreaking havoc in militarist prosecution of the war *for* drugs (Meeks 2006); spying and wiretapping Muslim-Americans in the North East (Democracy Now 2012c); sport hunting civilians (see US Department of Justice 2011; van Natta 2011) *inter alia.*

culture of public debate about policing in (liberal democratic) society, since what is radical is marginalized and that which affirms the status quo is lauded. This essay is an explicitly counter-colonial (Agozino 2003; Kitossa 2012; Tuari 2012) and materialist sociology of knowledge as it concerns policing studies. Through an assessment of selective major works, the aim is to examine the belief that policing studies is in crisis, especially since there appears to be agreement between what I will loosely describe as Consensus-Pluralist and Conflict-Marxian police theorists that this is in fact so. I suggest that when the claim of a crisis in police studies is examined closely, one sees nothing of the sort. To demonstrate this point, I will critically examine the work of Peter K. Manning (2010), Michael Raphael (2010) and Jean-Paul Brodeur (2010) on one hand with that of Sidney Harring and Gerda Lerner (1993) and Todd Gordon (2006) on the other.

Viewed from both a counter-colonial and materialist sociology of knowledge, what we have is really a lament from the left that the repressive apparatus has grown in power, and, from the "mainstream" and the slight left-of-center, intellectual contortions that confound their complicity with the status quo through obfuscations such as "democratic policing." On the contrary, there is every reason to believe that policing studies, at least from activist-scholars on the left, civil libertarians, hip-hop, reggae and folk-protest music, is as robust in its theory and empirical observations as it has ever been. I suggest that while new technologies (e.g. drones,

sound cannons and other military hardware
and software) and political autonomy have
moved policing in a direction parallel with 20th
century fascism, these are just that, the resonance of prior practices now concealed by
bourgeois obfuscations such as "democratic
policing." To make sense of this "new" reality of
policing, I suggest institutionalized policing
studies must fully develop theory that draws on
counter-colonial critiques of state repression[3] as
well as Conflict-Marxian studies of policing that
situate policing within the matrix of state and
society (see Brogden 1982). Through this *re-vi-
sion* and appreciation of critical consciousness
articulated by, for example, the Black Panther
Party (Heiner 2007), Marxist frames of knowledge production (Cornforth 1977) and Marxian
accounts of state formation and monopolization of violence (Tilly 1985), we find insights
that reveal the outlines of neo-liberal society
and a capitalist world order fitted for fascistic
policing.[4] While policing studies has always

---

[3] I opt for "repression" over "coercion," because the monopolization
of force is a political act intended for specific purposes rather than
an end in itself.

[4] In emphasizing repressive power, I am not unmindful of the
Gramscian equation - force of persuasion and persuasion of force
- elaborated by Stuart Hall's (1979) emphasis on the ideological
dimensions of policing. What must be conceded, however, is that
while this is a dialectic in the last instance, it did not begin as
such - indicating the possibility the equation is problematic. I
believe Charles Tilly, drawing on Arthur Stinchcombe, suggests
the plausibility of this critique: "Legitimacy...depends rather little
on abstract principles or assent of the governed: 'The person over
whom power is exercised is not usually as important as other
power-holders'" (1985, 171). It is for this reason that concessions
to inchoate mobs and organized rebellions are generally conceded
on two grounds: one, brief periodic concession to keep the "trains

been dominated by Consensus-Pluralist thinkers, decolonization practitioners and theorists and academic Conflict-Marxian theorists (however few, embattled and marginal they are), more accurately apprehend the ultimate uses of the policing institution in the matrix of maintaining power in the rush toward fascism.

THE DEBATE

Of what use and whose interests the police serve are questions raised at the instantiation of the triumph of the bourgeois revolution (Storch 1975). These questions are still being asked, but in full view of the conflict and tensions in the society they represent. The answers therefore differ, depending on one's relationship to those tensions and conflicts. Those on the front lines of dissent, those who are surveilled and infiltrated, live in occupied spaces or experience police coercion and repression, or are "organic" intellectuals representing the interests of the dispossessed produce critical inquiries that are in touch with the fundamental reality of policing in capitalist/colonialist society and the neoliberal universe (Balko 2013; Della Porta and Reiter 1998; Headley 1994; Lovell 2009; Sewell 2010; K. Williams 2007; C. Williams 2005; Websdale 2001; Nelson 2000; Pedicelli 1998). But in academic research on policing there is a debate about the state and health of policing studies. Indeed, in their mutual dissatisfaction with the

---

moving on time" and two, where there are sympathizers among the ruling class (Fox-Piven 2008). The question of theorizing enduring change, given the tortuous career of any social problem (Blumer 1971), is not within the scope of this paper.

state of policing studies, there appears to be a bridge between Consensual-Pluralist (Loader 2011; Brodeur 2010; Manning 2010) and Conflict-Marxian theoreticians (T. Gordon 2006; Harring and Ray 1999).[5] While there is no denying the import of empirical work and those that address the "scientific" elements of policing and its management, the concern among these theorists is that policing studies has taken a deeply "correctionalist"[6] turn. The result, it is argued, is that reflection and research on policing is a satellite of the policing apparatus' knowledge needs and this, consequentially, adds little to our understanding of institutional adaptations and practices to "changing" circumstances.

---

[5] There are those who assert, as José Dos Santos (2004), that it is policing itself that is in crisis. Interestingly, while Dos Santos admits the crisis of policing is traceable to neo-liberal generated social decay, he fails to explore this issue as a crisis of the state and that it is from this that both repressive policing and police crisis of legitimacy arise. Policing studies may, then, appear to be moribund precisely because policing and the state are in crisis and require forms of knowledge that seek to regain them their ideological legitimacy. Christopher Murphy's (1999) perspective on the problems with policing studies suggests that as goes the state's interest in policing research so goes academics' access to funding and a willing subject. Murphy is concerned with the implications of government and police foreclosure on research for efficiency, public policy and public education. Yet, an important preoccupation is the belief that the academic research cohort will decrease significantly from its already low number. Totally ignored by Murphy are academic Conflict-Marxian formulations as well a counter-colonial critique.

[6] David Matza (1969, Chapter 2) offers "correctionalism" as a moniker for a discourse that is hegemonic in institutional and scholarly approaches to "deviance." Its dimensions include: "crime" and "criminality" as objectively real, the assumptions that these have definite foundation in individual psychopathology or derelict social settings and relations and that deviance/crime can be gotten rid of.

There are two reasons for this "correctionalism," though the weight given by the theorists just noted differ, and, as I will suggest shortly, this fact has quite serious implications for whether and how policing studies can be imagined to stand apart from the state and its semiautonomous repressive apparatus. The aim of knowledge generated at a distance from the inner sanctum of institutionalized policing and the funding priorities of the state is to produce meanings that are analytically independent. Be it criminology, penology or policing studies, the subject matter is defined by the state—law, "crime" and its management. The struggle, from a Critical-Marxian perspective, has been to generate theory and research that treats the state's definition of reality as itself an object of critical study (Cohen 2007a; Hillyard and Tombs 2004; Agozino 2003; Visano 1998). With the foregoing in mind, the first epistemic problem is that policing is explored as an institutional form as though it can be abstracted from antagonistic social and political forces. Second, the broader function of policing as moral and social regulator, in terms of social and material conditions, and what this *means* for the emergence of certain policies, practices and the maintenance of social order is largely ignored by mainstream empirical and theoretical work. In sum, research that ignores these epistemic concerns is not concerned with policing as a social institution but with what can ensure that policing works "better."

In other words, the chief problem with detailing police management and organizational problems, "internationalization of policing," police functions and efficiency and use of force etc., is that the examination of these objects is not fully sociological. In most bourgeois empirical studies of policing, the nature of the state, political economy and historical materialist analyses of social formations[7] is emaciated. The point is not that there isn't theory in the "correctionalist" approach, it is that undeclared "correctionalism" is both a theoretical framework and an object for "improvement." How can one take as theory and one's theoretical start point the operations of the thing one wishes to "improve?" Naturally, such an approach will be rich in detail but what *meanings* it offers vis-à-vis a greater understanding of policing, state and society and how such detail can be meaningful toward economic and social democratization is difficult to approach. "Correctionalism" may find here and there improvements to be made, but it already presumes society is substantively democratic, as it does with institutional policing, and that there are only minor institutional defects in need of reform (see Cohen 2007b, 262). It is not implied by this criticism that "correctionalist" policing studies or reformism should be dismissed. Rather, my assertion, stated in a slightly different and more focused form than the complaints about institutionalized police studies, is that the "correctionalist'" study of policing should itself be an object of study vis-à-vis forms of knowledge in bu-

---

[7] "Social formations" is a Marxist concept that comprises the totality of economy, culture and ideology and the state and other things that make life possible and which shape the quality of human experience (see Greenberg 1993, 16).

reaucratic, class-based societies relative to ruling relations (D. Smith 1987) such as class, gender, race, sexuality and colonialism and imperialism. Another concern, long noted by insurgent sociology (Ladner 1973; Gouldner 1970; Mills 1948) and the emergent radical criminology of the early 1970s, is that "correctionalist" policing studies blur the lines between academicians, policy makers and practitioners (Manning 2010). The concern here is less about academic freedom, though this is an issue, and more about the ways "correctionalism" draws in and circumscribes scholarly inquiry to the concerns and needs of the police apparatus. Bill Fanell and Larry Koch, interestingly, suggest the issue is not merely "correctionalism" capturing academia, the process works also in reverse (1995).

While, analytically speaking, there appears to be agreement on the "problem" ("correctionalism" in policing studies), such consonance is superficial. At the start what must be avoided is the tendency to misperceive that where and when opposing theoretical perspectives are consonant in identifying a "problem," there can be a bridging of opposing theoretical approaches. For example, a unified theory of criminology (see Felices-Luna 2010; Huey and Pare 2010) that is value-neutral (Case and Farrell 1995) requires a sanitization of the relationship between contested epistemologies and the opposing social values and politics that underlies conflicts over knowledge, its production and the material basis of social organization. Thus there are serious limits to the view that opposing view-points, especially when demystified vis-à-vis their relationship to ruling relations such as class, gender, colonialism/imperialism, racism and sexuality are or can be congruent. We see that from critical examinations in the sociology of science, "science" is not the ground where uninterested and emotionally and materially uninvested truth-seekers mash together facts to arrive at true (consensual) knowledge (see Shapin and Shaffer 1985; Kuhn 1970). Science is heavily driven by politics (and culture), politics by economics and, historically, political economy by dominant social interests and the latter by a society's mode of production and cosmological view (Cornforth 1977). Another limit, but not for Conflict-Marxian theorists, is that the "correctionalist" view is not seen as *a* view, and the dominant one at that. Finally failure to appreciate that neutral views are not in fact so, abstract the researcher, knowledge and knowledge production from their embeddedness in prevailing social relations. Against claims that the researcher is outside it all, in the context of a society that reproduces capitalism, colonialism, homophobia, imperialism and patriarchy, proclamations of distance offer tacit complicity with extant social relations.

The point was made in another way by Howard Becker (1967) who asked "whose side are we on?". For Alvin Gouldner the answer, uncomfortable for many, went beyond "taking sides." The nature of institutions, he suggests, makes the point moot: institutions exist to maintain extant social relations and as such, so do the people in them (1979; 1970). This includes knowledge workers (a.k.a: academics, state institution researchers, journalists, novelists etc). To the extent the means of production are not socialized and bureaucracy is captured by an elitist cadre in defence of privileged allocations and ownership of productive property, the distinction is not between capitalism and socialism in ideal terms, but in the practical reality and contradiction of ownership and privilege in bureaucratic societies that exploit the masses of people (Chambliss 1993a, 30-32; Djilas 1973). The point is that forms of consciousness are structured by the interplay between social and material conditions and that some forms of consciousness—aware of itself, of social conditions and guided by robust theory—can more acutely see through conditions of existence and make transformative steps beyond reform. Others, whether conscious or unconscious of their allegiance to extant social relations, seek to conceal the structure of reality and the operation of order protecting institutions because of their embeddedness in the material conditions that produce a "hierarchy of credibility" (Becker 1967, 241; see also Sumner 1979). The nature of this embeddedness is the tendency and necessity of mystifying moves that treat reform as an end. Forms of knowledge that challenge hegemonic institutions, if they cannot be absorbed, are accommodated, marginalized, ridiculed, tolerated or structurally excluded as the case may be. But, since ideas are not independent of the people, classes, history, social and material conditions that produce them, it stands to reason that to take a stand against "correctionalism" in policing stud-

ies is also to self-consciously articulate a normative social theory that contributes to the struggle against ruling relations.

A Note on Theory

As to studies of policing, state and society, I
suggest social theory and its attendant values
fall into two rough-hewn categories: Consensus-Pluralism and Conflict-Marxianism. As I
have shown, the former constitutes the pre-
dominant mode of thought in liberal democratic social orders. What I suggest now is that
the Conflict-Marxian approach is far more robust in demystifying reality than Consensus-
Pluralism. Indeed, vital to Conflict-Marxian
theory is to account for contradictions that in-
here in the class conflict between the producers
of wealth and the owners of the means of production and the role of ideology as a cultural
and political force (Greenberg 1993). This fundamental distinction suggests these two approaches to epistemology agree differently on
the nature of the problem regarding policing
studies and thus what counts is their explanation of the problem identified. At the outset, we
are confronted with the paradox that "correctionalism" is a cul-de-sac created by this approach itself. Conflict-Marxian theoreticians are
not burdened by the latent necessity of explaining away contradictions inherent in social theory and the material conditions that sustain a
"correctionalist" viewpoint.

Now, none of this precludes slippages in the
Conflict-Marxianist approach, to wit one may
find, here and there, consensual-pluralism

seeping into its epistemology. For example, in accounting for theoretical accounts of coercive laws that are presumably inimical to the interests of the ruling class and assorted elites, Ron Hepburn shows that Willem Bonger, an early Marxian theoretician of capitalist law and its enforcement, unacceptably commits himself to "...reliance upon a certain degree of pluralism..." (1978, 78). Bonger's error was that he assumed the socially powerless occasionally gain proscriptive power to curtail ruling class practices incommensurate with the interests of the oppressed. This is not all surprising given, as Marx and Engels argue, the dominant mode of thought in any age is consistent with the interests of the ruling class—hence, the conception of bourgeois society. This means that ideology is more than the effort of the ruling class to indoctrinate subordinate classes. It is rather that in the very rhythm of life in a capitalist society, thought and action are constrained by forms of consciousness deemed permissible by the logos of bourgeois society. It is for this reason "bourgeois society" accurately describes the dominance of ideas that sustain the ruling class independently of their concerted efforts at indoctrination (Mepham 1979). Thus the power of the oppressed as "consumers, voters and members of voluntary associations" claimed by Bonger, to push the state to pass laws consistent with the interests of the oppressed, negates the fact that "solidarity" of sympathetic elites are required and that such laws themselves are either provisional or "gifts"[8] which negate and undermine

---

[8] See Manning's (2010) mystifying conception of "democratic" police "service" as "gift giving." Used variously throughout his

the necessity of more fundamental and on-going transformations (Hepburn 1978; Fox-Piven 1976). The central point is that without revolutionary and self-reproductive transformation, equilibrium-seeking actions taken by the state, ruling class and elites restore and conceal the fundamental conditions that generated moral outrage in the first instance (see Moore 1978). Theory must, therefore, be coherent, logically consistent with historical specificities, and, following Lenin's dicta, as "radical as reality itself" (see M. Smith 2003) in providing explanations of facts brought into question (Greenberg 1993; Segal 1971; Cabral 1966).

Consensual-Pluralism

What follows hereafter is not a thorough going critique and representation of Patrick Manning (2010) and Jean-Paul Brodeur's (2010) career summative works and less so of their prior scholarship.[9] One may turn to a cogent and just

---

text, "democracy" receives no thoroughgoing theorization. Any discussion of "democracy" must concede there are variants in both theory and practice and one particular meaning as opposed to others cannot be taken-for-granted but must be explicated (see MacPherson 1992).

[9] The prior scholarship of both authors differ in theoretical orientation. Manning's scholarship, while having a tendency toward conflict sociology, especially in the symbolic interactionist tradition, was also strongly pluralist in nature. While Brodeur's prior work on the other hand, in view of its more clear-headed conflict structuralist orientation, though very much in the domain of civil libertarianism, was uncompromising in its critique of the repressive power of the liberal state. To a large extent, therefore, Manning's position remains logically consistent, but Brodeur, perplexingly, seems to have modified considerably by moving toward an (uncertain) encounter with post-structuralism.

as problematically Consensual-Pluralist review of their work by Ian Loader (2011). (Nor following this will I engage in a full elaboration of Conflict-Marxian approaches to policing, state and society—this is a full and extensive literature I make no pretense of summarizing.) My purpose for this essay is restricted to stating manifest epistemological concerns and latent values that promote the demystification of institutionalized policing studies and the general "correctionalist" orientation toward it. It is hoped my brief but condensed remarks will not tend toward caricature but will suggest the Consensus-Pluralist statement of the problem of epistemology is inconsistent with its capacity to resolve the problem it identifies.

The Consensus-Pluralist approach is a continuum of theories that presume social contractarianism is the foundation for civil society. At one extreme lies the Durkheimian *conscience collective* which assumes fundamental and unmediated social agreement among atomistic individuals who "naturally," as though by some spontaneous creationist imperative arrive at agreement about morality and law.[10] By Durkheim's logic criminal and civil law are not the manifestation of social relations of production or dominant groups capturing legal legitimacy through a moral code consistent with

---

[10] To be fair, particularly in *The Rules of Sociological Method*, Durkheim's thought on law and morality opens toward a perspective more conducive to a conflict orientation. Yet, his consensualism was never divorced. On balance, Durkheim's more developed analysis, because of his rejection of Marxism, contained a hidden contradiction "resolved" by the dominance of consensualism.

their class interests. According to this view, both forms of law reflect pre-political moral awareness that sanctions are "doubly institutionalized," first by the *conscience collective* and then by the state.[11] The distinction that arises between criminal and civil law presumes that the former reflects what is most harmful and about which there is little disagreement in society. By this view, crime arises from moral failings and some groups seeking to opt out of the social contract to "take" what is not "theirs." Why this might be the case is never explored because it would undermine both the theory and its normative claims.[12] William Chambliss (1993a) demon-

---

[11] For a concise discussion of how the nexus between capitalist morality, law and the manufacture of consensus constitute and seek to impose habituations of (bourgeois) consciousness and action see Hepburn (1978), Moore (1978), Brogden (1982), Hall et al., (1979), Humphries and Greenberg (1993) and Spitzer (1993). All these work suggest that in class-based societies, consensus and morality are political rather than metaphysical in their constitution and playing out. Murder, rape and kidnapping are, for example, constituted, defined and enforced in ways consistent with certifying capitalist morality, private property and accumulation. Unless of course committed by state agents in service of those interests. As a notoriously sadistic CIA agent, George White, chirped: "I toiled wholeheartedly in the vineyards because it was fun, fun, fun. Where else could a red-blooded American boy lie, kill, cheat, steal, rape ad pillage with the sanction and bidding of the All-highest" (Cockburn and St. Clair, 1999).

[12] Making a similar point about the Classicism of the pan-*European Enlightenment* (i.e., Beccaria, Locke, Kant *inter alia*), Taylor, Walton and Young (1973: 4-5) demonstrate that this theory exhausted itself on the grounds of its own social and material conditions. For instance, founded on the economic theory of rational action, Beccaria admits, logically, that theft by the dispossessed can be accounted for rationally:

> He who endeavours to enrich himself with the property of another, should be deprived of part of his own. But

strates that Durkheim's conceptualization is complicit with bourgeois ideas. In essence, Durkheim ignored the fact that "political society is built on a foundation of repressive force" (Hepburn 1978, 72) where consensus is manufactured. To this end, one finds that in policing studies, Durkheimians such as Egon Bittner and James Q. Wilson *inter alia* (see Takagi 1979) are the theoretical substrate upon which pluralistic policing studies rest (see Manning 2010, accounting for his indebtedness to Bittner).

At the other extreme, Pluralists shed some of the empirically untenable aspects of European *Enlightenment* contractarian metaphysics by dabbling with conflict theory. Adopting the contours of a moderate left posture, they smuggle social conflict into their theorizing of criminal law without ever letting go of Durkheim's false dichotomy. This Pluralist view, then, admits conflict in society and that this is mirrored in the criminal law. Pluralists hold that society is

---

this crime, alas! is commonly the effect of misery and despair; the crime of that unhappy part of mankind, to whom the right of exclusive property (a terrible and perhaps unnecessary right) has left but bare existence."

While Beccaria sheds crocodile tears at the consequence of the "right of exclusive property", he accepts the double deprivation of those that would be punished by material loss, and pending none, their freedom by imprisonment. It is consequential for the sanitization of repression in consensus-pluralist policing studies that neither Beccaria *inter alia*, nor Taylor, Walton and Young for that matter, approach the issue of those whose person and labour was the property of others (i.e., chattel slavery) and so running away constituted theft, or those whose land was stolen from them (i.e., colonialism) under the specious logic of equality which admitted the colonial Other was less equal and thus any counter-colonial resistance justified punishment by, at the extreme, genocide (see Charles Mills 2006; Agozino 2003; Eze 1995).

composed of equally empowered and opposing groups and that the rationality of their claims determines their impact on law-making (Chambliss 1993a; Hepburn 1978). As articulated by Mike Brogden, with the state as the central node of its articulation, Pluralism regards the state as a "...citadel to be captured, or at least held and persuaded to favour sectional interests. Its power to make decisions is a prize to be striven for" (1982, 6). Law, then, is constituted by way of European *Enlightenment* reasoning as the end product of rational forces winning the day. Having then admitted conflict safely into its precincts, Pluralists take a more agnostic stand toward the "criminal." As asserted by David Gordon (1973) of liberals, Pluralists argue that the failure of some individuals/groups to achieve the material ideals of bourgeois society is a combination of their moral failings (criminogenicity and/or social disorganization) amplified by minor but adjustable defects in liberal democratic society.

Both Brodeur (2010), Manning (2010) and Michael Raphael's (2010) work can be located on the Pluralist end of the consensus-pluralism spectrum. Hence, their specific concern regarding the production of knowledge about policing, as noted by Loader (approvingly), concentrates on the fact "...that police research and policy are today in grave danger of forgetting the hard-won lessons of police sociology" (2011, 454). This notion begs from whom did police sociology win these hard-won lessons and what was the nature of the struggle? And since when was police sociology a monolith? It is instructive that in Manning and Raphael and Brodeur (and Loader) the insights of Conflict-Marxian social theorists and theory are nowhere to be found. This absence is important, since by this exclusion, Pluralism signifies itself as the theoretical counter-weight to hegemonic knowledge forms and presumes itself to be the basis for social struggle against institutionalized policing and thus takes credit for modest reforms (which were hard won by counter-hegemonic forces).

I: MANNING AND RAPHAEL

The foregoing is surprising since the Pluralist theorists give no account of their contradictions regarding the semi-autonomy of the police, the state's dominant role as force monopolizer toward sustaining capitalist social relations of production, and, of course the state's role in generating a surplus of ideology. Indeed, drawing on John Rawl's liberalism—the *veil of ignorance, justice* and *fairness*—Manning's vaguely defined conception of "democracy" obviates a historical materialist reading of struggles in liberal democratic society as well as self-conscious agency in demanding reforms of policing in lieu of a more finely articulated consciousness and action calculated to transform oppressive relations. He writes, "[r]eform efforts directed toward policing in the aftermath of the riots in the late 1960's, seeking to reduce social distance and to co-opt minorities into "partnerships," were visible and important, but they were never designed to alter the pattern of inequality" (2010, 244). The implicit assumption that reformism and the aspiration for social inclusion derives from relative deprivation (African Americans are jealous of Euro-Americans) is condemned by William Ryan as *blaming the victim* (1976) and by Robert Allen (1970) and Sidney Willhelm (1971; 1982) as subterfuge concealing the transformative nature of the rebellions against oppression. More explicitly, the rebellions, not "riots," were a rational response to African American exclusion from even the most meager benefits of capitalism and liberal democracy. And more to the point, the brutal repression by the police and National Guard, confirmed their useleness as a surplus population generated by outsourcing and the mechanization of capitalist accumulation (Bell 2000; Brand 1994; Kelley 2000; Willhelm 1971).

The post-rebellion *quiet* could not have been achieved without federal, state and local police, military complicity and political surveillance that assassinated radical and civil libertarian leaders; judicial complicity in framing and discrediting leaders that were not killed; the infiltration and disruption of labour, revolutionary, peace, social justice and reformist groups alike through spies and *agents provocateur*; and through the general practice of repression legitimated by the "law and order" complicity between the White political elite and racist police who operate as an occupying force in the lives of "redundant" African, Native, Latino and Mexican Americans (Daniels 2000; Kelley 2000; Churchill and vander Wall 2002; Greenberg 1993). Thus in view of the racist and violent police repression and their commitment to reproducing ruling relations, Manning's (2010, 248)

recitations of police work as dramaturgy is de-
contextualized and therefore depoliticized:

> [policing]...by many...features and practices...
> must of necessity remain backstage and out
> of sight. These are the practices that enable
> front-stage work and team work to go for-
> ward with *the public* (Goffman 1956). The po-
> lice are *feelings* oriented in spite of their
> protestations—they enact poetic and aesthetic
> actions... They enact *poetry*. [italics added]

It is the cruelest of jokes to suggest there is
anything "poetic," "backstage" or "out of sight"
about the bodies of poor, immigrant, people "of
colour" and students being bludgeoned, choked,
maced, tased, shot and surveilled.

In view of the racist history of policing, its
patrolling and surveillance practices connected
with slavery (Parenti 2008; Bell 2000; Kelley
2000; Hawkins and Thomas 1994), colonialism
(T. Gordon 2004; Fanon 1967; Anderson and
Killingray 1991; Enloe 1980), internal colonialist
containment (Wacquant 2008; Carmichael and
Hamilton 1972; Staples 1975), militarization
(Chambliss 1995b; Kraska 2007; Meeks 2006;
Klare 1974) and past and current social control
of the US/Mexican border (Parenti 2008), Manning at best mystifies the brutal and murderous
repression enacted by the police against the
poor, immigrants and an assortment of "surplus
people" and other "undesirables." Moreover, to
suggest that repression of targeted groups is no
longer a central objective of "democratic policing" in post-industrial society and that "trust",
"mutual obligation and reciprocity" arise between police and the governed wherein the po-

lice are Maussian "gift givers," grossly distorts reality at best and at worst is complicit with manufacturing consent. Clearly because he offers no theory of the state, Manning does not distinguish between the impossibility of "democratic policing" versus policing in a liberal democracy. Accordingly, power and violence are merely *significations* of police authority (Manning 2010, 249) rather than the reality of perceived "threatening" persons, groups and classes who are set upon by the state's repressive apparatus. Despite the obvious facts contradicting it, Manning (249) asserts the

> ...police give more than they receive, they resist provocation, and the response of the other cannot always be anticipated. Yet, a gift by the police, in this sense tolerance and patience in the face of uncertainty, creates an obligation to reciprocate (Mauss 1990). However, it is a problematic pattern of exchange and reciprocity because the gift is invisible.[13]

The choked and pock marked bodies of Mike Brown, Eric Garner, Philando Castile, Alton Ellis, Rekia Boyd[14] and so many others are hardly *invisible*, unless of course one accepts Ralph El-

---

[13] Given state authority and the personality of the police become merged in a uniform that manifests and symbolizes state monopoly on force in the maintenance of extant order, the police are "L'état, c'est moi." The practical result of the investiture of state power sets in place a prefiguring interactional dynamic in which the police regard both protest and *untermenschen* citizens/persons as threat to the state and social order. With this fact recognized, as Manning himself appears to do elsewhere (Terrill, Paoline and Manning 2003), risks concealing the dynamics of repression with talk of "gift giving." The ultimate danger of this approach, however, is that in individualizing the response of police to whatever context we lose the fact that the unalloyed function of policing is repression.

lison's proposition that African Americans are not worthy of sight, much less the right to exist. However troubling, it would be an error to dismiss these ideas as nonsensical, especially given Mannings' prior work that was critical in nature though it tended toward Pluralism (1971).

As with his earlier work there is certainly value in examining policing from a symbolic interactionist standpoint. Doing so, however, requires a theoretical framework that connects policing ideology (consensus making), moral regulation, social control and compulsion of the oppressed toward wage labour (T. Gordon 2006). The merit of a materialist approach is that it gives serious treatment to the state and society in ways that appreciate the relationship between resistance and social contradictions. It is little good, then, to seek as does Michael Raphael (2010, 255-258), Manning's protégé, the transformation of policing through semiotic tactics, as though by this Hegelian method of supposing ideas stand apart and are not determined by, though dialectical with, in the first instance, materialism. It is assumed that by changing the nomenclature of "policing" to "patrolling," the police apparatus it signifies is presumed to also change in reality[15]. Nor is it

---

[14] Kimberlè Crenshaw demonstrates that amidst the concerns over the police murder of African American men, African American women's experience of savagely equitable likelihood of being killed by police ought not to be diminished by its comparatively less prevalence (2015).

[15] Manning (2010) in general but Raphael (2010) in particular, suggest the "police" is a signifier too semiotically limited to make sense of policing in the post-modern context. In that context it is argued

meaningful to sustain undue faith in *Posse Commitatus*[16], as does Manning (2010) and Raphael (2010), when border militarization and the internationalization of the "war on terror" facilitates, through the Patriot Act for example, domestic policing by the military, the development of paramilitary/gendarmerie (e.g., rapid

> ...it is theoretically negligent to continue such significations. Thus, one must declare, by the power vested in the historically developed nature of semiotics and the English language, that from this forward, 'police' and its officers shall be referred to as agencies and agents, respectively, because they are agents of the people and their authority derives from the consent of the peopled governed and nowhere else. (24-25)

As I have been harping in this introduction there is much that is problematic about such statements in terms of its commitment to pluralism. Yet, my concern here is that this semiotic sleight of hand, intended to drain policing studies of the full spectrum of repressive practices from surveillance to truncheons and bullets in fact doubles on itself to reveal the very facts that are attempted to be concealed. Should then, Raphael seek to claim order is "patrolled" rather than "policed", then it would do well to remember that modern policing did not emerge merely from Peel's preoccupation with manufacturing consent. It emerged also from the fact that slavery was maintained by a patrol system that deputized the totality of all able-bodied white males of age and that it was regulated through a system of surveillance, metrics of biopower and homicidal brutality. Indeed, the emergence of modern policing in the US is intimately connected with the racialist program of the state, capital and White hegemonic society. It is vital to remember that the first forms of organized policing in the US were slave patrols and subsequently inclusive of the KKK terror campaigns which tightly forged classism and racism with capitalism and state brutality (see Hadden 2001; Bell 2000; Kelley 2000; Hawkins and Thomas, 1994). Moreover, a materially abstracted semiotics ignores that the police-patrol nexus are flip-sides of the same practice in the signal role policing had and continues to play in colonialism and imperialism (Anderson and Killingray 1991; Kelley 2000).

[16] The past decades in the US have seen the growth of private contract policing—basically mercenary soldiers. More relevant to

deployment units) and a whole range of military-police collaborations (Gillison, Turse and Syed 2016; Kelly et al. 2009; Parenti 2008; Kraska 2007; Lutterbeck 2004). Manning and Raphael's sanguine views can be counted as political naïveté, but a more rigorous explanation would be that they do not see the state in terms of class or colonial (and race) oppression but as a neutral arbitrator between factions defined by party rather than identity and interests. As a force in class warfare, always siding with the rights of the bureaucratic (in the case of socialist states) and capitalist class as the case may be, the state is not a politically neutral entity. So why then are police required? For William Ryan, the answer is classic, elegant and simple: "Presumably we hire them to do what they, in fact, do: arrest black people and poor people. In functional terms, it is hard to evade the conclusion that the major task we give our police is to control potentially disruptive or troublesome groups in the population" (1976, 208); basically, to seek, label and generate fear, isolate and destroy in the name and sake of protecting "society" (J. Miller 2011; R. Miller 1996).

Indeed as far as "crime" control and prevention goes the police may solemnly lament they can do anything at all about "crime." Yet to the extent criminal legislation continues to expand as do police on the streets in uniform and undercover, many hands make for light work of suppressing dissent, occupying ghetto commu-

the issue of *Posse Comitatus*, George W. Bush signed into law the Defense Authorization Act which grants the president executive authority to deploy the national guard and military, without consent of states, to quell civil disturbances (Morales 2006).

nities and stuffing prisons beyond their capacity. To the extent the neoliberal state is not a social democracy and in which citizens suffer forms of "social death," the state is deeply implicated in maintaining organized chaos through what David MacGregor calls "Machiavellian state terror" (2006). That is, through its ontology as a political-economic enterprise of exploitation and oppression, the "deep politics" of the state mandates the normalization of "evil" (MacGregor 2002) acts toward its citizens, and, in the case of imperialist states, upon the citizens of conquered and subordinated nations. Beyond state terror tactics, through the controlling practices implicated in the biopolitics of social "services," and many other methods of its repressive apparatus, the state regards its citizens as the enemy to be controlled and suppressed (Tilly 1985). Given the nature of ideology perpetrated by socializing agencies, at a deeper level by the Machiavellian state's pyrotechnics of "terrorism" and produced by the ontological facts of existence in a capitalist society, the state seeks to normalize "full spectrum dominance"; though, of course, not without resistance, even if inchoate. Thus, Alfred McCoy reminds us that in 2008 the Pentagon created Domestic Consequences Management Response Force (2010), the goal of which is to train and work with FEMA, the FBI and local law enforcement to anticipate civil unrest and crowd control. Finally, it is not feasible to claim as does Manning (2010) and Raphael (2010) that the police are not pawns of politics even as they are themselves political actors whose semi-autonomy, within definable limits, is conceded by plutocrats (Harring and Ray 1993; Johnson 1992).

II: JEAN-PAUL BRODEUR

Jean-Paul Brodeur's statement of the normative principles concerning the current state of policing studies is no less abstract than Manning and Raphael's. It's distinction, however, being more theoretically rigorous, is that toward identifying under-addressed areas and practices of institutionalized policing (2010, 185-6) the aim is to develop what Brodeur calls a "complete" theory of the institution of policing (8). For Brodeur, "...a theory of policing should strive to be descriptively complete, for only then can it aim for explanatory adequacy" (2010, 3).[17] Brodeur offers a theory of policing which views the policing institution and its fractious parts as a web. This theory, he argues, aspires to be all-encompassing, inclusive of the over-studied uniformed police and reforms directed almost exclusively toward it. While, ostensibly, looking at all dimensions of policing Brodeur claims his theory will be rigorously directed toward the dynamics and processes of criminal investigation. His approach claims to be mindful of how "innovations" from "...community policing to evidence-based policing...increased the gap between patrol and investigative units" (3) and it remedies organizational short-comings vis-à-vis the "...collection and analysis of criminal and security intelligence"

---

[17] By definition, theory aims to explain what is described. From the very inception then, the contradiction I describe that suffuses Brodeur's project is implicit from the very start.

(Ibid) manifested in "high" versus "low policing"
(223). Brodeur, however, specifies there are
boundaries to a complete descriptive theory.
Importantly, this boundary is not determined
by the postmodern attack on "grand narratives"—a problem in itself since postmodernism
also constitutes a grand narrative (Sardar 1999,
48). Rather, the boundary to a theory of policing
is determined by the magnitude of "...what
makes a society secure and orderly..." (Brodeur
2010, 4). Since the question is, by Brodeur's admission, too large or possibly monolithic to be
encompassed by a single theory of policing, the
degree of the theory's completeness is determined by the object it encounters. That is, a descriptive theory of policing must satisfy itself
with describing the elements that comprise the
web or *assemblage* of policing. Given "the various
components of the policing apparatus do not
form an integrated whole and generally operate
independently from one another, with few co-
ordinating mechanisms" (4), theory is determined by the facts *as they appear*. There are four
problems with theorizing policing in this way:
epistemological, ideological, normative and explanatory rigor.

First, for Brodeur, theory apparently extends
no further than what is visible. Taking presenta-
tion at face-value, theory is little more than a
camera image of reality and not itself an intervention on reality that not only describes but
also provides meaning. There are of course various meanings to theory (R. Williams 1983, 316),
but in terms of the social disciplines I am concerned with the ways theoreticians account for

their practice or ways of seeing the world. This fact is consistent with the most common meaning of theory, which is to provide, dialectically, an explanation of practice and to account for the way practice is informed by a philosophical worldview. To this end in developing a general account, the labour of the theoretician must not only explain practice vis-à-vis how human practices are organized, it must also account for the forms of consciousness and ideas that give direction to social experience. Social theory must therefore model the dialectical relationship between material conditions (thus the institutions that maintain these conditions) and forms of consciousness (both hegemonic and counter-hegemonic).

In the context of a social formation where the motive force of history *becomes* rather than *is* class conflict (Cabral 1966), a theory of policing that is not contextualized in terms of a more general model of "society," which is historically specific, is in fact not theory in the sense I have described it. Of course practice does of its own produce theory but this is not at all self-conscious theory; rather, it is ideology in the sense of obfuscation. As far as "theory" goes, Brodeur appears to elaborate a correctionalist perspective calculated to examine police practices for the purpose of increasing efficiency and/or to raise problematiques insofar as liberal democracy allows. Theorizing by this method, knowingly or not, makes the theorist complicit with the normalizing ideology generated by the state and its repressive apparatus.

Second, the ideological structure thrown up by liberal democracy, assuming "security" and "order" are synonymous with policing, ignores how policing itself generates insecurity and disorder and how capitalism (be it liberal democratic or state capitalism) does the same. The assumption that police are necessary ignores some basic facts that are historically and socially specific and which are suggestive of the manufacturing of consent. These are that: a) policing is *naturalized* rather than natural; b) the naturalization of repressive force requires the ideology that the police, as the state's sole executioner of civil use of force, are neutral of capitalist, colonial and imperial, racial and patriarchal interests; and c) that repressive force is necessary to maintain control, conformity and order in society (Pedicelli 1998, 13; see also Kelley 2000, 51).[18] Basically, structurally excluded from Brodeur's theory is that police are embedded in the social structure of capitalism, and, their *modus vivendi* is determined by that social structure even when their *modus operandi* modify over time. Given that "criminality," corruption and a broad range of other vices are constitutional to the enterprise of policing (even by law as noted by Brodeur 2010; see also Stamper 2005; Juarez 2004; Hibbert 1963), provided excesses are periodically investigated and ritually condemned, failure to imagine a world without police, hence the Westphalian state, is to fail to

[18] Both Pedicelli (1998) and Kelley (2000) argue the reasons for the failure of police reform is that this effort has been only to reform policing through public policy means within the context of the present social order. Given the role of police is to defend capitalist social relations, policing will not change without structural change toward social democracy in the least.

develop a social theory that is not determined by appearances.

Third, whereas the descriptive and methodological goals of Brodeur's theory of a policing web are clearly stated, its normative dimensions are not. One reason for this absence is that, presumably, the researcher stands apart from the object being researched. Taking this value neutral position, Brodeur claims theory has two objectives. First in a vernacular sense, theory is intended to give a "factual account of the whole range of the phenomenon" (4). Second, related to the facts of the phenomenon in question, by way of hypotheses, theory aims to identify the distinctive characteristics of the object of study and to explain its behaviour (4). This seems a classic statement of the scientific method. The chief problem here is that Brodeur ignores serious and unanswered criticisms against the European *Enlightenment's* tradition of generating and organizing knowledge as though the scientific method is amendable to moral philosophy (Douglas 1971; C. Wright Mills 2000).

Finally, based on the criticisms of social "science," there are serious limits to Brodeur's method, conception of theory, and, of course the explanatory rigor of his theorization. The notion of the researcher as distanced but through the scientific method made a priest of esoteric knowledge sequesters the researcher, their experiences and relationship from both institutional and societal policing: in effect the researcher is above it all. This then takes for granted the implication of consciousness being informed by history and the dialectic interplay between political economy and the ideological and cultural forms it makes possible. If the researcher is neutral, then so too is the theory, method and explanation they espouse an objective statement on reality. This is important because Brodeur's approach to theory implicitly sets parameters on what can be studied, how, as well as the broad range of economic relations and the forms through which authority and legitimacy are historically articulated and modified. For Brodeur, theory is open ended. It is basically an endless loop that explores the means of institutions but not ends. This is quite a serious contradiction: means but no ends! Claiming to follow Weber (minus confirming citations), Brodeur argues that as far as policing goes "...the state can only be defined by its means—coercion—since defining it by its ends would be a self-defeating task" (336).[19] What for Brodeur makes theory that takes *ends* as seriously as it would *means* a cul-de-sac is that a broad range of pressures within and without the police institution compel antinomies.[20] For example, as guaranteed by s25.1(2) of the Criminal Code of Canada, the police have a positive mandate to

---

[19] By delinking a critical inquiry of the ends-means connection, one would have to assume the state's *ends* are unproblematic and that what is needed, if anything at all, is reform of coercive tactics. But if we follow Weber's contention that it is "[n]ot ideas, but material and ideal interests, [that] directly govern men's conduct" (cited in Gouldner, 1975-76: 3), then the *ends* interested parties seek are precisely what should be made visible and assessed.

[20] That Brodeur elects to use a term that implies moral equivalency between the state breaking the law to uphold it is obviously a studied avoidance of the Marxist term "contradictions." A choice that legitimates the obfuscations of pluralistic theory and which presumably avoids the problem of choosing the side of one principle versus another reflects the hegemony of liberalism.

break the law to uphold it, provided, of all things, it is "in the public interest"; this is not merely because of capriciousness but because the criminal code establishes this practice as a right constitutive of "democratic policing" (6).[21]

The Canadian state is more circumspect in regulating its repressive apparatus in this regard than the US. For cultural and historical reasons having to do with state and capital formation rather than ethics, it allows on average two such operations in each province per year between municipal and provincial police forces. The issue, however, is not how many times the police legally break the law, but that they can do so at all. Rather than such a fact being "self-defeating" or a dead-end as theory goes, Brodeur neglects the first principle of the police: to defend the state that defends dominant class interests. The *quid pro quo* for playing this buffer role is that "[t]he state must obviously protect its protectors" (Reasons 1974, 270). Given that as John Hepburn argues "political society is built on a foundation of repressive force" (1979, 72), this is pretty straight forward since the least thing police are capable of doing is to prevent or solve state-defined crime; and, if so, it is not without massive information subsidies from an accommodating public. As a wedge between the colonized, immigrants, workers, students and oth-

---

[21] Other "antinomies" include "high and low policing", private vs public policing. The problem is that Brodeur provides no theory of society in which to ground these institutions and their practices. It is merely assumed and accepted that (liberal) democracy, hence capitalist democracy and its social organization vis-à-vis the repressive apparatus, do not need to be accounted for in its basic dimensions.

ers, the state creates a space of lawlessness to achieve its aims of defending extant relations of ruling class and elite domination by whatever means necessary (Agozino 2003; Liazos 1972; Ryan 1976).[22]

Indicating the limits of a Pluralist-Consensus theory respecting "antinomies," Brodeur gives no account of why the state would create law only to have its enforcers break it. By this convenience, the *ends* of the state escape theorizing not to mention confirming historical evidence. Moreover, giving lie to the myth that the purpose of the police is to prevent and solve "crime," the state, be it from the 16th to the 21st century, when not using its own agents, has routinely deputized proxy "criminals," "criminal organizations" and "terrorists" to flout the law by way of piracy, smuggling, drug trafficking, assassination and murder and "terrorist" attacks (Chambliss 1993b; Cockburn and St. Clair 1999; Naylor 1999; Tilly 1985). Eloquent testimony of the state's exceptionality to the law it creates by

---

[22] In the wake of retribution killings of police by African American army veterans in July 2016 for the police gangland-style execution of African Americans, the political establishment has called for solidarity between citizens and the police. Others, instead, have called for an explicit recognition of the fundamentally antagonistic relationship between the police and non-elite citizens (Van Westen, 2016). To this end, the UAW has called for the expulsion of the fifth columnist International Association of Police Unions from the AFL-CIO. Grounds?

> Historically and contemporarily, police unions serve the interests of police forces as an arm of the state, and not the interests of police as laborers. Instead, their "unionization" allows police to masquerade as members of the working-class and obfuscates their role in enforcing racism, capitalism, colonialism, and the oppression of the working-class. (UAW Local 265 2016)

inviting "criminal" proxies can be found in revelations that in 2011 and 2012 the FBI allowed its proxies to violate the criminal law, including murder, at least 5,658 and 5,939 times respectively (Reilly 2013). More spectacularly, not only do the DEA and ATF not track how many times its proxies break the law (Heath and Johnson 2012), the ATF ran—deadly for the Mexican and US public and one US customs agent in 2010— two Key Stone cops interdiction/surveillance US to Mexico gun smuggling operations between 2009-2011: "Wide Receiver" and "Fast and Furious." Not only did the ATF not follow up on credible indictable information or allow other agencies with more resources to assist in investigations, its field operatives, with knowledge of office command, induced gun smuggling to continue and failed to trace the guns or make substantive effort to set-up sting arrests (Office of the Inspector General 2012). Under these circumstances, how can one presume the ontological reality of "crime" and "criminality"—the apparent *modus vivendi* for the existence of police—to remain stable in social consciousness and institutional practice without recourse to a theory of "society" in which policing emerged and continues to defend inequities of power and private ownership of the means of production.[23]

---

[23] It may be tempting to regard "Wide Receiver" and "Fast and Furious" to be massive institutional failures, chalked up to the conflicting results of incompetence, agent careerism and/or inter-agency conflict etc. These are explanations that have validity, yet they must be subordinated to the wider context of a theory of capitalism and the state. Thus, gun manufacturers are complicit in the illegal trade of guns, just as tobacco companies and big pharma are complicit in the respective illicit trades of their

For Brodeur, the more obscure concept of "antinomies" is preferable to the more well-founded and rigorous Marxist conception of *contradictions*. For Brodeur, "antinomies" are built into the structure of policing in liberal democratic society; theory, therefore, cannot itself be unified because reality is discordant. Hence, theory based on the recognition of "antinomies" is "...unquiet and, at times, equivocal..." (2010, 8). The reason a theory of policing equivocates (and this is presumably a good thing) is because it is "affected by conceptual disturbances, unruliness, and pockets of ambiguousness that cannot be reduced to insignificance" (8). With such convolution, Brodeur claims his aspiration is to be *critical* rather than merely unquiet, since the former aims at "substantial reform of what it is critical of" (8). So deeply mired in confusion is Brodeur's approach to theory, however, that he seeks to rescue his "complete theory" from its incapacity to fully explain "antinomies." To do so, he concocts what he calls "self-discordant" theory (13).

---

products, because so doing is essential to the profit motive in the face of a crisis of profitability. Yet, taking MacGregor's (2006) theory of the Machiavellian state seriously, none of this is inconsistent with the state's complicity in failing to prevent mass gun killings in theatres and schools, as a pyrotechnic to justify a gun control strategy that would disarm its citizens. History is replete with the fact that where the "primary contradiction" is between the state and its citizens, feudal-fascistic regimes have always sought to disarm citizens who, if their consciousness becomes organized to create economic democracy, will sweep away the capitalistic state in favour of full democracy. As per note 17, the obverse is also true: that capitalistic states, as in the case of the 2nd US Constitutional Amendment's right to bear arms, was enshrined to protect the plantocratic regime of racial slavery, even at the expense of and with the consent of White labour.

The virtue of such a theory in which "antinomy" is embedded is that since policing is "ambivalent", theory cannot be "one-sided" because policing is too complex for this (13). Going back on his word that a theory of policing which is simultaneously "discordant" must aim toward criticality, we are told he eschews the very mode that enables reform because most of the time "... critical theory...is as dogmatic as what it purports to criticize" (14). So then, Brodeur eviscerates policing studies of the one possibility he claims it has to make reforms—criticality. At no point does Brodeur explicitly state what "critical" means. Hence to reject what is not defined compounds the problematic admission that his theory lacks the ability to explain "antinomies." One must, in the final analysis, wonder whether the so-called crisis of policing studies hinted at by Brodeur is not in fact deepened by "discordant" theory he proposes.

CONFLICT-MARXIAN PERSPECTIVE

Conflict-Marxian theoreticians are just as concerned about the "correctionalist" state of policing studies as are Consensus-Pluralists. Given the steady march of neo-conservative reclamation of public policy since the 1960s (Klein 2007; Harvey 2005), Conflict-Marxian theorists of policing have more to complain about. The error has been to assume that both the Soviet Union and China were indeed ideal manifestations of socialist theory. With their respective demise and capitulation to the liberal form of capitalism, left politics and theorizing has been thrown into disarray and (in general) capitulated to neo-liberalism (Proyect 2007; Petras 2001), though resistance abounds (Harvey 2011).[24] Concern about these facts, nevertheless, indicate the nature of Conflict-Marxian theorists' discontent with the state of policing studies is far from that of their Consensual-Pluralist counterparts. At the core of this distinction is that in substantive terms, Conflict-Marxian theories of society describe reality and articulate norms in ways that, among other things, do not take for granted the exclusion of knowledge production from social relations. The production of knowledge is, then, inherently material and political in nature. "Value neutrality" is, thus, not a possibility nor is it desirable. Theorizing policing, then, depends on a coherent theory of "society" rather than abstractification of the policing institution and its operations *from* the state and social formation that contain it. Indeed from this perspective, to the extent policing practices, ideology and branches of operation are modified, these are not only a function of the internal dynamics of policing but are relational to and informed by what is taking place in society.

From the vantage point of categorization, Conflict-Marxian theories of policing encapsulate a broad range of perspectives from Millsian "elite power" theory (a combination of Marxist and Weberian theory) through to a range of

---

[24] That the BRICS (Brazil, Russia, India, China, South Africa) have rushed toward neoliberalism as both development and counterbalance to the tendency of the rate of profit to fall, their intensive competition for geo-space and resources has intensified Western efforts to dominate and subordinate them.

more orthodox Marxist accounts.[25] For the purpose of this essay the disputations within this continuum are not relevant. Whatever their differences, which are not insignificant, there is also an external phenomenon that enables their categorization as a continuum in a unified conceptual field. That is, as a marginalized and often delegitimized epistemology relative to bourgeois knowledge, Conflict-Marxian theory is a knowledge form that through its descriptiveness and norm articulation, demystifies hegemonic social constructions of reality and offers a transformative vision toward a just and equitable world. It does do so through concepts that emphasize: a) historically specific conflict (among classes or groups) arising from, b) structural contradictions (incompatible interests in the ways classes and groups economically reproduce themselves) which are, c) articulated through the interaction between economy, ideology and the state.

---

[25] Orthodox Marxism should not be confused with "vulgar Marxism"—economic determinism (see Greenberg 1993, 15). Indeed, Cutler et al., argue that while Marx and Engels did not fully elaborate "non-class forces" such as parties and bureaucracy, orthodox Marxist accounts indicate Weberian conceptualizations of "non-class forces" were already anticipated by Marxist practitioners such as Lenin. Yet, the role of the economy in the final instance is not set aside; rather, it is that the idea of "non-class forces" as "representing" class interests is in error since, "...political practice...constitutes the interests which it represents" (Cutler et al. 1977, 237; see generally 231-238). This idea might enable Marxism to explain racism *if* racism is not merely a manifestation of capitalism but also exists as a cultural and non-economic force in which the White working class imagines itself and demands inclusion into a racial hegemony in which it concedes to class domination (see Charles Mills 2006; Willhelm 1980).

Though speaking expressly of Marxists, David Greenberg's observation punctuates my point: "...it is in the realm of *interpreting* research findings that Marxists will often find grounds for disagreeing with the work of their non-Marxian colleagues" [original italics] (1993, 20). Thus, the crucial point is not the pedestrian observation that there is something *really* wrong with policing studies because there is agreement from opposing viewpoints. It is, rather, the interpretation which is given to explain the "problem" of "correctionalism" in policing studies. Because of its internal contradictions, I have suggested the Consensual-Pluralist interpretation lacks both capacity and credibility to explain the nature of the problem it identifies. I will now sketch the Conflict-Marxian perspectives' statement of concern. Again, because this is not an exhaustive review, I will identify two representative complainants: Sidney Harring and Gerda Ray (1993) and Todd Gordon (2006)[26].

Harring and Ray (1993) recapitulate the history of Conflict-Marxian policing studies, its theory and empirical results—which are notably ignored by Brodeur (2010), Manning (2010) and Loader (2010)—and the social justice politics and manifestations of repression from which it articulates its normative claims. Importantly, Harring and Ray (1999) connect the production of ideas about policing to a sociological account of knowledge rooted in the Marxist conception of "social formation" (econ-

---

[26] Gordon's work neatly summarizes the radical left's concerns about policing studies.

omy, culture and ideology and the state). They note that despite critical interventions by an assortment of Marxian theorists and those involved in revolutionary struggles to end capitalist and state sponsored police repression, extrajudicial assassinations, spying, lying, *agents provocateur* and cycles and practices of corruption, research on the "...policing institution is bankrupt" (64). More to the point, they suggest, contemporary academic policing studies remain hopelessly mired in the evasiveness and equivocation of liberalism. The tendency toward mystification is inherited from the collusion between mainstream academia and the law and order judicial and political elite (63). Harring and Ray suggest that from Richard Nixon and his ilk through to Bill Clinton, Janet Reno and William H. Renquist, policing studies is dominated by the "law and order" agenda (63). The importance of their observation is that it alludes to the impact post-1960s neo-liberalism had on intellectual thought about the state and policing.

Significantly, Harring and Ray (1999) note, it was both against the inherent conservativism in policing studies and toward a critical research agenda that a fully sociological Conflict-Marxian perspective emerged (63).[27] Thus while Patrick Manning correctly observes that "[t]he systematic study of police by social scientists is

---

[27] The epistemic move toward Conflict-Marxian studies of the police was part of a general upsurge all over the Western world that derived its impetus from deinstitutionalization, prison abolitionism, radical criminology and radical grass-roots identity politics movements (see Cohen 2007a; Greenberg 1993; Lynch and Michalowski 2006; Inciardi 1980; Taylor, Walton and Young 1973).

a twentieth-century phenomenon...[that] indicates a coalescence of pragmatism and public
policy and to a lesser extent the internal dynamics of academic life and university politics"
(2010, 85), his error is one of over-generaliza-
tion. Equally problematic is Brodeur's reliance
on the U.S. National Research Council research
review that claims "the least researched in the
field of police studies were human rights, riot
control, police discretion, the use of firearms
and deadly force, and, finally criminal investigation" (2010, 185). Aside from being objectively
incorrect, if one factors in Conflict-Marxian
studies of policing, the point is that issues such
as criminal investigation, by the nature of police secrecy and proclamations of expertise,
limit scholarly research, and, especially from
the prying eyes of Conflict-Marxian researchers. The very structure of policing and
the mid-20th century emergence of its semi-autonomy from the state, political elite and the
citizenry, not only militates against critical examination of its routine practices, it gives Consensus-Pluralist complaints a ring of hollow-
ness.

The complaint that policing studies is in
moribund condition is all the more ironic since,
as Harring and Ray point out, "[p]olice work
may be more aggressively proactive now than it
was in the 1970s because the legal culture en-
courages aggressive police work" (1999, 78). At
the very time there should be robust theorizing
on policing and mass public protest about its

dominance in our lives, there is a chill wind.[28] Given the protective cover by the US Supreme Court and political elite's indifference when not collusion, the profligacy of the classist and racist character of abusive and death inducing police conduct ensures "...the bad policing work of the 1960s and 1970s became the good policing of the 1990s" (79). Interestingly, especially since the seemingly asymmetrical attacks on the US in September 1, 2001, the sundry wars on crime, drugs and immigration have metastasized into the war on "terror." Policing is now not only violently intrusive into citizens' private lives (Balko 2013) it has brought forward the state's concerns in the 1960s that urban spaces are war zones and must be policed as such (Kristian 2007). Harring and Ray (2010) suggest the violent nature of modern policing is traceable to prior preoccupations with the repression of labour (63). Hence, classism and racism are mutually reinforced in police practice and in the identification of problem populations (74). To what end? Harring and Ray suggest the objective of modern aggressive policing is to perpetuate extant and devolving class and racial inequality, especially through the discourse of moral hygiene (80).

Where Harring and Ray, however, do not fully explicate the relationship between policing studies, police practices and capitalism, at least in the paper cited, Todd Gordon extends this

---

[28] The sudden emergence of massive protests beginning with the slayings of Mike Brown, Eric Garner and Trayvon Martin and which have given life to the Black Lives Matter movement, suggest the dispossesseds' tolerance for police impunity has fully broken.

analysis following the propositions of the Open Marxist School (2003, 30). This is a position that explicitly locates theoretical and empirical work on policing vis-à-vis state power and capitalism's contradictory dependence on (living) labour and theft of the surplus profit it generates (T. Gordon 2003, 30). Within this context, Gordon completely ignores the pseudo-complaints of Consensus-Pluralists and instead debates conflict theorists whose analyses are approached from a non-materialist perspective. Gordon's central concern is that much of contemporary scholarship on policing assumes private policing and surveillance, instead of repression of labour and prospective "social dynamite," are the *sine qua non* of modern policing (and as such, is the proper preoccupation of policing studies). By ignoring the ways in which "surveillance" is itself a practice generated by the state, as though *agents provocateur*, brutality and repression etc are either minor defects of efficiency or are incompatible with what Brodeur calls "low policing" (2010), Gordon suggests critical scholars unwittingly commit to a pluralist view-point. The logical conclusion of these preoccupations gives the impression that repression is less manifestly required because there is general societal concordance that obviates the necessity for "low policing." Foucauldian and Eurocentric conceptions of the "post-modern," "post-industrial" and "post-traditional" alarm Gordon. He suggests the contemporary preoccupation with private policing tends to leave the impression that the objective of state repression, which for Gordon is inclusive of surveillance and the incorporation/subordination of private policing, is either not significant or where it arises, is surprising (Gordon 2003).

Gordon suggests Consensus-Plural policing studies is victim to its own success. It is a "servant of power" and as such, like bourgeois criminology more generally, lacks the ability to objectively examine the substance of its own enterprise. Quite specifically, by appealing to the Foucauldian discourse of *biopower* and a general preoccupation with surveillance as the new frontier of policing, Gordon suggests even critical police theorists have taken too seriously the notion that the state is in retreat or disempowered vis-à-vis capital. To the contrary, the state has abandoned both corporate regulation *and* modest defence of civil society while reinforcing its repressive capacities through the discourse of law and order, mass incarceration and the militarization of law enforcement (Chunn and Gavigan 2004; Harvey 2011; Klein 2007; Parenti 2008; Wacquant 2008). In practical terms, the legitimation of repression through the criminalization of protest and of alternative and non-wage forms of labour serve to force the working class back to the diminishing returns and discipline of the capitalist labour market (T. Gordo, 2010, Chapter 2).

There are, however, three related qualifications to the Open Marxist approach I believe are necessary for developing a rounded theory of policing, state and society. Todd Gordon is to be commended for taking gender and race seriously. While drawing on the Open Marxist approach, he admits it treats colonialism, gender, racism as relatively inert forces in capitalism and the operation of the state.[29] Yet, as he points out and seeks to elaborate, in colonialist, formerly chattel slave, immigrant exploitative and patriarchal capitalist societies, these ruling relations are essential pivots of state power (2003, 29-30). Especially regarding race, like Harring and Ray (1993, 74), Gordon avoids the familiar trap that racism is an ideology propagated by capitalists and the state; although to be sure, capitalists and the state do foment white supremacy. But Marxist labour theory exhausts itself when confronted with the historical continuity of colonial and racist discourse and prac-

---

[29] This does not of course deny that at points in 18th-19th century in Europe itself, *race* constituted *class* and vice versa (see Diop 1991, 128). Even for those on the left, such as Marx and Engels, this interpolation took on a character little different from European *Enlightenment* thinkers of the conservative persuasion. Marx was as dismissive of the "lumpen" as he was the racial Other, at least when the latter did not suit his morality or formulation of the "worker" (Avinery 1968; Moore 1974-75). When dealing with Others who were marked by colour and national-cultural differences, Marx's ideas too were shaped by: the supremacist imperialistic ethos of the age (Ani 1994) and the Eurocentric preoccupation with science as the mark of civilization, cultural superiority and "progress" (Sardar 1999). No doubt Marxist doctrinaires will balk at these ideas, as though Marx somehow managed to transcend the bourgeois order in which his ideas were framed and articulated. As noted by Joseph Schumpeter, "...there is no paradox in saying that Marxism [read: Marx's ideas] is essentially a product of the bourgeois mind" (2008: 6). The derivative difficulties of Marxist analysis with racism, this was not an anomaly unique to Marx's time—it is structural to the Eurocentrism of Marx's ideas and the school of thought following him (see Charles Mills 2006; Charles Mills 2003: Chapter 5; Cabral 1966; Fanon 1963: 40). This does not of course reject the essential insights of Marxist theory, but it does suggest both Marx's framing and those who have elaborated his theory were themselves constituted by the ideology of a capitalist, colonialist and racist society.

tice among the European working class as much as among the elite (Charles Mills 2006; Robinson 2000; Wilderson 2003; Willhelm 1980).[30] Moreover, Westphalian states, from capitalist to Marxist-Leninist, depend on expunging indigenous peoples *qua* indigenous peoples precisely because their historic methods of accumulation are pejoratively represented as either primitive capitalism or backward hunter gathering, and, because they must be made into elements within the discourse of "labour for itself" (Churchill 1992). Yet the point is not to deny the

---

[30] W. E. B. Du Bois, points out that "vanguard" White labour exhibited racist and pro-capitalist tendencies which were consequential for state formation and policing: "[White] revolt against the domination of the planters over the poor Whites... called for a class struggle to destroy planters, this was nullified by deep-rooted antagonism to the Negro, whether slave or free. If black labor could be expelled from the United States or exterminated, then the fight against the planter could take place. But the poor whites and their leaders could not for a moment contemplate a fight of united white and black labor against the exploiters. Indeed, the natural leaders of the poor whites, the small farmer, the merchant, the professional and the white mechanic and slave overseer, were bound to the planters and repelled from the slaves and even from the mass of white laborers in two ways: first, *they constituted the police patrol* who could ride with planters and now and then exercise unlimited force upon racalicitrant or runaway slaves; and then, too, there was always a chance that they themselves might also become planters..." [italics added] (1935: 27). Mirroring Du Bois, vis-à-vis the racism and militarism of contemporary policing, Chinweizu argues that as the West confronts serious challenge to its global dominance its

> ...ruling classes...[will]...rally their lower classes to defend [the Western order]. Their lower classes, who will in normal times be kept from full enjoyment of the fruits of the [capitalist] arrangement, will nevertheless be rallied through appeals to their racism, appeals asking them to defend *their* western civilization, *their* prosperity, and the superiority of *their* white race over all others. [original italics] (1974, 487)

salience of social class, but rather that race (whatever form it takes) and class are dialectical articulations of domination. The police themselves admit (without seeing it as problematic) that classism and racism are twinned. Racist stop and searches can be, and are, justified in class, gender and racial terms. So, inasmuch as Gordon recognizes the parallel and overlapping tracks of relations of ruling, there are three immediate problems and these affect how policing is studied from a Marxist perspective.

First, there is an apparent element of instrumentalism in the Open Marxist School's conceptualization of the state, or at least as it is suggested by Gordon. As shown by Ralph Miliband (1987, 10) the state has a semi-autonomous character from the ruling class and so at times it might oppose some fractions of that class to preserve its legitimacy and that of the capitalist system. Related to this, institutionalized policing also, though its mandate is structured by the state, operates semi-autonomously from the state, elites and the capitalist ruling class.

Second, the Open Marxist approach assumes the centrality of the category of the "working class." But, what happens, as has been the case for most indigenous people, who to this day, largely remain outside the class structure; or, African descended peoples in the Americas whose ancestors were "liberated" to join the wage economy but who technology and white supremacy precluded from equal inclusion in the "working class" (Gibson 2006; Willhelm 1970); or increasingly the White working class in the US who face disutility as they are disgorged from the class structure (Edsall 2012); or "Third World" peoples too poor to engage in consumerism or are simply "taking up space" on prime mineral concessions (Flanders 2012)? The basic question is whether the Marxist category of "working class" has the requisite analytical capacity to account for the economic disutility of large and increasing swaths of the so-called lumpen proletariat (Bauman 2004).[31] Can class theory, in view of overproduction, declining profitability, technification of production, off-shoring and massive disgorgement of people from the labour market contemplate the logic of genocide inherent to capitalism?[32] (see

---

[31] Ironically, following Adam Smith and David Ricardo, Marx's labour theory of value recognizes that capitalism tends to declining profitability made up, in part, by technological innovations in "constant capital" that aim to increase to redress the profitability crisis by making living labour redundant (see Huberman, 1963).

[32] Eloquent statements indicating the necessity of genocide come, not from the fringe but, from well-respected segments of the Western political elite. Zbigniew Brzezinski (2007), acknowledging the challenges to maintaining US global hegemony, recently argued among other things:

> For the first time in human history almost all of humanity is politically activated, politically conscious and politically interactive... The resulting global political activism is generating a surge in the quest for personal dignity, cultural respect and economic opportunity in a world painfully scarred by memories of centuries-long alien colonial or imperial domination. [emphasis added] (53)

Without offering objection, he next argues that the

> major world powers [Western], new and old, also face a novel reality: while the lethality of their military might be greater than ever, their capacity to impose control over the politically awakened masses of the world is at a historic low. To put it bluntly: in earlier times, it was ▸▸

Ford 2010; Gibson 2006; Leech 2012; Willhelm 1971).

Third, the preoccupation with "wage-labour" ignores that there are other social movements besides, but often related to, the working class struggle which threaten the state. As such, initiatives and organizations for civil liberties, the environment, peace, racial and social justice (especially against police brutality) are subject to a broad array of violent and disruption practices aimed at crushing political opposition rather than propagating compulsion back to wage-labour.

Finally, it is true the capitalist state has an imperative to criminalize alternate and underground forms of enterprise, thereby pushing social outcasts back toward wage labour and, by this means, depressing wages generally. Yet, the relationship between policing and the wage-

---

▸ easier to control one million people than to physically kill one million people; today, it is infinitely easier to kill one million people than to control one million people." (54)

Western powers already took this practical step before this speech in 2008. Henry Kissinger long anticipated the necessity for genocide in 1974:

> Populations with a high proportion of growth. The young people, who are in much higher proportions in many LDCs, are likely to be more volatile, unstable, prone to extremes, alienation and violence than an older population. These young people can more readily be persuaded to attack the legal institutions of the government or real property of the "establishment," "imperialists," multinational corporations, or other— often foreign—influences blamed for their troubles. (58)

Anxiety, fear and loathing continue as US military planners prepare to deal with a "youth bulge" as it prepares for the next 40 years of resource wars (see Clonan 2008).

labour thesis may not be all there is given the underground economy is necessary to neo-liberal capitalism even as it is criminalized and appropriated by the state (Neuwirth, 2011; Chen, 2007; Ruggiero 2000; Chambliss 1993b; Cox 1984). Criminalization of a subordinated illicit economy, broad though it may be and inclusive of a range of enterprises and services, enables the state to contain, selectively target and repress those populations surplus to the needs of a post-industrial capitalist society. Relatedly, the state itself strategically makes use of subordinated and illicit enterprises and services. This can be seen from state agencies' direct involvement in "criminal" activities such as narcotics, weapons and other forms of smuggling (Blum 2005; Web 1998; Chambliss 1993b). Or yet, when British, Dutch, French and US colonial governments contracted out to buccaneers the pirating of their competitors' ships, to the US government contracting mob hits on Fidel Castro, to the US giving the Cosa Nostra a free hand in post-World War II Italy as a bulwark against socialism (see Chambliss 1993b; Hamm 1993; Blum 2005), to the US training and setting loose Muslim "freedom fighters" (Al Qaeda) in Albania and Afghanistan, or to the equipping and training of paramilitary forces in East Timor and throughout Latin America. The "legitimate" law breaking by the police and their dependency on "criminals" also indicate the prosecution of "crime" is selective and strategic, even if the regulation of labour is consequential for maintaining extant relations.

None of the foregoing undermines the primary contentions of the Open Marxist perspective or Conflict-Marxian approaches more generally. It does, however, suggest the expressive
and instrumental purposes of policing, toward
maintaining the state and extant economic and
social relations ought not to be limited to one
manifestation: class control. It is not likely that
any one study can say all there needs to be said;
but, certainly, explicating particular dimensions
or aspects of policing within the context of a
Conflict-Marxist theory of society and state can
reveal the characteristics of particular practices
that are taken-for-granted. At the same time,
whatever the limitations of Conflict-Marxian
theories regarding policing and a historical materialist interpretation of the state and society, it
generates knowledge about policing that is, to
paraphrase Lenin, as radical as reality itself.

CONCLUSION

The limits of the Consensus-Pluralist view of
policing are its mystification of and servitude to
the state and its repressive apparatus. To this
end the consciousness and interests of the researcher are informed by the nature of her/his
epistemic enterprise—to provide a justifactory
framework for state repression. As such, Consensus-Pluralists are unable to be reflexive
about their consciousness and practices as ser-
vants of the state. Relatedly, Consensus-Pluralists have themselves engaged in bureaucratic
capture of the repressive state. Critical-Marxists
policing studies suffer no such defects; those
they have, from my view are of a different sort.

While the latter's emphasis is on the police and its repressive-surveillance tactics of maintaining order, their focus is not only on the "master institutions that produce...suffering" (Gouldner 1968), it is also on the bases of existence through which consciousness, practice, theory, classes and other sites of conflict and liberation are dialogic and come into being.

To a significant extent, what passes for the "crisis" of policing studies is not an absence of critical analysis and interpretation. There is an unbroken line of radical scholarship that extends the radical left analysis that burst forth in the late 1960's and early 1970's. Such analysis continues to explicitly chart the militarism of policing, the police-military blurring, crisis of the neo-liberal state and its blind defence of authoritarian capitalism and state power against the masses as directly relational to police activities such as: *agents provocateur*, surveillance and disruption tactics and, of course, repressive violence against dissenting social forces. Much is made of new technologies for repression such as police departments' use of drones or the appropriation of information technologies such as Facebook to track and surveil, but these technologies only enhance the reach of the state to target and discredit dissenters and terrorize the rest of the population. These are only new durable technologies toward the objectives of state repression (Austin 2013; Parenti 2008; Whitaker et al. 2013).

By way of concluding, a note of caution for the Conflict-Marxian side of the policing debate. Whether it is broadly theoretical in nature or emphasizes close grain analysis of police practices such as crowd control, "criminal" investigation or tendencies toward legitimate and extrajudicial repression, a good deal of quite excellent work on policing is impoverished by its *presentism*. The impression is created of "new Columbuses," as Stanislav Andreski (1973) and Pitirim Sorokin (1965) would call them, absent any sense of tradition, venturing boldly to the edge of epistemology within the five year citation cycle, despite the extensive volume of critical work beginning in the 1960's and 1970's that either details these issues, or at the very least anticipated them (one example is Platt and Cooper, 1974). In addition, a fulsome engagement with counter-colonial approaches to policing and the conception of "deep politics," would round out Conflict-Marxian epistemology of policing in historical terms.

Ultimately, the perceived crisis of policing studies is more than the sum of the parts thus discussed. The "problem" of policing studies in my view is at its core a problem for the sociology of knowledge. But here, knowledge is not an abstract exercise in pursuit of value neutrality. It is the pursuit of objective knowledge in social context. Thus any discussion about policing must not only be inclusive of the state and society, it should be guided by questions of political philosophy: what is the ethical and moral role of the police in a society where liberal democracy was stillborn the moment hegemonic forces brought it into being. In other words, what does it mean to police in a society where equality of opportunity is mandated by law when there is no room for equality of condition; but also, what does policing mean when the discourse of equality *is* the basis for uneven ownership of property, distribution of wealth and circulation of goods?

These moral-philosophical questions are especially urgent given that most criminologists and policing experts, unlike their leftist counter-parts (Shantz 2012), are not intimately connected to protest and social justice movements but are embedded within and wedded to "correctionalist" institutional settings. Overwhelmingly then, the "correctionalism" of policing studies bears the imprint of the social location of academics. But, as the police prepare to unleash a war of "full spectrum dominance" for which they have been preparing and quietly waging the last 40 years[33] on the discon-

---

[33] Since the early 1970s, RAND and other military research institutes have made policing a top priority in anticipating urban civil discontent and urban guerilla warfare. Contrary to the notion that the military and the police are distinct enterprises, military research and experimentation with social control suggests that in view of maintaining capitalism and the state, both military and police will play collaborative strategic roles within a whole. For example, a 2007 RAND research paper on counter-insurgency noted:

> Building strong police forces is also important—usually much more important than aiding the military. Police typically are far better suited to defeating small groups, because they know the communities well and are trained to use force discriminately... Not only must the police be strong and numerous, the laws they enforce must be suited for counterinsurgency... (Byman 2007, 28)

While Byman claims that US offers of training and assistance to foreign police forces have been historically weak (Ibid), assuming some optimal limit has yet to be reached, as early as 1974, Michael Klare (1974a; 1974b) and Joe Stork (1974) show this to be otherwise. The appearance of discontinuity and the supposed ▸

tented, displaced, "disemployed" and politically mobilized citizens of their nations, it is clear that Consensual-Pluralistic police studies will be as mired in ethico-moral malaise and mystification as it has always been. There is much work to be done as neo-liberalism moves forward and growing resistance along with it. But, along the way, it is important to recover and remember what the struggle for critical consciousness has already brought us in policing studies since there is nothing certain or inevitable about the present social arrangement.

▸ weakness of (urban) counter-insurgency training, preparation and cross-fertilization within and outside global hegemons is an obfuscation of reality. The US military, as that country devolves fully into neo-feudalism (Zafirovski 2007), is sanguine about the issue. Mike Davis (2007) cites Major Ralph Peters, author of the 1996 article "Our soldiers, Their Cities" written in Army War College journal *Parameters*, as follows:

> The future warfare lies in the streets, sewers, highrise buildings, and sprawl of houses that form the broken cities of the world...Our recent military history is punctuated with city names—Tuzla, Mogadishu, Los Angeles, Beirut, Panama City, Hue, Saigon, Santo Domingo—but these encounters have been but a prologue, with the real drama still to come. (cited in Davis 2007, 202)

Despite the willingness of Consensual-Pluralists to maintain the mythic separation between the police and the military and their faith in *Posse Comitatus* being inviolable, the facts are to the contrary (Army 2005; Morales 2000).

REFERENCES

Agozino, B. 2003. *Counter-Colonial Criminology: A Critique of Imperialist Reason.* London: Pluto Press.

Allen, R. 1970. Black Awakening in Capitalist America: An analytic history. New York: Doubleday Anchor Book.

Anderson, B. Imagined Communities: Reflections on the Origin and Spread of Nationalism. London: Verso.

Anderson, D and D. Killingray. 1991. "Consent, Coercion and Colonial Control: Policing the empire, 1830-1940." In D. Anderson and D. Killingray (eds.), *Policing the Empire: government, authority, and control, 1830-1940*. Manchester, UK; New York: Manchester University Press ; New York: Distributed exclusively in the USA and Canada by St. Martin's Press.

Andreski, S. 1973. *Social Science as Sorcery.* St. New York: Martin's Press.

Ani, M. 1994. *Yurugu: An African Centered Critique of European Cultural Thought and Behavior*. Trenton, New Jersey: African World Press, Inc.

Army, Department of. 2005. *FM 3-19.15 Civil Disturbance Operations.* http://www.fas.org/irp/doddir/army/fm3-19-15.pdf.

Austin, D. 2013. *Fear of a Black Nation: Race, sex, and security in sixties Montreal.* Toronto: Between the Lines.

Balko, R. 2013. *Rise of the Warrior Cop: The militarization of America's police forces.* New York: Public Affairs.

Becker, H. 1967. *Whose Side are We On? Social Problems* 14(2): 239-247.

Bell, D. 2000. "Police Brutality: Portent of disaster and discomforting divergence." In J. Nelson, (Ed.), *Police Brutality: An anthology*, 1st Ed. New York: W. W. Norton and Co.

Blum, W. 2005. *Rogue State: A guide to the world's only superpower.* Monroe, Maine: Common Courage Press.

Brand, D. 1994. *Bread Out of Stone.* Toronto: Coach House Press.

Brodeur, J-P. 2010. *The Policing Web.* New York: Oxford University Press.

Brogden, M. 1982. The Police: Autonomy and consent. London; New York: Academic Press.

Brzezinski, Z . 2009. "Major Foreign Policy Challenges for the Next US President." *International Affairs* 85, 1: 53–60.

Byman, D. 2007. *Understanding Proto-Insurgencies. RAND Counterinsurgency Study, Paper 3.* www.rand.org. Accessed 5 January, 2010.

Case, C and R. Farrell. 1995. "Myth, Allegiances, and the Study of Social Control." *The American Sociologist* 26, 1: 62-75.

Cabral, A. 1966. "The Weapon of Theory. Tricontinental Conference of the Peoples of Asia, Africa and Latin America." http://www.marxists.org/subject/africa/cabral/196 6/weapon-theory.htm. Accessed 14 August 2012.

Carmichael, S., and C. Hamilton. 1972. "White Power: The Colonial Situation." In Richard J. Meister (ed.), *The Black Ghetto: Promised land or colony?* Lexington, Mass: Heath.

CBC News. 2012. "South African miners keep striking after shooting." *The Associated Press.* http://www.cbc.ca/news/world/story/2012/08/20/south-african-mines-strikes.html.

CBC News. 2011. "Occupy pepper-spraying prompts university probe: University police chief, 2 officers placed on leave." *The Associated Press.* http://www.cbc.ca/news/world/story/2011/11/21/california-occupy-pepper-spray.html.

CBC News. 2007. "Undercover cops tried to incite violence in Montebello: union leader." http://www.cbc.ca/canada/montreal/story/2007/08/22/ot-police-070822.html.

Chambliss, W. 1995. "Crime Control and Ethnic Minorities: Legitimizing racial oppression by creating moral panics." In D. Hawkins (ed.), *Ethnicity, race, and Crime: Perspectives across time and place.* New York: State University of New York Press.

___. 1993a. "On Lawmaking." In William J. Chambliss and Marjorie S. Zatz (eds.), *Making Law: The state, the law, and structural contradictions.* Bloomington and Indiana: Indiana University Press.

_____. 1993b. "State-Organized Crime." In W. Chambliss and M. Zatz (eds.), *Making Law: The state, the law, and structural contradictions.* Bloomington and Indianapolis: Indiana University Press.

Chen, Martha. 2007. "Rethinking the Informal Economy: Linkages with the Formal Economy and the Formal Regulatory Environment. Economic and Social Affairs." http://www.un.org/esa/desa/papers/2007/wp46_2007.pdf.

Chunn, D and S. Gavigan. 2004. "Welfare Law, Welfare Fraud, and the Moral Regulation of the 'Never Deserving' Poor." *Social and Legal Studies* 13, 2: 219-243.

Churchill, Ward and Jim Vander Wall. 2002. *Agents of Repression: The FBI's secret wars against the Black Panther Party and the American Indian Movement*. Cambridge, MA.: South End Press Classics.

Coles, David. 2010. "Security operation or political theatre?" *Toronto Star*. http://www.thestar.com/printarticle/839199.

Chinweizu. 1974. *The West and the Rest of US: White predators, Black slavers and the African elite*. New York: Random House.

Clonan, T. 2008. "US generals planning for resource wars." http://iraqwar.mirror-world.ru/article/176035.

Cohen, S. 2007a. *Against Criminology*. New Brunswick: Transaction Books.

_____. 2007b. *Visions of Social Control*. Oxford, UK: Polity.

Coulson, M and C. Riddell. 1980. *Approaching Sociology*. London: Routledge and Kegan Paul.

Cornforth, M. 1977. The Theory of Knowledge. New York: International Publishers.

Crichlow, W. 2014 "Weaponization and Prisonization of Toronto's Black Male Youth." *International Journal for Crime and Justice*. https://www.crimejusticejournal.com/article/view/120

Cutler, A., B. Hindess, P. Hirst and Hussain, A. 1977. *Marx's 'Capital' and Capitalism Today, V. 1*. Boston: Routledge and Kegan Paul.

Davis, M. 2007. *Planet of Slums*. New York: Verso.

Della Porta, D and H. Reiter (eds.). 1998. *Policing Protest: The control of mass demonstrations in Western democracies.* Minnesota: University of Minnesota Press.

Democracy Now. 2012a. "White Plains Police Officer Who Used Racial Slur Before Killing of Kenneth Chamberlain is Suspended." http://www.democracynow.org/2012/7/24/white_plains_police_officer_who_used. Accessed 27 August 2012.

Democracy Now. 2012b. "Police Brutality in Anaheim Sparks Outrage After 2 Latinos Shot Dead and Demonstrators Attacked." http://www.democracynow.org/2012/7/24/police_brutality_in_anaheim_sparks_outrage.

Democracy Now. 2012c. "With CIA Help, New York Police Secretly Monitored Mosques, Muslim Communities Post-9/11." http://www.democracynow.org/2011/8/25/with_cia_help_new_york_police

Diop, C. 1991. *Civilization or Barbarism: An authentic anthropology.* Brooklyn, NY: Lawrence Hill Books.

Djilas, M. 1973. "The New Class in Communist Societies." In William J. Chambliss (ed.), *Sociological Readings in the Conflict Perspective.* Santa Barbara: University of California.

Douglas, J. 1971. *American Social Order: Social Rules in a Pluralistic Society.* New York: The Free Press.

Dos Santos, J. 2004. "The world police crisis and the construction of democratic policing." *International Review of Sociology: Revue Internationale de Sociologie* 14(1): 89-106.

Dubois, W. E. B. 1935. *Black Reconstruction: An essay toward a history of the part which Black folk played in the attempt to reconstruct democracy in America, 1860-1880.* New York: Russell and Russell.

Edsall, T. 2012. "The Hollowing Out." *New York Times.* Retrieved July 11, 2012. http://campaignstops.blogs.nytimes.com/2012/07/08/the-future-of-joblessness/

Enloe, C. 1980. *Police, military, and ethnicity: foundations of state power.* New Brunswick, N.J.: Transaction Books.

Eze, Emmanuel Chukwudi. 1995. "The Colour of Reason: The idea of 'race' in Kant's anthropology." In Katherine Faull (ed.), *Anthropology and the German Enlightenment: Perspectives on Humanity.* London and Toronto: Bucknell University Press.

Fanell, B and L. Koch. 1995. "Criminal Justice, Sociology, and Academia." *The American Sociologist* 26(1): 52-61.

Fanon, F. 1967. *Wretched of the Earth.* New York: Grove Press.

Flanders, L. 2012. "Talking With Chomsky: On OWS, Anarchism, Labor, Racism, Corporate Power and the Class War." *Counter Punch.* http://www.counterpunch.org/2012/04/30/talking-with-chomsky/.

Fox-Piven, F. 1976. "The Structuring of Political Protest." *Politics & Society* 6(3): 297-326.

Felices-Luna, M. 2010. "Rethinking Criminology(ies) through the Inclusion of Political Violence and Armed Conflict as Legitimate Objects of Inquiry." *Canadian Journal of Criminology and Criminal Justice* 52(3): 249-269.

Forcese, D. 2002. "The Future of Policing." In D. Forcese (ed.), *Police: Selected issues in Canadian law enforcement.* Ottawa: The Golden Dog Press.

Francescani, C., J. Roberts and M. Hicken. 2012. "Under siege: 'Stop and frisk' polarizes New York." *New York Times.*

http://www.reuters.com/assets/print?
aid=USBRE86205Q20120703.

Gibson, J. 2006. *Have They Decided to Kill Us Yet:
Global Black Labor Obsolescence and Manufactured
Black Genocide*. Kindle Edition: Kitabu Publishing
LLC.

Gordon, D. 1973. "Capitalism, Class and Crime."
Crime and Delinquency 19(2): 163-186.

Gordon, T. 2006. *Cops, Crime and Capitalism: The
law-and-order agenda in Canada*. Halifax:
Fernwood Publishing.

Gouldner, A. 1968. "The Sociologist as Partisan:
Sociology and the Welfare State." *The American
Sociologist* 3(2): 103-116.

_____. 1970. *The Coming Crisis of Western Sociology*.
New York: Basic Books.

_____. 1975-76. "Prologue to a Theory of
Revolutionary Intellectuals." *Telos* 3-36.

_____. 1979. *The future of intellectuals and the rise of
the new class: A frame of reference, theses, conjectures,
arguments, and an historical perspective on the role of
intellectuals and intelligentsia in the international
class contest of the modern era*. New York:
Continuum Pub. Corp.

Greenberg, D. F. 1993. "Introduction." In D. F.
Greenberg (ed.), *Crime and Capitalism: Readings in
Marxist criminology*. Philadelphia: Temple
University Press.

Hadden, S. E. 2001. *Slave Patrols: Law and violence in
Virginia and the Carolinas*. Cambridge: Harvard
University Press.

Hall, S., and C. Critcher, T. Jefferson, J. Clarke and B.
Roberts. 1979. *Policing the Crisis: Mugging, the state,
and law and order*. London and Bassingstoke: The
MacMillan Press, Ltd.

Hamm, M. 1993. "State Organized Homicide: a study of seven CIA plans to assassinate Fidel Castro." In William J. Chambliss and Marjorie S. Zatz (eds.), *Making Law: The State, the Law, and Structural Contradications*. Bloomington and Indiana: Indiana University Press.

Hawkins, H and R. Thomas. 1994. "White Policing of Black Populations: A history of race and social control in America." In E. Cashmore and E. McLaughlin (eds.), *Out of Order: Policing Black People*. London and New York: Routledge.

Harring, S and G. Ray. 1993. "Policing a Class Society: New York in the 1990s." *Social Justice* 26, 2: 63-81.

Harvey, D. 2005. *A Brief History of Neoliberalism*. New York: Oxford University Press.

Headley, B. 1996. *The Jamaican Crime Scene: A perspective*. Washington, D.C.: Howard University Press.

Heath, B and K. Johnson. 2012. "Crimes by ATF and DEA informants not tracked by feds." *USA Today*. http://www.usatoday.com/story/news/2012/10/07/informants-justice-crime/1600323/.

Hedges, C. 2010. "A Recipe for Fascism." *Truth Dig*, November 8. http://www.truthdig.com/report/item/a_recipe_for_fascism_20101108.

Heiner, B. T. 2007. "Foucault and the Black Panthers." *City* 11(3): 313-356.

Hepburn, John. 1978. "Social Control and the Legal Order: Legitimated repression in a capitalist State." In W. K. Greenaway and S. L. Brickey (eds.), *Law and Social Control in Canada*. Scarborough, Ont.: Prentice-Hall of Canada, Ltd.

Hibbert, Christopher. 1963. *The Roots of Evil: A social history of crime and punishment*. Boston: Little, Brown and Company.

Hillyard, P and S. Tombs. 2004. "Beyond Criminology?" In Hillyard, P., C. Pantazis, S. Tombs and D. Gordon (eds.), *Beyond Criminology: Taking harm seriously*. London; Ann Arbor, MI: Pluto Press; Black Point, Nova Scotia: Fernwood.

Huberman, Leo. 1963. *Man's Worldly Goods: The story of the wealth of nations*. New York and London: Monthly Review Press.

Huey, L., and P. Pare. 2010. "Bridging Divides in Canadian Criminology: Some thoughts on a possible future." *Canadian Journal of Criminology and Criminal Justice* 52(3): 237-241.

Inciardi, J (ed.), 1980. *Radical Criminology: The coming crisis*. Beverly Hills: Sage Publications.

Juarez, Juan Antonio. 2004. *Brotherhood of Corruption: A cop breaks the silence on police abuse, brutality and racial profiling*. Chicago: Chicago Review Press.

Johnson, B. 1992. "Taking Care of Labor: The police in American politics." In K. McCormick and L. Visano (eds.), *Understanding Police*. Toronto: Canadian Scholars' Press.

Kelly, T., S. Jones, J. Barnett II, K. Crane, R. C. Davis and C. Jensen. 2009. "A Stability Police Force for the United States Justification and Options for Creating U.S. Capabilities." RAND Corporation. http://www.rand.org/pubs/monographs/2009/RAND_MG819.pdf

Kelley, R. 2000. "Slangin' Rocks...Palestinian Style: Dispatches from the occupied zones of North America." In J. Nelson (ed.), *Police Brutality: An anthology*, 1st Ed. New York: W.W. Norton and Co.

Kissinger, H. 1974. "National Security Study Memorandum. NSSM 200. Implications of

Worldwide Population Growth For U.S. Security and Overseas Interests (THE KISSINGER REPORT)." http://www.lifesitenews.com/waronfamily/nssm200/nssm200.pdf.

Klare, M. 1974. "Policing the Empire." In A. Platt and L. Cooper (eds.), *Policing America*. Englewood Cliffs, NJ: Prentice-Hall, Inc.

_____. 1974. "Bringing It Back: Planning for the City." In A. Platt and L. Cooper (eds.), *Policing America*. Englewood Cliffs, NJ: Prentice-Hall, Inc.

Klein, N. 2007. *The Shock Doctrine: The Rise of Disaster Capitalism*. New York: Metropolitan Books, Henry Holt & Company Publishers.

Kraska, P. 2007. "Militarization and Policing—Its Relevance to 21st Century Police." *Policing* 1(4): 501–513.

Kuhn, Thomas. 1970. *The Structure of Scientific Revolutions* (Second Edition). Chicago: University of Chicago Press.

Ladner, J. 1973. "Introduction" In J. Ladner (ed.), *The Death of White Sociology: Essays on Race and Culture*. New York: Vintage Books.

Lefcourt, Robert. 1971. "Law Against the People" In Robert Lefcourt (ed.), *Law Against the People: Essays to demystify law, order and the courts*. New York: Vintage Books.

Liazos, N. 1972. "The Poverty of the Sociology of Deviance: Nuts, Sluts, and Perverts." *Social Problems* 20(1): 103-120.

Loader, I. 2011. "Where is Policing Studies?" *British Journal of Criminology* 51: 449-458.

Lovell, J. 2009. *Crimes of Dissent: Civil disobedience, criminal justice and the politics of conscience*. New York: New York University Press.

Lutterbeck, D. 2004. "Between Police and Military: The new security agenda and the rise of gendarmeries," *Cooperation and Conflict* 39, 1: 45-68.

Lynch, M., and R. Michalowsi. 2006. *Primer in Radical Criminology: Critical perspectives on crime, power and identity*, 4th edition. Monsey, New York: Criminal Justice Press.

McCormick, K and L. Visano (eds.) 1992. *Understanding Policing*. Toronto: Canadian Scholars' Press.

McCoy, A. 2010. *United States of Surveillance* [sound recording]. Boulder, CO: Alternative Radio.

McPherson, C. B. 1992. *The Real World of Democracy*. Toronto: Anansi.

MacGregor, D. 2006. "September 11 as 'Machiavellian State Terror'," *Research in Political Economy* 23: 189-221.

_____. 2002. "The Deep Politics of September 11: Political economy of concrete evil." In Peter Zarembka (Ed.), Confronting 9-11, Ideologies of Race, and Eminent Economists, Research in Political Economy, Volume 20. Amsterdam: JAI Press.

Mann, C. 1993. *Unequal Justice: A question of Color.* Bloomington and Indianapolis: Indiana University Press.

Manning, P. 2010. *Democratic Policing in a Changing World*. Boulder, Colo. Paradigm Publishers.

Manning, P. 1971. "The Police: Mandate, strategies, and appearances." In Jack Douglas (ed.), *Crime and Justice in America*. New York: The Bobbs-Merill Company Inc.

Matza, D. 1969. *Becoming Deviant*. Englewood Cliffs, NJ: Prentice-Hall, Inc.

Meeks, D. 2006. "Police Militarization in Urban Areas: The obscure war against the underclass," *The Black Scholar* 35(4): 33-41.

Mepham, J. 1979. "The Theory of Ideology in Capital." In John Mepham and David-Hillel Rubin (eds.), *Issues in Marxist Philosophy. Vol III. Epistemology, Science, Ideology.* Brighton: The Harvester Press.

Miliband, R. 1987. *The State in Capitalist Society: The analysis of the Western system of power.* New York: Quartet Books.

Mills, Charles W. 2006. "Modernity, Persons, and Subpersons." In Joseph Young and Jana Evans Braziel (eds.), *Race and the Foundations of Knowledge: Cultural Amnesia in the Academy* (pp. 211-251). Urbana and Chicago: University of Illinois Press.

_____. 2003. *From Class to Race: Essays in White Marxism and Black Radicalism.* New York: Rowman and Littlefield Publishers, Inc.

Mills, C. Wright. 2000. *The Sociological Imagination.* New York: Oxford University Press.

Morales, F. 2000. "U.S. Military Civil Disturbance Planning: The war at home." *Cryptome.* http://cryptome.org/garden-plot.htm.

Moore. Jr, B. 1978. *Injustice: the social bases of obedience and revolt.* White Plains, NY: M. E. Sharpe.

Morrison, T. 1995. "The Marketing of Power: Racism and Fascism." *The Nation* 26(1): 21.

Murphy, C. 1999. "The Current and Future State of Police Research and Policy in Canada." *Canadian Journal of Criminology* 41(2): 205-215.

Naylor, R. 1999. *Patriots and Profiteers: On economic warfare, embargo busting and state-sponsored crime.* Toronto: McClelland and Stewart Inc.

Nelson, J. (ed.). 2000. *Police Brutality: An anthology,* 1st Ed. New York: W. W. Norton and Co.

News 24. 2012. "Evidence shows miners shot first." http://www.news24.com/Multimedia/South-Africa/New-evidence-shows-Marikana-miners-shot-first-20120821.

Neuwirth, R. 2011. *Stealth of Nations: The Global Rise of the Informal Economy.* New York: Pantheon.

Nicolaus, M. 1969. "The Professional Organization of Sociology: A view from below." *The Antioch Review* 29(3): 375-387.

Office of the Inspector General, United States Department of Justice. 2012. "Report by the Office of the Inspector General on the Review of ATF's Operation Fast and Furious and Related Matters." http://www.justice.gov/oig/testimony/t1220.pdf.

Parenti, C. 2003. *The Soft Cage: Surveillance in America from slavery to the War on Terror.* New York: Basic Books.

_____. 2008. *Lockdown America: Police and prisons in the age of crisis.* New York: Verso.

Pedicelli, G. 1998. *When Police Kill: Police use of force in Montreal and Toronto.* Montreal: Vehicule Press.

Petras, J. 2001. "Left Intellectuals and the Desperate Search for Respectability: Accommodation with the status quo." *Z Magazine,* March 1: 54-59.

Proyect, Louis. 2007. *The Unrepentant Marxist.* http://louisproyect.wordpress.com/2007/02/22/a-reply-to-goran-therborn/.

Reasons, C. 1974. "Controlling the Controllers." In Charles Reasons (ed.), *The Criminologist: Crime and the criminal.* Pacific Palisades, CA: Goodyear Publishing Company, Inc.

Reilly, R. 2013. "FBI Allowed Informants to Commit More Crimes in 2012 Than Year Before."

Huffington Post.
http://www.huffington/2013/12/27/fbi-otherwise-
illegal-activity-report_n_4506385.html.

Robinson, R. 2009. "Is the U.S. on the Brink of
Fascism? Campaign for America's Future."
http://www.alternet.org/politics/141819/is_the_u.s
._on_the_brink_of_fascism/.

Ruggiero, Vincenzo. 2000. *Crime and Markets.*
Oxford University Press.

Ryan, W. 1976. *Blaming the Victim.* New York: Vintage
Books.

Sardar, Z. 1999. "Development and the Location of
Eurocentrism." In Ronaldo Munck and Denis
OHearn (eds.), *Critical Development Theory:
Contributions to a new paradigm.* New York: Zed
Books.

Segal, R. 1971. *The Struggle Against History.* London:
Bantam Books.

Sewell, J. 2010. *Policing in Canada: The real story.*
Toronto: James Lorimer and Co. Ltd.

Schumpeter, J. 2008. *Capitalism, Socialism and
Democracy.* New York: Harper Perennial.

Shantz, J. 2012. "Radical Criminology: A manifesto."
Radical Criminology: An insurgent journal, 1.
http://journal.radicalcriminology.org/index.php/r
c/article/view/1/html

Shapin, S and S. Schaffer. 1985. *Leviathan and the Air-
Pump: Hobbes, Boyle, and the experimental life.*
Princeton, NJ: Princeton University Press.

Smith, D. 1987. *The Everyday World as Problematic: A
feminist sociology.* Boston: North Eastern
University Press.

Smith, M. 2010. *Global Capitalism in Crisis: Karl Marx
& the Decay of the Profit System.* Halifax: Fernwood
Publishing.

_____. 2003. "Radicalism of the Left and Right are Equally Deplorable". In J. Blackwell, M. Smith, and J. Sorenson (eds.), *Culture of Prejudice: Arguments in critical social science*. Peterborough, Ont.: Broadview Press.

Sorokin, P. 1965. *Fads and Foibles in Modern Sociology and Related Sciences*. Chicago: Henry Regnery Company.

Spitzer, S. 1993. "The Political Economy of Policing." In D. F. Greenberg (ed.), *Crime and Capitalism: Readings in Marxist criminology*. Philadelphia: Temple University Press.

_____. 1975. "Toward a Marxian Theory of Deviance," *Social Problems* 22(5): 638-651.

Staples, R. 1975. "White Racism, Black crime, and American justice: An application of the Colonial model to explain crime and race," *Phylon* 3(1): 14-22.

Stork, J. 1974. "World Cop: How American built the global police state." In A. Platt and L. Cooper (eds.), *Policing America*. Englewood Cliffs, NJ: Prentice-Hall, Inc.

Sumner, C. 1979. *Reading Ideologies: An investigation into the Marxist theory of ideology and law*. New York: Academic Press.

Takagi, P. 1979. "LEAA's Research Solicitation: Police Use of Deadly Force," *Crime and Social Justice* 11: 51–61.

Taylor, I., P. Walton and J. Young. 1973. *The New Criminology: For a social theory of deviance*. Boston: Routledge and Kegan Paul.

Terrill, W., and A. Paoline and P. Manning. 2003. "Police Culture and Coercion," *Criminology* 41(4): 1003-34.

Tauri, J. 2012. "Indigenous Critique of Authoritarian Criminology." In K. Carrington, M. Ball, E. O'Brien, and J. Tauri (eds.), *Crime, Justice and Social Democracy: International Perspectives* (217-233). London: Palgrave MacMillan.

United States Department of Justice. 2011. "Investigation of the New Orleans Police Department." Retrieved May 7, 2012.

van Natta, D. 2011. "Race Issues Rise for Miami Police." *New York Times*. http://www.nytimes.com/2011/03/23/us/23miami .html?pagewanted=print

Visano, L. 1998. *Crime and culture: Refining the traditions*. Toronto: Canadian Scholars Press.

Wacquant, L. 2008. *Urban Outcasts: A Comparative Sociology of Advanced Marginality*. Cambridge, UK: Polity Press.

Webb, G. 1998. *Dark Alliance: The CIA, the Contras, and the crack cocaine explosion*. New York: Seven Stories Press.

Willhelm, S. *Black in White America*. Cambridge, Mass.: Schenkman Publishing company, Inc.

_____. 1980. "Can Marxism Explain America's Racism?" *Social Problems* 28(2): 98-112.

_____. 1971. *Who Needs the Negro?* Garden City: Doubleday books.

Williams, C. 2005. "To unnerve and detect: Policing Black activists in Toronto." In L. A. Visano (Ed.), *Law and Criminal Justice: A critical inquiry*. Toronto: Athenian Policy Forum.

Williams, K. 2007. *Our Enemies in Blue: Police and Power in America*. Boston: South End Press.

Williams, R. 1983. *Keywords: A vocabulary of culture and society*. New York: Oxford University Press.

Robinson, S. 2009. "Is the U.S. on the Brink of Fascism?" http://www.alternet.org/politics/141819/is_the_u.s._on_the_brink_of_fascism/

Stamper, N. 2005. *Breaking Rank: A top cop's expose of the dark side of American Policing.* New York: Nation Books.

Websdale, N. 2001. *Policing the Poor: From Slave Plantation to Public Housing.* Boston: Northeastern Press.

Whitaker, R., G. Kealey and A. Parnaby. 2013. *Secret Police: Political policing in Canada from Fenians to Fortress America.* University of Toronto Press: Toronto.

Zafirovski, M. 2007. "'Neo-Feudalism' in America? Conservatism in Relation to European Feudalism." *International Review of Sociology/Revue Internationale de Sociologie* 17(3): 393-427.

[arts & culture]

Selected Images and Commentary from Artact QC

In this issue of Radical Criminology, we are reprinting a small selection of digital paintings (created using Photoshop and a pen tablet) that were created over 2012-2013 by an anonymous artist(s) operating as **"Artact QC"** around the height of the student strikes and at a high point of street mobilizations in Quebec. [Permission from their homepage.]

Production Editor's note: We apologize for some translation errors from the (mostly) original French commentaries and can only hope that we've preserved some the sarcasm and wit of the original commentaries, which were written in the heat of a very specific historical moment. Further, we apologize for the grey-scale reproductions of very colourful art. If you are viewing this in our print version, please, you really must go check this feature out in colour online at:

http://radicalcriminology.org/issue6

On Our Cover: "Priorities" | June 2, 2012.

[Riot police clash with student demonstrators. The police act in front of--as if defending?--two billboards symbolic of Montreal capital: one depicting a large comedy festival and the other featuring a scantily clad woman watching a race car at the Grand Prix.]

Commentary[1]: Jean Charest, Quebec's current Prime Minister, said: "Those who were planning to disrupt the Grand Prix, they should rather abstain, out of respect for Quebecers."

Really? Really? Therefore sit back and allow the police to shoot rubber bullets into a crowd of demonstrators, allow them to throw an incredible amount of CS gas (which may under certain

---

[1] This comment came around the time of the public discussion about the Grand Prix held during the student strikes: https://en.wikipedia.org/wiki/2012_Canadian_Grand_Prix#Threats _from_student_protest_groups

conditions cause lung necrosis and second-degree burns) at the crowd, that's all very respectful of Quebecers.

But to allow the demonstrations to interfere with the Grand Prix of Montreal, that highly intellectual "activity" where you can enjoy the incredible opportunity to pay a large sum to be closed in near a circuit where multi-millionaires can break all the traffic laws during an afternoon, no, that is unacceptable. To others who would like to, it is not clear why, enjoy some quiet in one of the few parks of the island of Montreal, well, a solid fuck you very much, because it's a time to hear the wonderful roar of the engines and the subtle smell of wasted gasoline. And if you are not yet total insulted, the multi-millionaires who will arrive first after doing several times around the circle will then sprinkle around lots of expensive champagne jokingly. Hey, FUCK YOU, the poor!

We always ask the same segment of the population to be silent, for the good of the economy, while you shave the boreal [forest] to the root, while quietly privatising the health system, while selling all at discount for the cost of exploitation where the protection of the environment is left to the discretion of foreign companies. And the list is long.

At some point, we can wonder about the psychological integrity of the "silent majority" who not only supports this type of Government by its inaction, but that even worse I'm afraid, is preparing to re-elect him, because his summer of perpetual festivities might be disturbed by the clamor of a social consciousness that takes off.

"The System" | June 30, 2012.

[Two monstrosities toast with champagne glasses
over a barrel of oil and in front of a Quebec flag.]

Commentary: A judge has sentenced a young
protester to 7 months of prison without parole; the individual has been described as
part of a group that would have terrorized
downtown Toronto during the G20 summit

in 2010 (think of poor downtown Toronto and especially the poor, poor windows!)[2] Another judge, his eminent splendor François Rolland[3] (*"Birdie" Frank* to his buddies) has determined that an in-depth debate was necessary before weighing the suspension of law 12 (stemming from Special Law 78).[4] Don't you all feel like *"Big Shots,"* discussing about indentures and terminology like that? Personally, I am so thrilled to know that my life is well regulated by writings that I have never really had the time to read, but have been ruled as valid by tanned golfers with necromancer robes and magical hammers. I am 200% convinced that the judge, immediately after announcing his verdict, headed straightaway towards another room to quickly examine and debate the legality of this law.

During the student strike some students challenged the decisions of their General Assemblies by asking the courts for temporary injunctions forcing their professors to teach them even if they would be alone in the classroom. By opposition to their counterparts who wore the red square as a symbol of the strike (from the saying "squarely in the red" in reference to being heavily indebted), the injunctions students adopted the green

[2] 1- http://www.sabotagemedia.anarkhia.org/2012/06/g20-in-saint-jerome-quebec-a-comrade-is-sentenced-to-7%C2%A0months-in-prison/)

[3] François Rolland is the Chief Justice of the Superior Court of Quebec. (http://www.tribunaux.qc.ca/mjq_en/c-superieure/bienvenue.html)

[4] English: http://www.cbc.ca/news/canada/montreal/quebec-court-rejects-bill-78-injunction-request-1.1279630

square as their emblem and created a group called *Socially Responsible Student Movement of Québec*, a faction against the strike, for the tuition hike, and closely related to the ruling government of Jean Charest (the group was set up by *Young Liberals*). Even if not numerous, the "greens" ended up hindering the justice system with all their injuctions demands.

Chief Justice of the Superior Court of Quebec François Rolland, eventually decided that all student injuctions demands would go through him and he approved every single one of them. Hence, the conflict was not merely political anymore but became judicial as well. Confronted with the fact that his injunctions were not respected by the red students (they blocked the doors of their schools or disturbed classes), Chief Judge Rolland added the threat of harsh penalties to his injunctions (prison up to a year, and fine up to 50 000$ for anyone who would prevent green students to attend classes). He also ordered involved colleges to use police forces as needed, as well as called upon the Attorney General of Quebec (Jean-Marc Fournier) to enforce the law and make sure that the rights of the green students would be respected.[5] Indeed, there were "muscled interventions", as mainstream media calls it, where police tried by force to break the red students staking lines, for instance at College de Rosemont on May 14 2012[6] and College Lionel-Groulx on May 15th 2012. In this last case, the red stu-

---

[5] http://tvanouvelles.ca/lcn/infos/regional/montreal/archives/201
2/05/20120511-072058.html

dents had an additional opponent, a Conservative senator, Claude Carignan, who personally helped the green students obtain their injuctions (two of his children being green students at this college). On May 15th then, the SQ (*Sureté du Québec*), our provincial police riot squad, showed up in Sainte-Thérèse, a small city north of Montreal, with the mission of liberating a path for those who have been identified by many, as scabs. To be successful, the SQ would have to confront concerned parents who were present forming a line of their own, a group of professors opposed to the hike and the red students who stood by the doors.[7]

---

[6] Rosemont College May 14th 2012: students have been pepper sprayed, hit with batons and one student suffered a head injury.

[7] SQ at Lionel-Groulx College May 15th 2012 (http://www.youtube.com/watch?v=K_BGel1ltZ8)
Also that day, a bus heading towards Cegep Lionel-Groulx (from Montreal) was intercepted by the SQ and the 18 people inside were illegally detained under the Canadian Criminal Code Article 31. For a critique of police use (or misuse) of Article 31 (which was also applied in Victoriaville and at the Formula One event in Montreal), see: English:

(http://www.quebecprotest.com/post/26562409433/by-order-of-article-31-i-am-placing-you-under-arrest); for the arrest itself, see: (http://www.youtube.com/watch?v=9TQy9FKKVaQ); for criticism by retired police officer René Forget of this illegal detention as well as other police behavior, see:
(http://www.quebecprotest.com/post/23769940349/open-letter-to-police-officers-sent-from-a-retired)

On May 31st, a collective of professors from Cegep Lionel-Groulx, co-signed an open letter in the newspaper Le Devoir. This letter, exposing their side of the story, retraces the

Besides the fact that it is ridiculous to give vol-
leyball, theatre, or any kind of course that requires debates between students to a unique
individual, the granted injuctions raised the
question of the legitimacy of Students General Assemblies as well as the right of this
portion of the population to vote a strike.
Very quickly in the mainstream media there
was a campaign to call the strike a *boycott* instead, proponents claiming that the notion of
strike doesn't apply to students under the
law.[8] Clearly a tactic to discredit the student
movement and rip them from any kind of
leverage.

On another note, as referred in the text above,
Chief Judge Rolland didn't seem uneasy to

---

events that led to the violence of May 15th, and compares
the role played by the direction of the Cegep to the one of
the "executive agent manipulated by authority" in the Stan-
ley Milgram experiment. English: (http://www.que-
becprotest.com/post/24470574512/the-violence-at-lionel-
groulx-our-side-of-the-story); Original in french:
(http://www.ledevoir.com/politique/quebec/351265/violence-
a-lionel-groulx-voici-notre-version). Following the publication of this letter, the direction of Cegep Lionel-Groulx imposed disciplinary measures on the eleven signatory professors who were accused of displaying a lack of loyalty to
their institution. Condemning this attack on free speech, a
petition is asking for the withdrawal of the disciplinary
measures:

(http://www.avaaz.org/fr/petition/Levee_dune_mesure_dis-
ciplinaire_contre_11_enseignantes_et_enseignants_du_Col-
lege_LionelGroulx/?fiUFrab&pv=1)

[8] For the opposite position, I suggest: *The student strike is not
a simple boycott: history and perspectives* (http://ajpque-
bec.org/?p=167).

reject an emergency injunction that was requested, this time, by the major student organizations, in collaboration with trade unions and others, against the Special Law 78.[9] The judge is following in the footsteps of the *Quebec Council of Employers* and *The Board of Trade of Metropolitan Montreal*, who have given their support to Bill 78, in tacitly defending the controversial law instead of rallying behind advocates of constitutional and human rights.

"Spécisme" ("Speciesism") | June 10, 2012.

A row of pigs with batons blocks entry for two (protesting) young people visibly wearing red squares pinned to their clothes, while the guards part to allow entry to the club district to two other well-heeled patrons.

---

9 http://en.wikipedia.org/wiki/Bill_78

◄**Commentary**: Last night I was watching the transmission CUTV (fortunately they exist as I was getting tired of hearing LCN weep over the fate of windshields of police cars). You could see the police restrict access to Crescent Street, ever using their excellent judgment. So we could see some people could enter smoothly, as if they were invisible to our proud peace officers. In just a quick look, you could tell that they let go by a certain physical type (no chance to the bearded with long hair, the exceptional big open brothel that is Crescent Street does not want you), but an incident caught my attention. Two young women were denied the right of way, apparently quite normal. But one of them starts to warm up and scolded the security guard with a delightful verve. And that's when I understood the trick that the gatekeepers use to detect the Communist villain who believed they could deceive their vigilance by not wearing the red square (which makes political profiling work much easier, admittedly): the activists are unable to feign the blank and glassy eyes of passersby who themselves are able to ignore a bloody social crisis in order to go have a drink to the health of billionaires who refuse to pay the bill.

This observation was, in my humble opinion, confirmed when I witnessed a short clip that showed three individuals wearing the red square handcuffed to hurry down the sidewalk, flanked by some showy policemen, and yet these people were ignored by the masses who wandered along safely, protected as they were from this threat embodied by these various "despicable people" with their slogans that invite to see the world from a perspective that is not necessarily to the advantage of established power.

Imagine a world where we should all actually do our "fair share,"[10] not paying, but contributing something valid.

---

[10] The expression "to do its fair share" (*faire sa juste part* in French) is the motto used by media in Quebec to sell the concept known, in Europe and elsewhere, as "austerity measures." One might note the manipulative quality of this slogan though, implying that nothing unreasonable is asked from the people: far from taking fraudulently from them, austerity policies are simply a contribution portrayed as "equitable". The focus is therefore diverted from the definition of "fair" to the questioning of the integrity of those who would challenge such a virtuous maxim. [Translator's note: This footnote explanation of the "fair share" phrase was the artist's comment provided, in English, on another piece, "Capital" http://artactqc.com/?p=636]

Le Drame ("The Drama") | June 11, 2012.

[A bureaucrat holds up a piece of the broken glass window of an investment corporation. While other suits and the media focus is clearly on the broken window, in the background riot police are bludgeoning student strikers with truncheons and making arrests.]

Commentary: "48th night demonstation: broken windows and forceful dispersion." Thus the Press describes the event last night. Further, it was reported that the windows were broken at the *Caisse de dépôt et placement du Québec,*[11] where was gathered all the economic upper crust of the province, along with the Governor of the Bank of Canada and the President of the Bank of France. It seems there was a reception inside, but the article does not say what exactly was being celebrated. Anyway, no care about that, what we want to know is how many windows were shattered by the anarcho-communists. Think of the windows, the damn WINDOWS!

---

[11] CDPQ is a large pension plan investment and insurance company.

The press article also teaches us that a window was broken at the headquarters of the National Bank (heartless band!) And harm was committed on innocent patrol cars and other vehicles.

But here I have a little on my hunger, because the title spoke of forceful dispersion; usually when our extraordinary media uses the euphemism "muscular," it means that an ambulance left with someone who has received too much love from the brave policemen. And the article does not really mention what happened to the protesters. Ah well, I guess this is incidental compared to the incredible expense we will assume the poor banks have to undertake to replace the windows. Such trouble, but we know who we really have to blame when we will pass on the bill as arbitrary increase in user fees.

"Dêmokratía" | September 30, 2012.

[A defiant student demonstrator gives the finger to on-coming riot police threatening baton-beatings.]

Commentary: Well, it's over!? We can go back to our activities and let politicians run our lives? Was it something that not everyone wanted? Because Christmas is coming and you need to get there early if you want to enjoy the best discounts. Not to mention that the fall timing of succulent Quebec television should begin shortly, "Occupation Double Académie" and "Cooking with Trucmuche."

Prosperity, in the capitalist system, always comes at the cost of a certain violence outside the area of abundance. This violence must be, as far as possible, on hidden recipients that could, you never know, develop a humanitarian conscience that would drive them to confront the binding system to reorient a certain share of violence usually reserved for "other" in order to eliminate any threat to its survival.

This system, it is us, our laziness, our materialistic desires. We are always looking for the easy solution, and what could be easier than the simple act of scribbling a piece of paper before placing it in a box. Here, the citizen's duty has been accomplished, say 10 "Hail Mary" and you will be absolved of any responsibility for the next 4 years.

Tomorrow, we exchange the chairs. Handshakes are complicit dinners in the capital too. A smell of rancid ties floats in the air. A suit going on, another will replace fear not.

"L'Embarras du Choix" ("Spoiled for Choice") | November 21, 2012.

[After speaking about how the awful the choices in the election were, especially to the poor..]

Commentary: ...That sigh of ease in the journalistic sewer, we will be able to return to focus on the erosion of the collective intellect by selling the notion that it will be much better for everyone if we privatize the health system ... We can just afford it, we'd better do as the States, as the American case. It'll just be beneficial to the health insurance department Powercorp, worse for you investors, put your money on it, there is a lot of money to make the denial of human dignity these days.

In my view, democracy has failed because of the human factor, as all political philosophies. It depended too much on the corporate media to inform enough to participate in the process, so that the vote be based on relevant and critical thinking. But it was not counting concentration corrupt media that guides this reflection to the interests of a ruling class. And yet, as with hypnosis, it only works with participants who are willing.

"Le Sommet de l'Éducation" ("The Education Summit") | February 10, 2013.

[In an airy, colourful meeting room filled with skeletons in suits, a couple of students point to a red square placed on the conference table.]

Commentary: Is it that you tremble with excitement in anticipation of the education summit, trembling with impatience and salivating at the prospect of many in-depth debates, which will undoubtedly take place between intelligent people who have a vision for the future—and the rectors accompanied by their supporters of the government and employers? Finally fall silent the evil spirits who said that in Quebec, the elections it was pile-on to determine the mascot who would come stay the course towards the beautiful neo-Liberal society that have planned for us our benevolent masters of finance, with the option to vote for the qsl for those who have difficulty reading the instruction manual. [...]

"Répression Rétrograde" ("Retrograde Repression") | February 17, 2013.

Commentary: I watched the documentary "DÉRIVES"[12] this week. What I found more repulsive wasn't the behaviour of the police, which I considered quite normal in their role as agent of repression (we don't dress up in killer robot gear to go chat with a crowd disarmed); Neither was it the poisonous rhetoric of the chroniclers disguised as journalists for the occasion, this too was part of a logic of social division which should surprise no one except the most naive and/or stupid of us. No, what shocked me, it was the testimony of women who helped evacuate one seriously injured.

In front of the indifference of "peace officers", these women carried him off, to avoid being trampled, in a residential street on private land. And here, they tell us that people were out on their balconies screaming at them to leave, that the demonstrators in rout had no business here. Ah, the beautiful example of depth of soul of these good people that teem in Quebec, these people who, instead of stopping to inquire about the state of health of the victim, are worried about their beautiful lawn decorations. City boy, you're guaranteed a good future well prosperous. You've a level of humanity enough to be functional, but not high enough to make a difference. It's nice to see that bloom in the spring, the trees in blossom, so well it serves your children. And since most of the mass media are supporting this individualistic approach, we don't have to feel even the little shame usually relevant to such a cowardly act; after all, we pay our taxes, we consume, we close our mouth,

---

[12] By 99% Media: https://youtu.be/9iZdAdczrGk

why do we have to have more to worry about who's next, especially that he was probably looking for it, they are all like that the "artistic Christs of cheapskate guitars and red squares." You're my Adonis, I can't even say I hate you. I don't even despise you either. It just gives me a profound discouragement, to know that you and your clones probably form the majority of the public in the province. Makes me well aware that I'm part of a minority, an aberration in this well oiled system. But it's not my fault, I feel it viscerally, when I see these images of brutality and of (from my point of view completely stupid) injustice, I have a surge of adrenaline and a blind rage that burns in my belly. I know I'll require a few Prozac pills in order to find it quite awesome your world.

"Chatons de Saule" ("PussyWillows," February 17, 2013)

[Two young people carrying black flags—one with a red bandana, the other's black—hold hands and stand defiantly against a sea of riot police.]

Commentary: I took a quick pass over a Jean-Jacques Samson column, one of the great chroniclers of the fabulous *Journal de Montréal*, the newspaper which one reads while snacking on a nice plate of junk food (with the advantage of being able to wipe our shiny fat fingers without fear of losing the thread of the narrative). It put forward an intriguing good title: "Parasites of the ASSE."[13] [...]

It reminded me of reading in an American alternative newspaper an article about what the author called an eliminationist speech (the belief that a political opponent would be the equivalent of a cancer that should be eradicated). Whenever I read an article which generalizes the "red square," I think that it is not so far from that. Rarely would one use the term "parasite" to refer to a valid interlocutor. In fact, a parasite is something that one has no remorse to crush, to kill, to eradicate under a big shiny riot cop boot. Ah, it was something last year to see the media treatment of the events; It was still streamlining police brutality (poor sprouts, they were insulting, they were tired at some point to be there like idiots every night without being able to romp on something), then they invited retired police officers to give another point of view when the images were too difficult to justify. Even better, it spoke simply.

In the end, there were elections and democracy has survived narrowly, but this latent hatred of those who think differently remains. But you, who is delighted to see a hairy student to be abuse by a group of police officers: if one day your child, your daughter, say, was found in one of these events, because she has friends, because she is young, because she has a heart still beating while yours is dried by years; and if your daughter was wounded in the head, if she

---

[13] Striking students union.

lost an eye, if a police officer had a little fiddling of breasts while arresting her; and if you were told by way of explanation that you had only to better educate him, that she didn't have to be there, if there is nothing wrong, if it only happens to us, it's nothing. Will you be among those who will add to the reproaches, or will you come to share my anger?

Please visit **http://artactqc.com** to see these pieces and many more in vivid, searing colour. (For example, once you take a peek at their rendition of the Queen getting off her toilet, found @ http://artactqc.com/?p=1171, you'll know you cannot un-see this artwork.) Or visit: http://facebook.com/ArtactQc2.0

ALL EYES ARE UPON US

Mother, mother
There's too many of you crying
Brother, brother, brother
There's far too many of you dying

--Marvin Gaye

... then they stomped

     John Willet

as he lay on the sidewalk
hands cuffed behind his back
and shot

     Michael Brown

who was on his way this fall to college

    Stop and frisk
    Stop and frisk

and used a chokehold to kill

     Eric Garner

who sold cigarettes one-by-one
on the street in Staten Island
and punched again, again
in the face
great-grandmother

     Marlene Pinnock

as she lay on the ground
then they stood around while
an angry bartender
pushed vet

William Sager

down the stairs to his death;
maybe they helped hide
the security videotape
then it was
unarmed

Dillon Taylor

in Salt Lake City, and
homeless

James Boyd

in Albuquerque

and   Darrien Hunt

in Saratoga Springs, Utah--

how about that grandmother
92-year-old

Kathryn Johnston

shot to death in a SWAT team raid
gone bad?

then it was
unarmed, homeless, mentally ill

Kelly Thomas

clubbed to death by three Fullerton cops
left with pulp for a face

in '73 in Dallas

Santos Rodriguez

was marked by officer Cain
who played Russian Roulette
with the handcuffed 12-year-old
in his cruiser—
till the .357 fired; Santos' blood
all over his 13-year-old handcuffed
brother David

and those cries of
19-month-old   Bounkham Phonesavanh
in whose crib
the flash-bang grenade exploded—
his nose blown off

> *Shelter in place*
> *Shelter in place*

or 41 police gunshots at immigrant

              Amadou Diallo

who died
right there
in the doorway
of his Bx. apt. bldg.

and that cop who shot and killed
7-year-old

              Aiyana Stanley-Jones

as she slept

and those Cleveland cops who shot
12-year-old

              Tamir Rice

who had a BB gun
and gave him no first aid--
watched him die

all those police
with gas masks and helmets in

        Ferguson, Missouri

telling the people

don't be on the streets after sundown

        Ferguson—still a sundown town
        maybe soon like a town near you

with M-16's, MRAP's,
armored personnel carriers—
in this war against the people

    Lockdown
    Lockdown

                                  Gene Grabiner

[book reviews]

Crashing the Party: Legacies and Lessons from the RNC 2000
by Kris Hermes
Oakland: PM Press, 2015.

**Reviewed by— Irina Ceric, Kwantlen
Polytechnic University, February 2016.**

Just as activists tend to take the availability of legal support for granted, so have both social movement writers and scholars tended to ignore the work of providing radical legal support, particularly the contributions of non-lawyers. In *Crashing the Party*, long-time activist and legal worker Kris Hermes takes on two tasks aimed at overcoming these erasures. This unique book provides what is arguably the first in-depth examination of radical legal

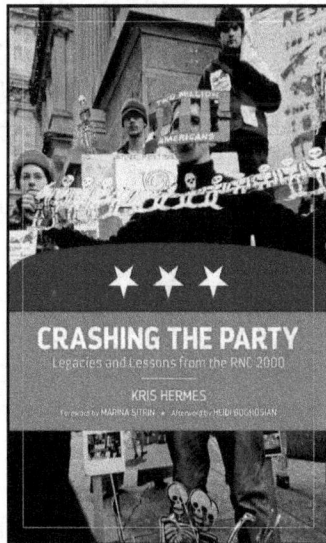

support in North America, an analysis framed by his meticulous recounting of the mobilization against the Republican National Convention [RNC] held in Philadelphia, Pennsylvania in the summer of 2000. To tell both stories, Hermes recounts the organizing that culminated in days of creative and diverse actions against the RNC as well as the repressive police tactics deployed against the protesters, tactics which continue to serve as a blueprint for protest policing. What makes *Crashing the Party* distinctive, however, is its focus on the court solidarity organized by the R2K Legal Collective, a group made up of legal workers, lawyers, law students, defendants and activists. As a result, Hermes documents the emergence of jail and court solidarity and radical legal support as forms of collective action, neglected legacies of the global justice movement.

That the 2000 RNC protest was undoubtedly one of the all too brief series of mobilizations that made up what we now refer to as the global justice movement—a moment that continues to exert a hold on the imagination of the North American left, particularly as younger generations of activists (re)discover this history—is one reason to publish (and read) a book about a now 15 year old struggle. But the 2000 RNC protest was also— and remains—a unique example of radical legal organizing, one we can and should learn from in order "to preserve our shared legacy of political and legal resistance", as Hermes argues. (8) These lessons would be even more accessible if the book's depiction of the 2000 RNC was not so detailed. *Crashing the Party* is almost too ambitious, combining an exhaustive, action-by-action retelling of that summer's resistance while also discussing many aspects related to movement history in the US more generally (e.g. histories of surveillance, infiltration, and judicial intervention in policing practice and policy—sometimes going back decades). Nonetheless, the result is a work that ought to be read by a wide audience, activists themselves as well as academics interested in social movements, policing, state repression, and critical legal studies.

Hermes' central argument is that "[b]ecause of mistreatment on the streets and in jail, as well as the excessive charges applied to hundreds of protesters, the RNC 2000 arrestees sought vindication in the courtroom, spurring a court solidarity strategy that began with a mass refusal to accept plea bargains and a mass demand for trials." (7) More contentiously, he contends that the tactics underlying this strategy ("activists staging political trials, overcoming charges, exposing widespread surveillance and infiltration, raising unprecedented funds for legal defense, and using media to shift public opinion") have never been used together since. (8) Recent examples in Ontario (the 2010 Toronto G20) and Quebec (student strikes and anti-austerity protests since 2012) suggest otherwise, as most if not all of these court solidarity tactics were used in fighting charges arising from these recent mobilizations. This oversight is at least partly due to the book's US focus, although Canadian law collectives are included in the list of radical legal collectives compiled by Hermes.

Regardless of the uniqueness of R2K Legal's strategy, however, *Crashing the Party*'s comprehensive account of radical legal support from the perspective of legal organizers is not only valuable as movement history but also provides a glimpse into the political tensions underlying activists' interactions with law and the state. Hermes engages with issues long debated by progressive lawyers and legal scholars on the complex dynamics between legal and political activists, particularly questions of strategy, knowledge, and decision-making power that inevitably arise during interactions between legal professionals and the movements they support. The book contains many instructive, grounded stories of such interactions, not all of them pleasant or productive. The civil suits that resulted from the RNC arrests however, do illustrate a successful attempt at creating "a new way for activists (both plaintiffs and supporters) and lawyers to work together collectively" through the use of consensus decision making and extensive discussions in which everyone affected would be heard. (201)

Crashing the Party also explores key questions that anyone who has participated in direct actions will immediately recognize. For instance, how do we challenge legal support fatigue or a lack of faith in jail solidarity (suspicion that often threatens to become a self-fulfilling prophecy)? (232) He reminds us that it is "crucial that we assess the state's resources, strategies, and tactics, as well as its limitations and vulnerabilities" when thinking about legal responses, offensive and defensive. The 2000 RNC protest serves as a potent example of how movements can grow and develop new capacities not despite repression, but in resistance to it, learning "ways in which we might gain collective strength against the state." (12) As someone who has been involved in providing radical legal support for the better part of two decades, such reminders, especially coupled with Hermes' critical yet hopeful analysis of the promise—and perils—of radical legal activism, serve as a much-needed validation. Legal support is no one's favorite organizing role, but the work is both necessary and generative: "Arguably, it is in the realm between the legal world and the world of political organizing where, when boundaries are pushed, unexpected results can occur." (228)

□ ◊ □□ ◊ □□ ◊ □

Who Killed the Berkeley School? Struggles Over Radical Criminology

by Herman & Julia Schwendinger
with foreword from Jeff Shantz

Surrey: Thought|Crimes Press, 2014.
220 pages.
http://thoughtcrimespress.org/BerkeleySchool

Reviewed by—*Aaron Philip*
Criminology student, Kwantlen
Polytechnic University, March 2015

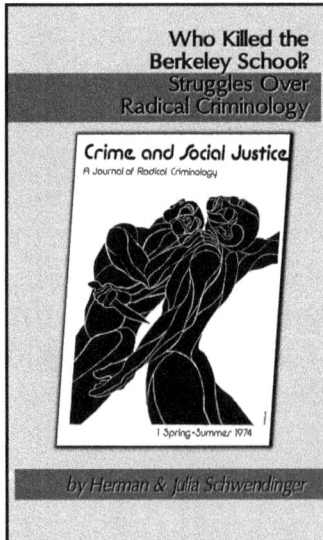

*W*ho Killed the *Berkeley School* is a story of struggle and tragedy, as the name suggests. The struggle is against what Jeff Shantz calls one of Ronald Reagan's forgotten "frontal assaults on dissent and resistance."[1] It was in 1977 that the Berkeley radicals school was defeated, as Ronald Reagan, the Regent of UC Berkeley, Governor of California and soon to be the next President of the United States acted against them. Told from the perspective of central participants,

---

[1] Foreword i

Julia and Herman Schwendinger, the book reads partly as a historical account and partly as a eulogy, chapter one details an "autopsy conducted after an assassination"[2] The book's goal seems to be to provide insight into what happened at the University of California—Berkeley and provide lessons for contemporary radicals and activists. On this basis, the book will be reviewed, for how well it meets this goal.

The impact of the Berkeley school is made very clear from the foreword by Jeff Shantz "The Berkeley School radicals identified the real sources of social harm in society—state, military and corporate actions. They also insisted on calling these harms by their proper name—crimes." [3] Shantz goes on to declare that the Berkeley school is a model which critical criminology should strive toward.

MAIN ARGUMENTS AND INSIGHTS

Based on the titles of the chapters and the foreword, the book sets up a narrative of uncovering and exposing the "friendly fascists" that are all around us and seeing the deeper meaning behind power relations in society and how they leads to oppression. The academic institution is joined with the community as the Berkeley school offered means of resistance for students and community activists.

---

[2] Page 3

[3] Foreward 1

Early on, the book identifies the enemies of the Berkeley school as government and university officials, including faculty whose senses had been dulled by McCarthyism and the Cold War.[4] It seems to be a constant feature of politics that blind patriotism will allow otherwise rational and educated people to rationalize the images of war and support their government in campaigns of repression and terror.[5] Also in chapter 2, the powerful regents are introduced, the American elites who own or sit on the board of directors for many transnational corporations. The beginnings of the theory of overlapping nodes of power, a central feature of critical theory are to be found here, what Dwight D Eisenhower first called "the Military-Industrial complex." Regents sitting on the Lockheed Corporation, Institute for Defense Analysis, amoung others set the stage for a confrontation when the radical school of criminology at Berkeley decided to resist the powerful capitalists. To suppress this development the book provides a logical account detailing how the regents attempted to silence the critics of the state-crime empire by "seizing the power to veto tenure recommendations—a power traditionally given to UC chancellors."[6] Throughout the book, footnotes are engaged to add additional background information and detail.

---

[4] Page 9

[5] Page 12

[6] Page 14

The Berkeley School fights the stereotype of radicals as "'extremists' and 'utopians' with ultra-left aims."[7] The book argues that the radicals were of diverse backgrounds and interests but were brought together by a mutual awareness of the unjust oppression endemic to a corrupt capitalist society and a desire to be a part of the social movements that characterized this period of history.

A point that is pertinent today, in the age of mass uprisings around the world, including the Arab Spring of 2011, Occupy Wall Street protests, and uprisings in Brazil and other countries plagued by inequality and corruption, is the comparison of how violence is being used. The protests organized by Berkeley were largely peaceful, and the odd violent protestor, acting outside the intent of the majority gathered through "gratuitous, spontaneous and disorganized violence" "pales in comparison with the organized and systematic clubbing and beatings by the police."[8] Often the message of a protest can be lost when violence enters the debate. Most people who may otherwise be sympathetic to an oppressed group's movement now have an excuse to ignore them. The right-wing critics of Fox News cannot however ignore the approach taken to violence by either side in this case, as the example of October 18, 1967 saw 200 police officers who must have been pumped up on testosterone "kicked, clubbed

---

[7] Page 33

[8] Page 35

and beat 4,000 unarmed and nonviolent demonstrators."[9] The book features press, physician, police and protestor accounts which include amoung them the description of a "massacre."[10] An open letter in the *Daily Californian* condemning the police for brutality and violations of the law can be seen as a model for resistance for contemporary citizens disaffected by police actions and seeking an avenue for resistance. Although the Berkeley School is no longer as it once was, the legacy can be used to continue to resist, as videos emerge like the most recent police shootings of civilians.

General Strengths

Much of the book focuses on how the Berkeley School engaged the community and offered avenues for resistance. One of the most pertinent examples is the first anti-rape group in the United States, *Bay Area Women Against Rape.*[11] This group identified a gap in the criminal justice system and lobbied for humane treatment of rape victims while taking initiative to establish support networks and disseminating information related to rapists' *Modus Operandi,* as well as advocating a victim-oriented approach and providing sen-

---

[9] Page 36

[10] Page 36

[11] Page 31

sitivity training to police officers who would handle rape cases. [12]

Descriptions and explanations of the radicals themselves were major strengths of the book, as it succeeded in portraying radicals as regular folks, who held the strength of their conviction and are relatable people, reacting to events unfolding outside the school. The effect is to build credibility and empathy. Rather than appearing as scary radicals out to burn the constitution and blur all lines of familiarity, the book portrays the Berkeley School as rooted in the liberal culture of the San Francisco Bay Area, and as attempting to bring about more "equality, justice and participatory democracy."[13] They were trying to make the United States into the place Americans already think it is.

The fact that the book is available freely online is also a strength, as it seems the authors are more concerned with releasing their story, than with making a profit. The credibility of the argument is solidified through this.

CRITICISM

Although the book engages a dramatic style and tells the story with flair, the excessive detail and understandably numerous characters involved make it more difficult to sort through the details to find the core of the narrative. Although footnotes were used to pro-

[12] Page 32

[13] Page 34

vide additional information, further versions could be edited down for readability and flow.

Overall the book meets its objective of providing insight into the assassination of the Berkeley school and stands up to critical review. Other possible criticisms may be centered around a biased account of the historical events, but this is to be expected given the book is authored by participants rather than neutral observers or researchers.